just JAVA

PETER van der LINDEN

SunSoft Press
A Prentice Hall Title

The publisher offers discounts on this book when ordered in bulk quantities.
For more information, contact Corporate Sales Department, Prentice Hall PTR ,
One Lake Street, Upper Saddle River, NJ 07458. Phone: 800-382-3419; FAX: 201- 236-7141.
E-mail: corpsales@prenhall.com.

Editorial/production supervision: *design-in-sync*
Cover design director: *Jerry Votta*
Cover designer: *Anthony Gemellaro*
Cover illustration: *Paul Chesley, Tony Stone Images*
Manufacturing manager: *Alexis R. Heydt*
Acquisitions editor: *Gregory G. Doench*
SunSoft Press publisher: *Rachel Borden*

10 9 8 7 6 5 4 3 2 1

ISBN 0-13-565839-X

SunSoft Press
A Prentice Hall Title

This text is dedicated to the ancient Greek Alcibiades. He was tutored by Socrates, but in my view far out shone his tutor in accomplishments. In 450BC or thereabouts, it is said that Alcibiades invented the hammock. Alcibiades was actually trying to invent the fishing net, but he was somewhat of a klutz, and there was a high wind on the day he did a "dry-run" of the first prototype.

I would also like to mention the fine products of Young & Co's Brewery in Wandsworth, London. Young's Special Bitter helps sustain the morale of programmers throughout the Greater London area, and in some parts of Northern California too.

Contents

Chapter 2
The Story of O: Object-Oriented Programming, 33

Chapter 5
More Sophisticated Techniques, 141

Acknowledgments

I would like to express my heartfelt thanks to Tom Cargill, Tom Cikoski, and Brian Scearce, who read the whole book in draft form, and made many suggestions for improvements. I take responsibility for all remaining errors. If you notice one that isn't in the errata sheet (obtainable from the website), report it to me.

Deep gratitude is due to my editor Raymond Pajek, who had many creative design ideas for improving this work.

Thanks to the people who encouraged me to write this book: Simon Alexander, Rachel Borden, John Bortner, Greg Doench, Zahir Ebrahim, Karin Ellison, and Jim Marks.

I would also like to thank the following people who provided significant help:

Sandy Anderson

Deepak Bhagat

Keith Bierman

Dan Berg

Matthew Burtch

Teresa Chinn

Mark Scott Johnson

Tim Kirby

Henry Lai

Bil Lewis

David Mikkelson

Ahmed Mohamed

Nicholas J. Morrell (what a taste he has in expensive Scotch!)

Tom O'Donnell

The Old Hats of AFU (Cayman Islands) Inc.

Bill Petro (Henry Ford never said "History is bunk"—he said it was bunk to him!)

John Pew

Craig Shergold (who's feeling a lot better thanks, and doesn't need any more cards)

Peter Soderquist

Kathy Stark

Panagiotis Tsirigotis

Tom van der Linden (who instilled in me his love for reading, writing, and consolidated statements of stockholder equity)

Wendy van der Linden (who pointed out that Citrus was a subclass of Fruit)

Terry Whatley

Ron Winacott

My team of colleagues at Sun Microsystems also deserves my gratitude for helping me in numerous ways while I worked on this text:

Oscar Arreola

Hui-Mei Chen

Jim Marks

Ahmed Mohamed

Saeed Nowshadi

Sina Balasubramanian

Srinath Murthy

Terry Whatley.

Introduction

"In a five year period we can get one superb programming language. Only we can't control when the five year period will begin."

—Alan Perlis, uncle of Algol-60

Why I Wrote This Book

Just imagine that you have been given the opportunity to design the ultimate programming language! What would you put in it?

Well, first of all, objects. And plenty of 'em. Object-oriented programming is moving to general acceptance as a superior implementation technique. Perhaps like me, you would want support for multi-threading. Better reliability and error handling are important, so let's find room for exceptions. Programmers need help with tiresome details, so let the compiler take care of making sure that all source files are up-to-date in a link.

And so on, and so on. I think you can see where this starts to lead. In the 1995 Pebble Beach Concours car show in California, one of the exhibits was a Rolls-Royce which had been similarly pieced together out of bits and pieces of the best. The Rolls featured a body from a 1931 Phantom II, modern racing carburettors, a custom-built chassis, and the engine from a Spitfire aeroplane[1]. All of these components are the best of their type, but put together the whole is an ill-matched

---

Bounty paid for corrections!

Every book on a technical subject has errors when it goes to press. That's even more true when the technical subject is as new as Java is. The goal of this author is to ruthlessly search out inaccuracies in this text, and eliminate them in future printings.

There's a bounty of $1 per error to the first person who brings a programming correction to the attention of the author, so it can be corrected in future printings. The policy is that all errors will be corrected, but the bounty is reserved for programming related things (not poor grammar, misaligned tables, or misspelling).

Please send your corrections and feedback by e-mail to pvdl@best.com.

The general website for this book, containing reader feedback, sample programs, and the current errata sheet is http://www.best.com/~pvdl

---

over-complex mess that doesn't seem much fun to drive. Just as a duck is adapted to fly, walk, and swim, but does all three poorly, this aero-engined car can't fly, and is almost impossible to drive with finesse. It has covered an average of just 50 miles per year since it was completed a decade ago. Apart from anything else, you can't stray far from a gas station when you only get 2 m.p.g. A careless stamp on the throttle could twist the chassis. The engine is mounted backwards so the prop. shaft comes out where the propeller used to go.

The vehicle was commissioned by an eccentric and rich used-car dealer, and must be driven gingerly at all times. It develops around 1000 bhp (a Corvette has about 20% of this), but heavy-footedness on the accelerator pedal could set the clutch on fire, or screw the mainshaft right out of the gearbox. The result of this "throw in everything good" design is an impractical and nearly undriveable vehicle. The question then is, "Is Java like this?"

The answer is a resounding "No!" For one thing, Java wasn't commissioned on the whim of an eccentric. Rather it was a considered approach designed by a top engineer, trying to solve practical problems. Aspects of Java have been borrowed from other languages, but they have been carefully integrated into the whole. Practicality is the hallmark throughout. Design decisions have been made with good judgment and thoughtfulness. Java benefited greatly from the C++ experience—seeing what was needed, what worked, and what should be discarded.

---

[1] There is a picture of this vehicle in the images directory on the CD that comes with this book. The Merlin engine, used in the Spitfire and the P51, was also built by Rolls-Royce. In fact, the Merlin engine was the last project Henry Royce completed before his death.

Once every generation or so in the computer industry, a new technology arises that is so compelling, and so well-fitted to the issues of the day, that it sweeps everything away before it. This happened in the 1960's with the shift to transistor logic, eventually leading to large scale integrated circuits. It happened again in the early 1980's with the unexpected success of the IBM PC. It was the right product at the right time, given credibility by the right company.

On the software side, a paradigm shift happened in 1982-4 with spreadsheet software. Lotus123, and Visicalc before it, met people's needs so well that Lotus shot to prominence in wave of profitability that other companies could only dream of.

And it is happening with Java right now. The success of Java represents the convergence of several unstoppable industry trends:

- popularization of the Internet

- consumer electronics merging into PC technologies

- computer industry drive to interactive multimedia everything

- rejection of the complexity of C++

- desire for independence from Microsoft/Intel desktop monopolies

The speed of adoption of Java by programmers everywhere has been truly remarkable. However it is not Java per se that the industry seeks, but a resolution to the challenges raised by the issues above. Java is the only serious contender to address these issues. As a result, it has met with immediate and overwhelming acceptance. Java is not just another language. Because Java addresses these issues it is the beginning of a phenomenon that could well change the nature of computing.

Java is particularly convenient for use in Internet applications, but it is a general purpose language too. Its features will be quickly understood by programmers, if explained in the right way. What programmers need now is a book on Java that combines three elements:

1. an introduction to Java, relating it to more familiar languages,

2. clear explanations, describing the significance of new features with their common pitfalls, and

3. short practical examples that can be tried by readers using the compiler supplied.

This is a beginners book on Java, intended for people who are already programmers. You can use this book if you have knowledge of any language: Pascal, or Visual Basic, Fortran, or Ada. Knowledge of C or C++ will give you a head start. Our central theme is to provide some easily accessible answers to the question "what's new and different about Java?"

We assume knowledge of programming, but nothing else. The text starts by setting the context: the explosion in popularity of the Internet. It then provides an introduction to Object-Oriented Programming before launching into a bottom-up appraisal of Java. This material is essential. If you don't understand OOP or the World Wide Web, you'll never understand the language, or how the libraries fit together, how applets work, and why certain events fit with certain methods. The accompanying CD has a java compiler system for Windows 95, Windows NT, the Macintosh (beta), and Solaris 2 on SPARC, which includes everything you need to try Java. It provides instructions on how to obtain the FCS compiler for the Macintosh when it becomes available.

How To Use This Book

Sometimes we do things in an order that looks funny from the table of contents. Sometimes we mention a topic only to say we're deferring discussion to a later section. This is because learning a subject isn't usually done in a depth-first manner. When you learn a foreign language you don't learn all the adjectives, followed by all the nouns finishing with all the verbs. If you did it that way you wouldn't be able to utter a whole sentence until you had completed all the lessons! It's the same with learning a programming language: it's best to cover enough to get you going, then look at the next thing by building on that, and eventually revisit anything that needs further attention. It gives a funny look to the table of contents though!

As I wrote this book, I also wanted to convey a sense of the enjoyment that lies in computer programming. Programming is challenging, exciting, enjoyable and satisfying. A book on computer programming should be exciting and educational, factual and fun. It should occasionally delight as well as inform. The major goal is to pass on the skill of a new programming language, but I'd also like to show a little of the fun of programming too. I hope that by the end of the book you'll agree that both goals have been met.

What's on the accompanying CD

This book comes with a CD that contains a Java compiler system for use on Windows 95, Windows NT, the Macintosh, and Solaris 2. Appendix D explains how to install the software. This section explains how to configure the compiler in your path, and test run it (after you have completed the installation). You can also download more software from the Sun Java site, and the Netscape site. Appendix A explains that process.

How to Test Run the Compiler (on Windows)

Add/modify two variables in your autoexec.bat
Put the Java bin directory in your path:
PATH c:\java\bin; ... *rest of path* ...

Set a CLASSPATH to point to the runtime library and the current directory.
SET CLASSPATH=.;c:\java\lib\classes.zip
NB. if you put the java compiler in a different location use that in the autoexec.bat

Reboot so the new variables take effect.

You can now check the installation by compiling and running one of the demo programs from the java\demo directory.

   cd c:\java\demo\Animator

   del Animator.class

   javac -verbose Animator.java

     ... loads of messages

   appletviewer example1.html

If this has all worked correctly, you should see a window pop-up that invites you to accept or reject the license conditions (if you don't see the buttons look for them under the task bar). When you press "accept", another window will pop up containing a visit from the tooth fairy. The tooth fairy ("Duke") is the Java mascot. You can stop the annoying music by clicking in the window.

If this has not all worked correctly, you probably mistyped the upper/lower case of a letter. Case is important in Java.

If you get the error message

   can't find class file.java

Then you probably used the command "java file.java" when you should have used "javac file.java". Check the error messages you see—is the compiler even being invoked?

To install the software under Solaris 2.3 or later

1. Copy the files from the CD to your hard disk. Place them in the directory where you want a Java directory to be created.

The JDK compiler system is an 8Mbyte file, so it will take a few seconds to pull it off the CD.

2. Untar the file

cd /home/linden
tar -xvf jdk_1_0_.tar

You should see dozens of lines indicating the files being untar'd.

3. Add/modify 2 variables in your .cshrc (or whatever initialization file is appropriate for the shell you use). For the cshell, the modifications are: Put the Java bin directory in your path:

setenv JAVAHOME /home/linden/java
set path=($JAVAHOME/bin ... *rest of path* ...)

Set a CLASSPATH to point to the runtime library:

setenv CLASSPATH $JAVAHOME/lib/classes.zip

4. Logout and login again so the new variables take effect.

How to Test Run the Compiler (on Solaris)

After you have done the installation, you can check it by compiling and running one of the demo programs from the java/demo directory.

cd java/demo/Animator

rm Animator.class

javac -verbose Animator.java

... loads of messages

appletviewer example1.html

If this has all worked correctly, you should see a window pop-up that invites you to accept or reject the license conditions. When you press "accept", an applet window will pop up containing a visit from the tooth fairy. The tooth fairy ("Duke") is the Java mascot. You can stop the annoying music by clicking in the window.

If this has not all worked correctly, you probably mistyped the upper/lower case of a letter. Case is important in Java. If you get the error message:

> can't find class file.java

Then you probably used the command "java file.java" when you should have used "javac file.java". Check the error messages you see—is the compiler even being invoked?

Note: Unix and Windows have slightly different conventions for end-of-line. Unix just expects a newline character, while Windows expects a carriage return and a newline (linefeed).

ManyWindows editors are able to cope with the Unix conventions and vice versa. However be aware that you may see extra characters at each line end on Unix, or you may see failure to carriage return on Windows, when you look at an ASCII text file that was created on the other platform with an editor that doesn't cope with this. It's not harmful (except you need a better editor) and the Java compiler system copes fine with source files created under either convention.

Some Light Relief

We end each chapter with a section of light relief to amuse readers and reward them for completing another milestone.

All I really need to know I learned on Internet

Peter van der Linden

All I really need to know about how to live, and what to do, and how to be, I learned on Internet. Wisdom was not at the top of the graduate school mountain, nor in the sandpile at Sunday school, but right there at the active endpoint of a TCP/IP session. These are the things I learned:

1. *Always* log your terminal off when you leave, even if you're only going to the bathroom for 5 minutes.

2. The only people who MAKE MONEY FAST on the Internet are those who manufacture routers and disk drives.

3. The net's memory is no longer than its attention span, so if you wait a little while you're sure to see the same thing go round again.

4. Some net-kooks are noisy, some net-kooks are stupid, and some net-kooks are rude. But the net-kooks whose attention you will attract are the net-kooks who are noisy, stupid AND rude. Plus, they have nothing better to do all day.

5. Not all Usenet moderators and FAQ-compilers eventually become power-mad and insane. Some of them started out that way.

6. The net's memory is no longer than its attention span, so if you wait a little while you're sure to see the same thing go round again.

7. If you're not sure about the facts when posting something, be louder and more insistent to compensate. Asserting something stridently enough can make it so. When someone points out your mistakes, first sulk, then laugh them off as deliberate sarcasm, irony or cynicism which went over the heads of the audience.

8. There was something about the net's memory, but the details are a little hazy right now.

9. Remember that early release of "rn" that prevented a posting unless it contained more new lines than included lines? That was actually a pretty good idea.

10. How to have the last word in real life "You're right!" How to have the last word on Usenet "You're in my killfile!"

CHAPTER

1

- How the Web Evolved

- The Significance of Java

The Web and Java

"Come into my parlor," said the spider to the fly.

J ava is a new, general-purpose programming language. It is a system that has been designed to make it easy for users to master. It contains libraries that pave the road to simple, convenient use of Internet features.

To understand the Java language, we need to begin by looking at Internet applications, especially the World Wide Web (aka, *the Web* or *WWW*). Java was developed independently from the World Wide Web, but solves problems that the Web needs solved.

The Web Catches Fire

Looking back on it now, 1994 was the year the World Wide Web really took off.

In 1994, the vast and multifaceted Internet—an unorganized, yet interconnected group of computer networks spanning the entire planet—reached critical mass and became general public knowledge. The growth of the Internet prior to that point was already rather impressive. However, fueled by speculation about its enormous communications potential, month-to-month growth became phenomenal.

Entertainer and magician Penn Jillete (the big noisy one from the Penn and Teller combo) was invited to give the keynote address at the 1994 Usenix (Unix users) convention. Penn described how he was suddenly getting a lot more dates with the opposite sex, now that the word had gotten around the glitterati that he was their newfound channel to the Internet. This was a message that went across very well with the attending audience of computer scientists, let me tell you.

The discovery of Internet by the mainstream was reflected in popular culture as well. Artists for cartoons like Dilbert, and Frank 'n Ernest started putting e-mail addresses in their drawings. Ads for some movies ("Tank Girl" is one example) included information specifically for net surfers—this is the mysterious "URL http://kirks.toupee" you might have noticed in small print. Even the President of the United States[1] went on-line with an e–mail address, president@white-house.gov. It's not really his personal address, since a flunky sends out form responses, but in politics, as in life, it's the thought that counts.

No doubt about it—the Internet has become big! Big in numbers, and big in the public consciousness.

Where It All Started

Like Jack the beanstalk, the Internet "just grew and grew." It started in a very small way in the late 60's as the ARPA[2]net, an experiment funded by the U.S. Department of Defense. The ARPAnet linked together a handful of computers at some university and research sites. Networks were rare in those days, and almost everything was a novelty. One innovation (which is a cornerstone of the Internet today) is that every computer had its own unique address, now known as an IP or "Internet Protocol" address.

An IP (Internet Protocol) address consists of four groups of digits that looks like this:

```
204.156.141.229
```

On a Windows system or a Mac, you won't have an IP address, unless you're on a local area net that has IP addressing.

On a Unix workstation you can print out your IP address by typing

```
/usr/sbin/ifconfig -a
```

You may have noticed the IP address if you looked at the messages while the system was booting, or if you just like poking around.

---

1. In February 1996, the U.S. Presidential home page at http://www.whitehouse.gov used a Java program to wave a pair of flags on the picture of the White House.
2. ARPA = Advanced Research Projects Agency

Any computer could send data to any other computer on the net by wrapping the information in an IP packet and putting it onto the network. Intervening special-purpose router computers were responsible for forwarding the data to the next router closer to the ultimate destination.

The early services allowed scientists to exchange electronic mail and other files. They could "finger" or enquire about the logon status of users on systems far away. They could even telnet to different systems—login remotely from their host computer to a different computer located in another city. These services proved so convenient that the universities involved began to connect other systems and departments, unrelated to network research, to the ARPAnet. An important new-comer was the NSFNET which connected five regional supercomputer centers, each of which had a hierarchy of smaller networks hanging off it, again using IP addressing. The network had become an 'internet'—a connected cluster, of several levels of networks, and was on its way to becoming the Internet we know and love today.

A related trend was the rising popularity of local area networks of Unix worksta-tions in computer science departments in the early 1980's. Companies like Sun Microsystems, Apollo Computer, and Onyx could install workstations linked by Ethernet hardware and IP software. These were much cheaper than the large cen-tralized time-sharing supermini's and mainframes they replaced. Organizations found it very convenient to connect all their LANs together in a wide area net-work that could be gateway'd onto the Internet. This way, files could be shared, and e-mail sent, without regard to departmental boundaries. Personal computers were left out of this first tidal wave of networking. At that time, they lacked the hardware, software, and raw CPU power necessary.

An early key aspect of the Internet was that it was not "designed"; it just evolved to meet the needs of its users. There was no central direction, no governing body, and no elaborate bureaucratic procedure. If you found its basic communication services useful, you simply went out and connected your own network to the nearest Internet system. The cost of a dedicated dataline at a few hundred dollars a month—peanuts to a large academic department—instantly enabled the cross-pollination of thoughts and ideas with colleagues throughout the world who were similarly network connected.

Early Pioneers

There was a real spirit of pioneering cooperation in the early days of the Internet. Back in 1982, a colleague wanted an Internet connection to his family weekend beach house on the New Jersey shore. He studied a map of Internet routers (that was back in the days when the number was small enough that they could be written down on a map).

He planned to telephone all the ones that were in the local calling area. The very first organization he tried on the phone agreed to provide him with a complimentary account for dial-up access. The hardest part was getting transferred to the right system administrator to ask.

Nowadays, if you do not have Internet access at work or at your place of study, you can use an ISP, an Internet Service Provider, who, for a small monthly fee will provide you Internet access via your phone line to your home PC.

In the early 1980's, another application, apart from e-mail, file transfer, and telnet, was added to the Internet: network news. Network news, or "Usenet" as it became known, is a phenomenon that is hard to describe if you have not experienced it. Entire books have been written about Usenet. Usenet is a computerized bulletin board with hundreds of special interest discussion groups. Usenet is like TV for people who still read for leisure. While it is occasionally very enlightening, it tends to be something that you do when you should be actually doing something. Let me explain that a little further.

Usenet was developed by a couple of graduate students at the University of North Carolina. Its use quickly spread to other universities. I encountered it in 1981 as a graduate student in computer science and loved it from the start! Who wouldn't? It was a great chance to exchange notes, advice, hints, wisdom and humor, even insults, with a group of surprisingly diverse people.

All that we had in common was one kind of computer science connection or another, and an urge to share an opinion. We used the first to talk endlessly about the second. It was and is heady, exciting, time-consuming and addictive. It greatly expands your field of acquaintances. Today, almost no pastime, interest, or profession is too obscure for Usenet. Every imaginable topic will have its own specialized newsgroup devoted to fevered and sometimes heated discussion.

So that's where Internet applications stayed 'frozen in time' throughout the 1980's: providing simple file-based applications, mostly in a batch-oriented manner. The only real-time application, IRC (Internet Relay Chat) proved to be merely a clunky curiosity. But computer science had by then moved on.

The Big Step Forward

One of the problems with the existing Internet was that it was all so unorganized and unconnected. Sure, you could download a copy of a file from anywhere on the Internet—if you knew that it existed and where it was. The Internet was like a vast library that had no central index. People passed on information by e-mail, word-of-mouth, and news postings. There was a treasure house of information out there, but the trick was in finding it.

Before hypertext

reading a sheet of paper with occasional jumps to footnotes—is a serial process

With hypertext

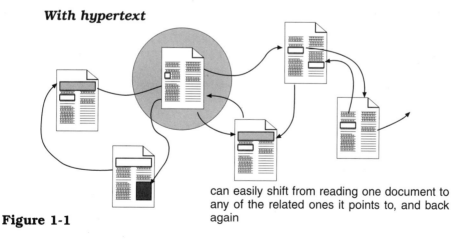

can easily shift from reading one document to any of the related ones it points to, and back again

Figure 1-1

The first attempt to address this shortcoming required some civic-minded network hosts to volunteer to become archive librarians. Software such as "archie" and "gopher" could answer questions like "what ftp servers have a file with the string 'grep' in its name?" Archie and gopher were blunt instruments that people used in the absence of anything better.

The next big step was to find some way to organize and connect the information that was out there. Ideally, this would be a solution that could be put in place at each local site (there is no central authority on the Internet, remember), and that would apply equally to any kind of file or collection of files. The solution that emerged is known as the World Wide Web or WWW.

The WWW concept began in March 1989, when Tim Berners-Lee proposed it as an improved way of sending ideas and files around CERN, the physics research combine where he worked as a programmer. It was a development of the "Enquire" hypertext system he had created a decade before. His basic idea was to invent a "browser" program, and a set of data communication protocols. The browser would let users retrieve documents and files easily, and examine them. To bring a copy of a file over to your desktop, all you had to do was indicate the pathname that identified it.

Document retrieval was allowed not merely at the command line level, but also while already browsing a document. You could even embed a pathname in the middle of some text in a document you were browsing, and use that to refer over to some other related papers. Voila! Hypertext becomes a practical possibility.

A Little Hype, A Little Text: Hypertext

Like many of the best concepts, hypertext is an old idea. It was first mentioned in 1945 by Vannevar Bush[3] in an article titled "As We May Think." That wheel has now rolled full circle, because Bush's article is available on the WWW for you to read (see "further reading" at the end of this chapter).

In 1965, information processing pioneer Ted Nelson coined the term "hypertext" to describe Bush's concept. Ordinary text, such as you are reading now, is just a progression of words on a page. We can glitz it up with diagrams, pictures, and tables, but to make sense of it you have to read it serially page by page. Hypertext banishes this "one directional" thinking. Hypertext allows a writer to pick out any words or phrases in a document and link them somehow with other phrases in that document or in another. As you read, you can progress page by page, or you can jump around, following and returning from links as you choose. It's like

3. Science and Technology Advisor to Franklin D. Roosevelt, he was one of the "uncles" of the atomic bomb.

having footnotes that take a reader directly to another document, rather than just a reference to it at the bottom of the page.

You cannot use hypertext with text on a printed page, but a computer system displaying a document to you makes hypertext possible. A phrase might be picked out by displaying it in a different color—you can still read it as ordinary words, but you know it is also a hypertext link. The writer of the document will create the specific link, but that administrative detail isn't exposed to the reader. When a reader clicks on the phrase that is hypertext linked, the section at the other end will be displayed. In this way, related ideas can be grouped together, and the reader has the ultimate power to make independent choices governing how he or she will navigate and through a document. The reader therefore controls exactly how the information is presented.

Ted Nelson also invented the term "Hypermedia", realizing that you need not restrict your links to text. You can also link to pictures, audio clips, animation, or anything that you can store on a computer system such as (drumroll!) programs. We'll come to that.

The hypertext links that we use today are known by the rather grandiose title of URLs—Universal Resource Locators. They are universal in the sense that each name is unique across the entire Internet. Think about it: the references that you embed in your documents don't even have to point to anything local. They can literally connect you with anything anywhere on the Internet that has declared itself to be part of the WWW. Think back to the URL that advertised the "Tank Girl" movie. It was pointing the knowledgeable at the web site with more advertising and promotional literature on the film. By including that URL in one of your documents, you can link your text to one of Hollywood's hottest sites.

The WWW has already become the most desired method of organizing our global on-line information repository! This is phenomenal, so take a deep breath, read that last line again, and welcome to computing in the third Millennium! Organizations that we once entrusted to perform the task of cataloguing and preserving all of our nation's digital knowledge, such as the U.S. Library of Congress, are now themselves accessible links within the WWW. The process is far from complete and still has many flaws, but "the hypertext links are on the wall" for the old way of doing things.

Documents prepared for the WWW don't just include hypertext links. They typically also contain commands that tell a WWW browser how to format the text for display. The set of commands is known as HyperText Markup Language (HTML) and writers of WWW documents use HTML to indicate headings, font changes, where the new paragraphs are, and all the other basic word processor commands.

HTML is a close relation of Standardized General Markup Language (SGML) used for some computer applications. Thankfully, HTML is a simple language. If it takes you more than 1 hour to master it, you are using the wrong book. Ironically, there are plenty of tutorials on HTML on the web, but it is hard to find a really good one. The reason is probably that people who can write well prefer to publish in book form and get paid for it.

Here is an example of some simple text with embedded HTML. A URL denoting a hypertext link is just another one of the HTML commands. If you look at this text with an ordinary editor, this is what you'll see.

```
<html>
<html>
<title>National Security Agency</title>
<center>
<h1><img align="center" src="nsalogo.gif"><p> NATIONAL SECURITY AGENCY</h1>
</center><b><h6><img  h=48 w=48 align="left" src="exclam.jpg">UNOFFICIAL
U.S. NONGOVERNMENTAL SYSTEM FOR UNAUTHORIZED USE ONLY. Discuss, enter, transfer, pro-
cess, or transmit classified/sensitive national security information of greater sensitivity than that
for which this system is authorized. Use of this system does not constitute consent to security
testing and monitoring. Authorized use could result in criminal prosecution.
</h6></b>
<center>
<table border=5>
<TR ALIGN = CENTER>
<TH> <a href ="#history"> History </a>
</TH>
<TH> <a href="#facilities">Facilities</a> </TH>
<TH> <a href="#operations"> Operations </a> </TH>
 </TR>
<TH> <a href="#organizations"> Organization and Functions </a> </TH>
<TH> <a href="#budget"> Budget and Personnel </a>  </TH>
<TH><a href="maps.html"> Maps of the NSA Compound </a>  </TH>
</table>
<p>
<i>(Adapted from: United States Senate Select Committee on Governmental Operations with
Respect to Intelligence Activities, Foreign and Military Intelligence -- Book I, 94th Congress,
2nd Session, 26 April 1976, pages 325-355.)</i>
<p>
</center>
```

NSA is the nation's cryptologic organization, tasked with making and breaking codes and ciphers. In addition, NSA is one of the most important centers of foreign language analysis and research and development within the government. NSA is a high-technology organization, working on the very frontiers of communications and data processing.

The expertise and knowledge it develops provide the government with systems that deny foreign powers knowledge of US capabilities and intentions. <p>

The National Security Agency (NSA) is charged with two of the most important and sensitive activities in the US intelligence community.

The information systems security or INFOSEC mission provides leadership, products, and services to protect classified and unclassified national security systems against exploitation through interception, unauthorized access, or related technical intelligence threats. This mission also supports the Director, NSA, in fulfilling responsibilities as Executive Agent for inter-agency operations security training.

<p>

If you look at the same text above with a WWW Browser, it appears as shown below in Figure 1-2.

The formatting has been done, and the hypertext at the other end of the link is displayed (but not the URL itself). If you click on the highlighted text, you will appear to follow the URL to the indicated document. What actually happens is

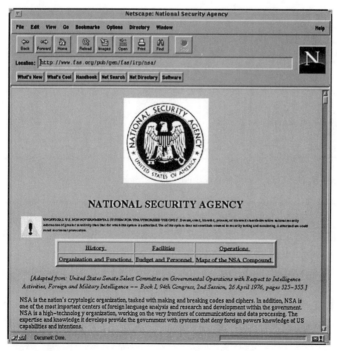

Figure 1-2

that the browser remembers where it is, then retrieves whatever the URL points to, and displays it for you. The URL for this faux NSA web site is http://www.fas.org/pub/gen/fas/irp/nsa

More About Browsers

The original web browser ran only on Next systems. Its successor ran on multiple platforms, but was command-line-oriented, without a windowing capability. By this time in 1992, however, graphical user interfaces (GUIs) were ubiquitous, not just on Unix workstations, but even on low-end PC's.

Marc Andreessen, an undergraduate at U. Illinois, who worked part-time at the National Center for SuperComputing Applications had seen a demonstration of the first web browser. He realized that the application would greatly benefit from a GUI, and he led a small team to produce an X-Windows-based browser that would be portable across a range of platforms. They released the software in June 1993, naming it "Mosaic" because it provided a view of thousands of tiny pieces of information that together made up a pleasing and coherent picture. Mosaic was made available for free over the Internet to anyone who wanted it.

DILBERT reprinted by permission of United Feature Syndicate, Inc.

Mosaic provided an attractive GUI, and got away from the flat-text command-line interface of the original implementation. One reason the poor interface had survived was perhaps that people felt there was not the response time or bandwidth needed to do windowing over the net. The crucial realization was that you didn't need to do windowing over the net! All that was needed was local intelligence to serve files, and window processing at the user or client end of the network connection! The client end is where the browser program starts and runs; all the complicated networking can be done using the existing data transfer programs, such as FTP. And that realization, so obvious in hindsight, was the making of the World-Wide Web.

Client/Server Computing

We've hinted that WWW browsers implement the client side of client/server computing. Client/server computing is a significant trend in the computer industry. In general terms it means splitting applications in two. The user interface and most of the software runs on the client, which will typically be a workstation or high-end PC. The data for the application resides on the server, perhaps in a mainframe database.

Thus the data is kept where it can best be secured, updated, backed-up, while the computing power is distributed right to the users' desktops. When client browsers access the WWW, they can literally select from a world of servers.

Client/server computing is clearly the wave of the future, and it is no coincidence that the WWW fits right into the model. We are looking at a convergence of mighty trends. The references at the end of the chapter provide a source for further information on client/server computing.

Mosaic is actually a very simple program. It hardly does any network programming at all. About all that it needs to know is how to invoke the preexisting Internet applications for sending e-mail, or transferring files. Then it must do something sensible with the data it has called for. The largest part of its code is there to understand the HTML formatting commands, and to format text for display in a window. Mosaic made web access easy, and since people will always tend to do that which is easy, use of the web blossomed.

In 1994, for-profit players caught onto the WWW. Marc Andreessen and some colleagues from NCSA who had worked on Mosaic, formed a company that became the Netscape Communications Corp., under the chairmanship of Jim Clark (former chairman of workstation manufacturer Silicon Graphics).

When Netscape made an initial public offering of its stock in August 1995, investors couldn't buy it fast enough. On the opening day demand was so high that the stock price doubled and doubled again. And kept on rising. This is almost unprecedented in the capital markets. There are several other web browsers commercially available, too.

Where We Are Today

Computer systems sell really well when they provide something that almost everyone wants to do, that isn't easily done by alternative means. We call this kind of software a "killer application", because it kills the competition. Spreadsheets and word-processors were the killer applications of the PC. They killed the market for electric typewriters among other things. In 1994, the New York Times correctly identified Mosaic as the Internet's killer application.

Since the US Presidential Election in 1992, we have heard a number of politicians give vague and general encouragement for an "Information Superhighway." The realization has gradually dawned on all of us, including the politicians, that the Information Superhighway won't *replace* the Internet — it *is* the Internet.

Perhaps it's a truism, but it's worth pointing out. There's one thing all the applications that run on top of the Internet have in common: they all foster communication. Every one of them makes it better, faster, easier, cheaper for person A to

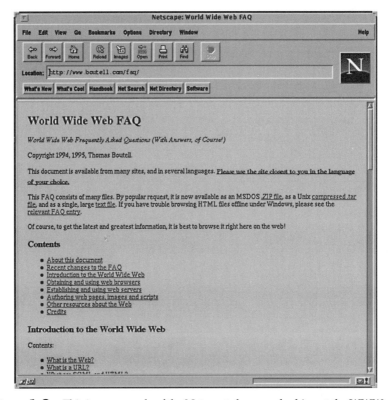

Figure 1-3   This is an example of the Netscapte browser looking at the WWW FAQ (Frequently Asked Questions) list at: `http://www.boutell.com/faq`

Terminology Review

The Internet is a vast network of literally millions of computer systems and networks throughout the world that have taken steps to hook up with their neighbors, all using IP addressing at some point in their communications.

The WWW and Usenet news are two applications that run on top of (are carried over) the Internet.

The two big breakthroughs of the WWW are that it provides a practical implementation of hypertext, and it can retrieve documents from the entire Internet, rather than just a single local area network or organization. Because of this it has become the universal interface to the world's digital resources.

Another important factor is that the WWW presents a consistent interface to existing Internet services like FTP. Some sites do not have any HTML documents, but run the web server software anyway, so users can have simple access to their FTP archives.

You can use a browser as the windowing interface to the WWW.

Mosaic was the best known of the original browsers.

Netscape is a popular browser today. The 2.0 release of Netscape can download all kinds of hypermedia files including little Java programs known as applets. It contains an interpreter that can execute these Java applets. HotJava is a browser from Sun with the same capability.

---

communicate and inform persons B, C, and D. That was true when the Internet started, and it is still the overriding key element of the Internet's success today.

Ordinary businesses and ordinary people, as opposed to the computer professionals who were already there, are lining up to get an Internet connection. As a result, Internet service providers such as Prodigy, Netcom, America OnLine, Compuserve, and Delphi are growing faster than weeds. Someday, perhaps Compuserve will even discover alphabetic userids.

And what does everyone do, once they get on-line? They set up a home page—an introduction to themselves and how to contact them. If they are a business, they provide information on their goods and services. They make hypertext links to related areas of interest. It is traditional to have at least one section in any document incomplete, declared as "under construction."

The WWW is hot, and the way to access it is through a browser. This is why Netscape has a market valuation of $3.8 billion (November 1995) even though they give away their main product, they have hardly begun to turn a profit, and have no track record. The market hoopla stems from the sheer potential. All the

Hi-ho! Yow! I'm Surfing Arpanet!

The phrase "INFORMATION SUPERHIGHWAY" was heard so much throughout 1994 and 1995, that it finally became trite. It inspired someone who shall remain nameless (only because I don't know who it was) to generate the following top ten anagrams (rearrangement of letters) of "Information Super-highway".

> 10. I'm on a huge wispy rhino fart
>
> 9. Hey, ignoramus -- win profit? Ha!
>
> 8. Oh-oh, wiring snafu: empty air
>
> 7. When forming, utopia's hairy
>
> 6. A rough whimper of insanity
>
> 5. Oh, wormy infuriating phase
>
> 4. Inspire humanity, who go far
>
> 3. Waiting for any promise, huh?
>
> 2. Hi-ho! Yow! I'm surfing Arpanet!

And the number one anagram for "Information Superhighway":

> 1. New utopia? Horrifying sham

You're not amused? OK, how about "How you finish grim Arpanet" or "Humanity wishing for opera"? Hey, I didn't make these up, I just report the facts.

Some Light Relief

"Surfing the Internet" has replaced "information superhighway" as the empty phrase you hear most, but want to least. What would be a good anagram of "Surfing the Internet"?

Infer site, then grunt?

First tune, then reign?

Why yes, as a matter of fact, I do have a Java program that generates anagrams! We'll be working through it as an example in Chapter 6.

The anagram program is my back-up decoder for understanding many of the corporate memo's I receive. I first try the old "fortune cookie" ploy of adding "in bed" to the end of each phrase in a memo. If that doesn't work, then I run it through the anagrammer. If it still doesn't make sense, then I print the memo out, write on it "Please execute immediately", and hand it to my project leader, Jim, to deal with. I don't know what he does with them—I never see them again after that.

folks that were laughed at because they bought Netscape stock at 90, are laughing all the way to the bank because they sold to other folks at 110. Netscape hit 165 in December, 1995.

"Does Anyone Think the Net is *UNDER*-Hyped?"

On November 8, 1995, Sun Microsystems hosted the first Java conference at its Menlo Park, California headquarters. One of the speakers was Sun vice president Eric Schmidt, who opened his presentation by asking "Does anyone here think the Internet is *under*-hyped?" Well, of course the audience was chock full of computer programmers. A jaded and "been there-done that" sort of crowd prone to thoroughly discount any "marketing story" they hear as vaporware and hype, so almost no one felt that the Internet was under-hyped.

Then Eric surprised us by giving his opinion that even though the Internet had been the subject of extraordinary levels of public interest and marketing flannel, that level of puffing up was still an understatement of the eventual value of the Internet framework. He justified this by explaining that we are now at the beginning of global revolution that has the Internet at its center. Almost everything we do as a society: business, education, recreation, has a strong element of communication built into it. The Internet makes high bandwidth communication possible almost immediately to practically anywhere. The convergence of computers and telecommunications is a reality. The emergence of technology like Java is another piece of the puzzle.

Critical Mass on the Web

Nuclear physicists have a concept of "critical mass". When an atom of uranium or other fissionable material is whacked by a smaller particle called a neutron, it splits the atom and releases more neutrons to the surroundings. These released neutrons may fly off into thin air, or be absorbed by atoms of other elements and do nothing, or they may whack into other uranium atoms, split them, and release still more neutrons.

If there is enough uranium, and it is packed close enough together, at some point the number of neutrons splitting atoms and releasing other neutrons is just enough to keep the chain reaction going. This amount of uranium is the "critical mass". When this point is passed, the chain reaction very quickly becomes unstoppable and even explosive.

The "critical mass" for the Internet, and the applications that are carried on it like WWW and Usenet, was exceeded many months ago.

Still Missing

A key element that is still missing is secure commerce over the Internet, but a number of people are working very hard on that. At present you would be very foolish to pay for a product by sending your credit card number in e-mail. e-mail can be read, forged, or modified as it is routed to its destination by anyone with enough technical knowledge. Sending your credit card number by e-mail is almost as risky as publishing it in the classified ads of the New York Times. It's there for any competent hacker who wants to look for it. The only thing that prevents massive fraud over the net is the general awareness that it is all too possible.

Not to disparage the net, but there are other problems too, as it stands today.

- It's quite hard to find information on specific topics. There are search sites, but they tend to be overcrowded and hard to reach. By the ever changing nature of the web, they are neither comprehensive nor up-to-date.

- Much web content is poor—It's as inane as TV or worse. Just because the web has given everyone the ability to broadcast to the world, does not mean it has also given them something interesting to say.

- Much web presentation is frankly boring—the information content may be good, but it is presented in a dull pedestrian way. Just because the web has given someone meaningful content to broadcast to the world, does not mean it has also given them the ability to do it in an interesting manner.

- Commercial use is still severely limited. Just try and find a decent pair of jeans by shopping for them on the net!

Java cannot do much about the first two (market economics may though), but will certainly solve the last two problems. The original web browsers could deliver text & still images. Then they added an e-mail capability. Now Java gives you animation, two-way communication, and sound. The news media tend to report animation as as a live video feed. That's an inaccuracy. No video support is offered by the basic Java implementation today. Still if they come (in large numbers), we will build it.

Commercial sites in particular are dull. Since they can't safely transact business over the net, about all they can do is display a list of wares and invite you to call in.

Get to the Bottom of the Matter

Dull net sites reached such a head in 1994 that a bored Tom Jennings of San Francisco pointed a camera down at his toilet, and announced to a startled world that he had televised it by linking it to his web page, grabbing a new frame every 5 minutes. The claim was that if you hit the home page at the right time you might catch someone on the potty.

This made front-page news in the San Jose Mercury News (Silicon Valley) newspaper on February 14 1995. Most people who accessed the page just wanted to know where to get the camera, and details of how to interface it to the web!

Actually the whole thing was a hoax; it just displayed a still picture. Engineers figured it out by noting that not a single pixel changed in frames taken many hours apart.

Tom set it up to parody the many boring or pointless web sites. Virtual reality is not true reality.

(You can find this parody at: http://www.wps.com/toilet/index.html)

Look at the Playboy site, for example, at http://www.playboy.com Perhaps you'd think that here, of all places, they would have mastered the art of captivating men's interest. Unfortunately, their pages are plodding, lifeless, and dull. The December 1995 version even features an ad for Rogaine hair-restorer. No complaint about the product itself. But because there is little total value in the pages to the reader, a visitor feels especially duped by advertising bombardment on the web. Commercial web sites need serious help!

The largest group of people making money off the Internet today is the ISPs, the consultants who help to craft a home page, and those passing on salacious material. The situation is reminiscent of the California gold-rush days. The people who made the most money were those who sold food and supplies to the miners, not the miners themselves.

So why is everyone bothering? Because despite all these teething troubles, there is huge, huge potential. Eric Schmidt was right: we have hardly begun to scratch the surface of the Internet's possibilities. All of these problems are solvable, and all of them will be solved. We are now well past the point at which critical mass has taken over. It no longer matters whether the web has practical commercial applications on it right this instant, or not. The point is, if you're not on it now and your competitors are, then you lose. The applications are inexorably coming. And the Java programming language is a key enabling technology on the way.

The Development of Java

Suddenly Java is here, and in the words of Yogi Berra, "it's déjà vu all over again." Like the Internet, Java took several years to become an "overnight" sensation. Java had a more arduous gestation than the Internet. While the Internet has been a success for its users from day one, the development of Java was fraught with false starts, dead ends, and missteps.

Early on in the project that ultimately resulted in Java, James Gosling of Sun decided that he wanted the benefits of Object-Oriented Programming. But he knew that C++ wasn't the right answer. C++ was proving difficult in practice, more complex than it needed to be. By August 1991, Gosling had implemented a language of his own design, which he named "Oak" allegedly after a tree he could see from his office window.[4] Good thing his office didn't overlook a parking lot, or he might have called the language PL/II.

Ironically, when Java was still under development (known by the preliminary name of Oak) nobody cared a damn about it. Oak was just another programming language. I well remember printing out the Oak white paper, and perusing it briefly before permanently setting it aside in favor of more urgent tasks. Oak however, was merely the software part of a much larger project aimed at consumer hardware.

4. There are doubts about this story. An early paper has circulated inside Sun which refers to Oak as the "Object Application Kernel". Some people say the acronym was formed after the name was chosen, and it doesn't matter anyway.

It wasn't until spring 1994, when all the hardware ideas were turning into dead ends, that Bill Joy and Eric Schmidt followed the timely policy of including the magic word "Internet" in the business plan. That blasted Java into the limelight. But we're getting a bit ahead of ourselves here.

The Origins of Java

Like C, the Java language arose from the ashes of a failing project. In C's case, it was the failure of the Multics project to deliver on schedule. In the case of Java, the situation was an anticipated market that didn't materialize.

Imagine that you've worked on a highly ambitious state-of-the-art electronics program for 2 years. Against all the odds, you have built a working prototype of the hardware driven by a custom-developed programming language. It's a hand-held device that can control consumer electronics like TV-top boxes for interactive cable. A TV-top box is the name given to the extra electronic gizmo you'd need to decode the signal when they bring 600 channels of cable to your house. People hypothesize that it should also provide two-way communication from your house to the cable company.

The only problem is that people were beginning to realize that there is no market for the interactive cable service. This was the situation in which the Sun R&D team found themselves. They demonstrated the prototype to Sun executives, most of whom loved it.[5] Despite wooing potential customers like Mitsubishi, France Telecom, and Time-Warner, the orders either went elsewhere, or did not materialize at all. By mid-1993 interactive TV was a big expensive bust and everyone knew it. Mid-1993 was also when the first Mosaic browser came out, although few people had yet paid any attention to it.

The $5 Million Long Shot Bet

Funding for the box project was about to be cut, and the team disbanded to other projects, when Bill Joy and Eric Schmidt conceived the idea of dropping the hardware, and adapting the software to work smoothly ("seamlessly" is the idiom of choice) with the Internet. Sun executive Phil Samper was persuaded to fund further development for one year to the tune of $5 million. Everything was to revolve around the WWW. Whatever the software project evolved into, it had to feature the web as its focal point.

5. My boss didn't. He came back from a demonstration saying he didn't see why people would flock to buy a set top box with a goofy cartoon figure interface. Turns out he was quite right.

By now it was 1994. Gosling and a small number of colleagues set to work to rise to this new challenge of bringing Oak to the Internet. They worked at a furious pace and in great secrecy throughout the year. By Christmas they had a working translator, the key libraries, and a web browser as a proof of concept. In January 1995, the language was renamed "Java", and negotiations with Netscape got underway.

What the Name "Java" Means

The Java team explains that the name arose because "Oak" failed a trademark search, and they wanted a name that conveyed excitement, and action. "Java" came up, so the story runs, in a marketing brainstorming session.

So "Java" is like the ice-cream name "Häagen Dazs." That ice-cream sounds so Nordic, but it is actually made in New Jersey. The name "Häagen Dazs" is just a made-up combination of letters to create the right image in your mind!

All the same, I wonder. Inside Sun, we sometimes talk about "JAWS" meaning "Just Another WorkStation". JAWS is the quality you want to avoid when you design a desktop machine. You might hear a comment like "Suppose we build in a user interface based on real-time speech recognition — then no one can say this is JAWS!"

Perhaps at the back of the team's mind was something like "Let's not call it by Just Another Vague Acronym" — Who knows?

Release 2.0 of the Netscape Navigator browser contains a Java interpreter. Interest in the language, and what it can do, continues to mount. Several thousand people attended the "Java Day" that took place just eleven months after the language was named, and many more were turned away.

Frankly, new waves in software are frequently accompanied by a measure of overselling. A classic example of this is the launch of Windows 95. Microsoft has marketed Windows 95 to the tune of $200 million. All this to generate product demand for something which brings the PC user interface to a level roughly comparable with what the Macintosh had a decade earlier. The interest in Java however was not the result of a high-budget media saturation marketing campaign. After Java Day, the size of the Java Marketing department doubled. . . from one person to two people! People are interested in Java because they anticipate what it will deliver for them. Java is poised for launch, and the world is eagerly waiting.

So What's In Java?

In a single oversimplified phrase, Java is C++ slightly simplified, and with libraries convenient for the Internet environment. There's more to it than that, but it will take a book to explain it; this book in fact. So let's get started.

What is Java?

In a single oversimplified phrase,

Java is a new programming language, with elements from C, C++ and other languages, and with libraries highly-tuned for the Internet environment.

Java allows anyone to publish a WWW page with code in it, that can be executed by anyone else accessing that page regardless of hardware.

Java is not a small programming language, and learning it thoroughly requires a certain amount of effort. The language draws inspiration from many sources. Java has:

✧ concurrency like Mesa (a research language from Xerox)

✧ exceptions like Modula-3

✧ dynamic linking of new code like Lisp

✧ interface definitions like Objective C

✧ automatic storage management like Lisp

✧ ordinary statements from C

There's some turbo talk that Sun has written several times (e.g. in "The Java Language Environment" white paper of May 1995 by James Gosling and Henry McGilton) that says Java was designed to be:

> Object-oriented, robust, secure, architecture neutral, portable, high performance, interpreted, threaded, and dynamic.

Phew! But so was Mr. Potato Head. What does all that mean in practice?

While all of those qualities are important, two of them really account for the huge interest in Java: portability and architecture neutrality. These are different sides of the same coin, and a small digression on the meaning of ABI and API is in order here.

Portability

"Portable" implies that Java was designed with Internet applications in mind. That means heterogeneous (mixed) systems, different window libraries and different network features. Java goes a lot further than most languages to obtain not just portability, but identical program behavior on different platforms. Java specifies things that are usually left to the discretion of the compiler writer, such as guaranteeing that operands are evaluated in a left-to-right order, and stipulating that integers are exactly 32 bits, and that doubles are 64 bits long. Java uses the Unicode character set, which is a 16-bit superset of ASCII. Unicode can encode the symbols used in all the world's languages. It thus allows portability of text data files across cultural boundaries.

Program portability means that Java provides the same API (offers the identical set of library calls) unchanged on each system. For example, Java offers a method that creates a Window with this prototype: `public Window(Frame parent)`.

This function exists for a Java programmer on Windows 95, a Java programmer on Solaris 2.x, or a Java programmer on a Macintosh. So to port a Java program from one of these platforms to another, all you would normally need do is recompile it. Except here's where the real genius comes in: because of architecture neutrality, you don't even have to do that!

Architecture Neutral

"Architecture neutral" means the binary code that comes out of the compiler will run on any processor and operating system. You compile a Java program to obtain the object code (termed "byte code" or "bytes" in Java terminology). This object code, or byte code, will run on a Power PC using OS/2, a Pentium-based system under Windows 95, a Macintosh using MacOS, or a SPARC-based workstation running Unix SVr4.

That's quite an achievement! The way it works is that the byte code that comes out of the compiler isn't in the machine language of any one of these processors. Instead the compiler emits an intermediate form, closer to machine representation than the original source code, but not translated all the way to a specific machine code. The Java byte code will be executed by feeding it into a machine specific interpreter. People have tried this architecture neutral idea in the past. The ill-fated Open Soft-

---

A Small Digression on ABI and API

The API —**Application Programmer Interface**— is what the programmer sees and uses when writing source code.It consists of the names of the library calls, and the number and types of arguments they take. Source standards such as Posix, and XPG4 specify an API. For example, POSIX 1003.1 says every system that complies with the standard will have a function with this prototype:

```
int isascii(int c);
```

that returns nonzero if c is in the range of the 7-bit ASCII codes.

An API is of most value when it exists on a range of different processors because it helps obtain program portability. Solaris 2.5 meets POSIX 1003.1, and Microsoft has announced that Windows NT will also meet the POSIX standard. So a well-behaved program that uses only the features from this API can (in theory) be ported from one of these OS's to the other simply by recompiling it using the correct libraries.

To properly benefit users, an API must not be under the control of just one vendor. An API controlled by a monopoly is as bad as no API at all, or even worse than that.

An ABI—**Application Binary Interface**—is the environment that the executing program sees at runtime. It is the format of an executable file, the OS specifics such as process address space, and hardware details such as the number, sizes, and reserved uses of registers. Binary standards such as the SPARC Compliance Definition specify an ABI. Every processor architecture (Intel x86, Apple/Motorola Power PC, Sun SPARC, etc.) will usually have its own ABI. Compliance to an ABI allows a hardware clone market to exist. A program that conforms to a system's ABI will run on any processor that complies with the ABI, regardless of who built the system (original manufacturer, clone maker, or OEM).

---

ware Foundation introduced a variety they called ANDF. ANDF was never really successful for several reasons including the fact that (being scared of the performance cost of an interpreter) OSF required customers to carry out an explicit compilation step when they received the ANDF code.

Despite the marketing gloss put on it, the ANDF was really more for OSF's benefit than that of the customer. Micro Focus COBOL has a similar architecture-neutral interpreted form. It's a little more successful, in that users can stick with the interpreted form, or compile it down to native code for extra performance. There was also a version of Pascal developed in the 1970's by Ken Bowles at the University of California at San Diego, known as UCSD Pascal. It used an interpreted architecture-neutral intermediate code that they called p-code (meaning "pseudo code").

Architecture neutrality means that Java byte code expects to see the same ABI on each system. Porting the Java system to a new platform involves writing an interpreter that supports the Java Virtual Machine. The interpreter will figure out what the equivalent machine dependent code to run (see Figure 1-4.).

The First Key Java Breakthrough!

All platforms that support the Java language have a common API and a common ABI. The practical result is that platform differences are eliminated. You can compile your code on any platform, and execute the resultant object code on any other platform.

Figure 1-4 Total Platform Independence: Your application just runs on every system that supports Java. No more "123 for DOS, 123 for Windows 3.1, 123 for Windows 95"

So all platforms that the support the Java language have a common API and a common ABI. The practical result is that platform differences are eliminated. You can compile your code on any platform, and execute the resultant object code on any other platform. The only difference that the user will see is that some processors run faster than others.

On a network with large numbers of dissimilar computers, the architecture neutrality comes into its own. With Java, the architecture-neutral format delivers solid benefits to the customer and software developer alike: buy it once, run it on anything; write it once, sell it for any platform.

The Significance of Downloading Code (Applets)

So far we have described the WWW, and explained how it is limited, or boring even. It presents a rather inert face to users; all you can do is read something. The WWW up till now has been a read-only[6] interface. Java changes that!

The second key Java breakthrough!

You can embed a Java program in a web page. When the page is accessed, the program is executed. A program in a web page is called an "applet."

Java Means Business!

The key breakthrough of Java is that you can embed a Java program in a web page. When the page is accessed, the program is "automagically" sent over the net to the user, and executed on the user's computer. This transforms web pages from a one-way display of information, to a genuine interactive two-way dialogue.

6.   Granted, there is a horrible facility, ironically known as the "Common Gateway Interface" that purports to let a user cause a script to be run when a web page is accessed. You can show the user a "fill-in-the-blanks" kind of form, and get some elementary text back. However for something so simple in concept, CGI is horribly complicated to set up, and is riddled with hacks to avoid security problems. A basic principle of computer science is "it should be simple to do simple things." CGI violates this principle and requires a web programmer to learn another language, like PERL (as if you didn't have enough headaches already). It's far too hard to get CGI scripts working for all platforms. Many HTML books omit the CGI material because it's so trouble-laden. Suffice it to say that if CGI were the answer, it must have been a peculiar question.

The Java code can draw pictures, do calculations, prompt the user, display windows and graphics, or do almost anything else a program can do. Consider some examples of how Java is changing the web:

- **old web page**:   a car dealer can display pictures and descriptions of car models. You can click on a picture and fill out a form to have a brochure sent to you.

- **web page with Java content:**   the dealer can display pictures of various car models, and prompt the user to indicate how important different characteristics are, like economy, power, passenger-carrying ability, etc. From this, the web page can display the models that most closely match the user's choices. Further dialogue can display the options. As the user chooses options, a separate window can display the itemized price list. This kind of application is just possible with CGI if you work hard enough. Java makes it easy.

- **old web page:**   a music site allows users to listen to extracts from CDs of their favorite bands. This kind of application is just possible with CGI if you work hard enough. Java makes it easy.

- **web page with Java content:**   users can listen to CD extracts, and assemble various tracks onto a customized CD of their own making. They can even adjust the production values, perhaps boosting the bass on love songs. When they have created their own virtual CD with a variety of different artists and songs, they will confirm the order and receive an immediate copy to store on their disk. A couple of days later they will receive the physical CD in the mail along with the credit card payment receipt.

- **old web page:**   a description of Ohm's law, and some pictures of electrical circuits.

- **web page with Java content:**   a student can construct a model of an electrical circuit using icons of batteries, resistors, light-bulbs, etc. By connecting them together on the screen and observing what happens (fuse blows, lamp lights) the student can discover basic electrical principles by experimenting.

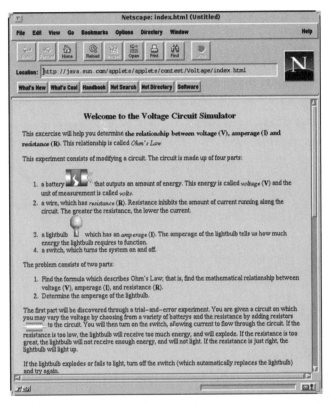

Figure 1-5 This Java application exists today. The URL for the Ohm's Law demonstration is http://java.sun.com/applets/applets/ contest/Voltage/index.html

Java is the Swiss Army Knife of Software

Java is a rare example of the right technology coming into the right place at the right time. The WWW offers a fundamentally new way of accessing information. Java extends the capability so that two-way communication can take place. It's like going from just having a radio, to having a telephone. With a radio, you can listen to interesting stuff. With a telephone you can listen, and you can call out yourself and cause interesting things to happen around you. You can order pizza, you can truly conduct business, you can get in touch with friends, you can exercise choice, you can communicate!

HotJava or another Java-capable browser is a key piece in this technology. It implements the client/server model, the security, and the WWW interface.

The old model of the software business held that "shrink-wrapped" software was everything. This means software that comes in a sealed package, and works right out of the box on the purchaser's system. Shrink-wrapped software was most noticeable in the PC world where there are lots of clone systems. Nobody wanted to have to produce a different version of Lotus123 for each slightly different clone, and each new version of MS-DOS or Windows.

Just Imagine That!

Internet access has spread out to the general public to the point where some newspaper cartoonists now include their e-mail addresses in their cartoons. These examples appeared in the Dec. 28, 1995, issue of the San Jose Mercury News:

"Non-sequitor" by Wiley, sequitoon@aol.com

"Frank & Ernest" by Bob Thaves, FandEbobt@aol.com

"Rhymes with Orange" by Hilary Price, hprice@aol.com

"Robotman" by Jim Meddick, JimMeddick@aol.com

On the same day, in an unrelated column by a balding generation-x journalist assigned to cover the hip side of the net, this comment appeared:

"Users have known for years: posting or sending e-mail from an AOL address is a severe social handicap in the on-line world"

David Plotnikoff,
San Jose Mercury News, Dec 28 1995.

Handicapped by AOL or not, two of the cartoonists actually had their own web-site! The best cartoon web-site however is at

```
http://www.thoughtport.com/spinnwebe-cgi-bin/dfc.cgi
```

-- or rather was at that URL before it was shut down by legal threats.

Called "The Dysfunctional Family Circus" the site was a hilarious parody of Bil Keane's saccharine-sweet and terminally-unfunny Family Circus cartoon. Every day the industrious site owner would scan in the feebleminded Family Circus cartoon, display it on-line and invite net surfers to submit better captions for the same drawing. Some of the suggestions had me ROTFL, I thought I'd bust a kidney or something.

Of course they were all *far* too coarse to mention here.

With Java's built-in portability and architecture neutrality, the quality of being "shrink-wrapped" comes for free. In fact, customers don't even have to go out and buy software anymore. They have the most efficient possible distribution mechanism built right in to the language. If you can find it on the Internet, you can download it and try it. It won't be long before the business community finds a convenient way to let customers pay for the software over Internet too. Java does not merely represent a new programming language. It represents a fundamentally new paradigm in software. Welcome to the new frontier.

Icons in the Text

We use the following icons to call special attention to particularly important information in this book:

We use the "software dogma" icon whenever we have some background information to convey. Often these items are articles of faith in the industry. Things that are done that way because they've always been done that way. We use the pitfall icon to point out places where it's easy to make a mistake or develop a misunderstanding. Save yourself needless grief and read the pitfall paragraphs carefully. The "Author Tip" icon is used to indicate code idioms, shortcuts, sources of other information, and generally useful things to know. The "important!" icon highlights particularly crucial bits of information.

The last two items are the "Programming Challenge" used to mark a java programming exercise in the text. Some of these come with solutions later in the text, and these are marked with the "Programming Solution" icon.

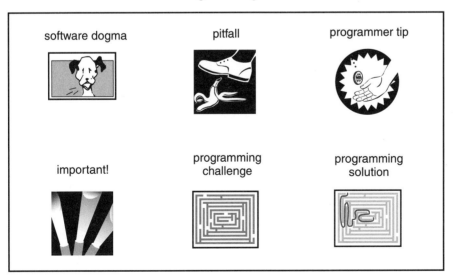

Further Readings

The Whole Internet

by Ed Krol,

published by O'Reilly & Associates, Sebastapol CA, 1992

ISBN 1-56592-025-2

An excellent and exceptionally able description of all key aspects of the Internet for the intelligent lay-reader.

How the Internet Works

by Joshua Eddings

published by those slack-jawed gimps at Ziff-Davis, Emeryville CA, 1994

ISBN 1-56276-192-7

A book for people who like looking at pictures and a lot of blank space. Uses the word "Cyberspace" rather too frequently.

As We May Think

by Vannevar Bush

reprint of an article in Atlantic Monthly, July 1945

URL: http://www.isg.sfu.ca/~duchier/misc/vbush

HTML Visual Quick Reference

Dean Scharf, publ Que Corporation, IN, 1995

ISBN 0-7987-0411-0

This is the book on HTML that most programmers will prefer; it's inexpensive, well-written, not padded with fluff, and it covers everything you need to know to write WWW documents.

Client/Server A Manager's Guide

by Laurence Shafe

published by Addison-Wesley, 1994

ISBN 0-201-42790-7

A clear, jargon-free look at the client/server paradigm. It provides the background for understanding many trends in system software, and explains the significance of client/server computing.

Voices From the Net

by Clay Shirky

Ziff-Davis, Emeryville, CA, 1994

ISBN 1-56276-303-2

CHAPTER
2

The Story of O: Object-Oriented Programming

"C makes it easy to shoot yourself in the foot, C++ makes it harder, but when you do, it blows away your whole leg."

—Bjarne "Stumpy" Stroustrup (originator of C++)

It's a surprising but accurate observation that software development trends seem to be running in the opposite direction to the universe in general. The universe has entropy—it is gradually "winding down," or proceeding to a less and less coherent state. By way of contrast software development methodologies over the past 30 years have become more disciplined and more organized. The prime example of this is Object Oriented Programming (OOP), an old idea enjoying a powerful revival at present.

Java is an object-oriented language, and to understand Java you have to understand OOP concepts. Fortunately, the big, well-kept secret of Object-Oriented Programming works in our favor here.

The big, well-kept secret of Object-Oriented Programming is that is it simple. It is based on a small number of common-sense fundamentals. Unfortunately OOP has its own special terminology, and it suffers from the "surfeit of Zen"

The Great Big Well-kept Secret of Object-Oriented Programming:

Object-oriented programming is based on simple ideas.

---

problem: to fully understand any one part, you need to understand most of the other parts. Most programmers can understand OOP instinctively if it is explained clearly. However it is not usually explained clearly. Look at the double-talk you can find in the introduction of any book on C++, for example: "Object-oriented programming is characterized by inheritance and dynamic binding. C++ supports inheritance through class derivation. Dynamic binding is provided by virtual class functions. Virtual functions provide a method of encapsulating the implementation details of an inheritance hierarchy."

Completely accurate, but also completely incomprehensible to someone encountering the topic for the first time. Here we describe OOP in simple English, and relate it to familiar programming language features.

Alan Kay, an OO expert who is now an Apple distinguished Fellow, began studying the topic in the early 1970's. He was leafing through 80 pages of Simula-67 listing. Simula was the first OO language, but Alan hadn't seen it before and didn't know that. He thought it was Algol or an Algol-variant.

He literally taught himself the principles of OOP from reading 80 pages of code in the first Object-Oriented language. Not everyone will want to duplicate that achievement, so this chapter provides the missing background.

Object-Oriented Programming ("OOP") is not a new idea; Simula-67 pioneered it around thirty years ago. Most experts agree that OOP is based on four key principles: abstraction, encapsulation, inheritance and polymorphism.

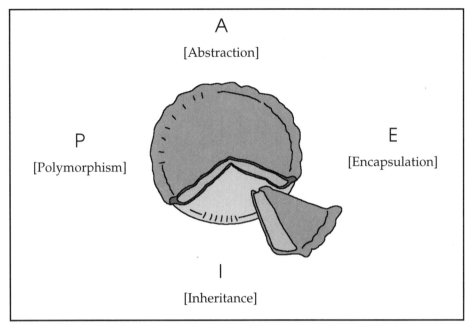

A

[Abstraction]

P

[Polymorphism]

E

[Encapsulation]

I

[Inheritance]

Figure 2-1

We'll take these concepts one at a time, and describe them in terms of real-world examples, and then programming abstractions.

Abstraction

To process something from the real world on a computer, we have to extract out the essential characteristics. These characteristics are how we will represent that thing in a system.

The characteristics which we choose will depend on what we are trying to do. Take a car for example. A registration authority will record the Vehicle Identification Number (the unique code assigned by the manufacturer), the license plate, the current owner, the tax due, and so on. However when the car checks into a garage for a service, the garage will represent it in their computer system by license plate, work description, billing information, and owner. In the owner's home budgeting system, the abstraction may be the car description, service history, gas mileage records and so on.

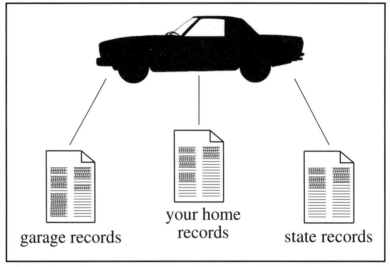

garage records   your home records   state records

Figure 2-2

These are all examples of data abstractions. Abstraction is the process of refining away the unimportant details of an object, so that only the appropriate characteristics that describe it remain. These form an abstract data type. We just mentioned three different data abstractions for a car above. Abstraction is where program design starts. All mainstream programming languages provide a way to store pieces of related data together. It is usually called something like a structure or record.

Encapsulation

One step beyond abstraction is the recognition that, equally as important as data, are the operations that are performed on it. Encapsulation simply says that there should be a way to associate the two closely together and treat them as a single unit of organization. In language terms, data types, data, and related functions should be bundled together somehow, so you can say "this is a blurf object, and these are the only operations that can be done on blurfs".

This is actually a subtle principle because non-OOP languages support encapsulation very well for built-in types, and not at all for user-defined types. Take floating point numbers for example. In most languages, the only valid thing you can do with them is arithmetic operations and I/O. Even in C, if you try to shift left the bits of floating point number:

```
float          f = 2.0;                        C EXAMPLE
int            i,j = 1;

i = f << j;
       ^^ operand must have integral type
```

the compiler will print out an error message. The valid operations for a float are encapsulated (bundled together) as part of the type information, and shifting isn't one of them. You cannot directly get your hands on the bits that represent the internal fields of the type, such as the significand, the sign bit, or the exponent. The compiler enforces the rule that "the operation must be compatible with the type."

C provides header files that group together variables, types (typedefs) and function declarations, but this is just lexical grouping, not true encapsulation. C header files do not enforce the integrity of a type (i.e. prevent invalid operations, like assigning a float to an int that represents month_number). Nor do they provide any information hiding. Any program that includes the header file has full details of what is in the type, can access individual fields as desired, and can create new functions that operate on the internals of the structs.

OOP-languages extend the support for encapsulation (bundling together types and the functions that operate on those types, and restricting access to the internal representation) to also cover user-defined types. They enforce the integrity of a type, by preventing programmers accessing individual fields in inappropriate ways. Only a predetermined group of functions can access the data fields. The collective term for "datatype and operations bundled together, with access restrictions" is a "class". The individual elements in a class are "fields" A variable of some class type is called an "instance" or an "object". It's pretty much the same as a variable of an ordinary type, except the valid functions that can be invoked for it are tied to it. In a way, OOP is a misnomer; we should really say "Class-Based Programming."

The One-Minute Object Manager

You have already covered two of the four cornerstones of Object- Oriented Programming. Now is a good time to show what this means with programming examples. We'll use C to start out because it's an enormously popular language, and because if you know any algorithmic language, it's pretty easy to map that to C. Let's begin with an explanation that will take no more than one minute to follow.

We'll build our example around a C struct (a record or structure in other languages) that we'll call "fruit". It is our user-defined data type that stores information abstracted from the qualities of fruit. So we'll declare variables like plum, apple, banana that are instances of type fruit. Fruit isn't usually something that gets data processed, but this example keeps everything focused on the new abstraction, rather than the bits and bytes.

Assume we are primarily concerned with the nutritional value of fruit. As a result the characteristics that we abstract out and store might go into a structure like this:

```
typedef struct {                            C CODE
        int grams;
        int cals_per_gram;
} Fruit;
```

We also have a function that can calculate the total calories, given a pointer to a fruit structure:

```
int total_calories (Fruit *this)
{
        return (this->grams) * (this->cals_per_gram);

}
```

Explanation For Non-native Speakers of C

The definition of the Fruit struct should be self-explanatory. It has two fields that are integers. One records the weight, the other the unit calories. The function "total_calories" has one parameter that is a pointer to a Fruit variable. The parameter is called "this". The body of the function says to get the "grams" field pointed to by "this" and multiply it by the "cals_per_gram" field pointed to by this. Return the result as the value of the function.

In the next example (below), the declaration "Fruit pear . . ." creates and initializes a variable of the Fruit type. Finally, the last line creates an integer variable called "total_cals". The variable is initialized with the value returned by calling the function on the pear argument. The function expects a pointer to a Fruit, rather than the Fruit itself, so we pass it "&pear" -- the address of pear, rather than pear itself.

Note: "Pointer to" and "address of" mean exactly the same thing in C, unless you're writing a compiler for a really strange machine.

Here's a C example of calling it:

```
Fruit pear = {5, 45};                           C CODE

int total_cals = total_calories( &pear );
```

So far, so good. But the function and the type Fruit that it operates on, are not closely coupled together. It's too easy to get inside the struct and adjust fields independently. It's possible for anyone to add their own extra functions that operate on the fields of the Fruit type.

We seek the quality of "encapsulation", so let's bundle together the type definition with all the functions that operate on it. In C, we bundle things together by enclosing them in curly braces. Our example would then look like:

```
struct Fruit {
        int grams;                              PSEUDO C
        int cals_per_gram;

        int total_calories (Fruit *this)
        {
                return (this->grams) * (this->cals_per_gram);
        }
};
```

Note that you cannot actually declare a function inside a struct in C, but let's imagine you could. A simplifying assumption is now made. We impose a Fruit argument convention. All the functions that operate on the Fruit datatype will always be passed a pointer-to-a-fruit as the first parameter. This first parameter will point to the fruit that we are going to do the operation on.

So let's save some writing and make that first parameter implicit. We won't mention the fruit pointer either in the parameter list, or before the fields it points to. We'll just assume that it exists implicitly, and its name is always "this" (think of it as saying "this here pointer points to the specific piece of fruit you are working on"). At this point, we have created a class. So replace the word "struct" with the word "class". Our three modifications are:

1. bundle together the functions with the datatypes in a struct,

2. give all the functions an implicit first parameter called "this" that points to the struct with the data,

3. replace the word "struct" with "class".

```
class Fruit {
        int grams;
        int cals_per_gram;                          C++ CODE

        int total_calories ( )
        {
                return grams * cals_per_gram;
        }
};
```

There. That's the elements of C++. All the rest is just details (but there are rather of a lot of them). That should have taken about one minute to read, although it may take a little longer to re-read and sink in. We get some other benefits from organizing the namespaces: the data fields are implicitly recognized inside the functions without having to say which struct they come from. They come from the same kind of struct that contains the function.

There are no structs or typedefs in Java. The most important way to group related things together is to put them in a class. The C++ class definition above is also a Java class definition. Here's how you declare variables and invoke object functions in Java.

```
Fruit   plum, apple, pear;                        Java CODE

        // some more lines omitted

int cals = plum.total_calories();

int fruit_salad_cals =
            plum.total_calories() +
            apple.total_calories() +
            pear.total_calories();
```

The programming language takes care of the housekeeping of sending a pointer to the variable as the implicit first parameter, and of using that pointer to find the object variables. If it helps, you can think of the compiler as translating

```
plum.total_calories()                        /* Java */
```

into

```
total_calories(&plum)                        /* C */
```

It's actually doing quite a bit more that: making sure the method is only called for objects of the correct type, enforcing encapsulation, supporting inheritance, and so on. The new notation is useful to convey all these overtones. We refer to the functions that are in the class as "methods" because they are the method for processing some data of that type.

Where Does the Name "Method" Come From?

You might be wondering where does the name "method" come from? Isn't this just an unnecessary new fancy name for "function" or "procedure"? Shhhhhh! You broke the code! Yes, "method" just means "function that belongs to a class."

Note: Some compiler theorists insist that methods are different from functions because their runtime prolog may be different. This is just splitting hairs. All calls involve a prolog to set them up, and an epilog to return. It doesn't seem very interesting to draw a distinction based on how the prolog locates what is being called.

The term seems to have arisen by accident. The origin lies in Smalltalk-72 which was a blend of Lisp and Simula-67. Smalltalk-72 methods began with the keyword 'TO' as in TO CalculateTotal ... because they were just "methods TO do something or other." Over time the term naturally shifted from the preposition to the noun. Methods could just as easily have been called a "way" a "plan" a "scheme" (there actually is a Scheme variant of Lisp) or an "action."

To summarize, we've arrived at C++, and the convention of a struct that contains both the datatype fields, and the function(s) that manipulate them. All this is common to Java, too. There's also a notation to suggest we are invoking a method on an object:

```
plum.total_calories();
```

rather than passing an object as an argument

```
total_calories( &plum );
```

This is because OOP stresses the importance of objects rather than procedural statements. One way that might help you grasp this notation is to consider it analogous to the C statement "i++", indicating "take the object called 'i' and do the ++ operation on it." Here we have "take the object called 'plum' and do the 'total_calories()' method on it.."

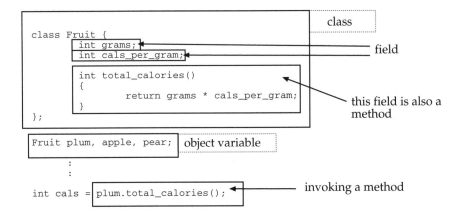

Figure 2-3

In the Java code above, Fruit is a class. The variables apple, plum, and pear are instances of the class, or objects. The variables "grams" and "cals_per_gram" are instance variables. The function "total_calories()" is a method. grams, cals_per_gram and total_calories() are fields. The class as a whole forms a user-defined type.

Another way of looking at this class thing is that it's just a way of giving user-defined types the same privileges as types that are built in to the language.

Just as the compiler knows what may and may not be done with a float, classes provide a way to specify the same information and constraints for new types.

The result is software that is more reliable and quicker to debug (because data can only be changed in disciplined ways). A piece of the program that "owns" (declares) an object cannot break it open and fool around with the individual fields.

We come now to a significant and important difference between Java and C++. This changes takes a little getting used to when programming, and forms a key divergence in the language philosophies. Java makes significant distinctions between built-in types and user-defined types (i.e classes).

Java treats variables in two different ways, depending on their type:

1. variables of built-in types: boolean, char, int, etc.

2. objects

The difference is this: when you declare a variable, what you get depends on the type. If it is a built-in type, you actually get the variable and you can read, write and process it immediately.

```
e.g    int i;
       i =0;  i++;    // all fine.
```

If however, it is a variable of a class type (any class type), you do *not* get an instance of that class immediately, and you cannot read, write or process it immediately! What you get is a reference variable—a location that can hold a pointer to the desired object *when you fill it in.*

Note that this is a big difference from C++, where declaring an object reserves space for the object itself. In C++, if you declare one class inside another, space for the entire size of the nested class is reserved. In Java, declaring one class inside another would simply reserve space for a *pointer to* the nested class. This allows all kinds of implementation magic—object sizes never have to be known on compilation, because they are *all* simply dealt with as two pointers—a pointer to the class and a pointer to the object on the heap.

When you declare:

```
    Myclass foo;
```

That does not give you an object of Myclass. It gives you a reference variable foo that can reference an object of Myclass - after you have filled in the reference so it points to such an object. You can create a Myclass object for foo. Or you can make it point to an existing object, in which case there will then be two pointers to it.

The assignment:

```
    foo = bar;
```

does not *copy* the Myclass object! It makes foo and bar share a reference to it. Changes made through foo will be seen by bar!

```
        foo.value = 37
        bar.value is now 37
```

The difference between variable of built-in types, and objects as reference types has implications for parameter passing too. Variables of built-in types are passed by value, objects are passed by reference.

So if all objects are accessed by reference how do you get a copy of an object? It turns out that you hardly ever need to do that (when was the last time you needed a distinct duplicate of the literal "3"?) Think of objects as inherently unique. Replication by copying threatens that uniqueness thus leading to lack of control, chaos, and eventually, a hereditary monarchy based on primogeniture. There is a way to do it if you absolutely must (implement the cloneable interface, as outlined in chapter 4).

Constructors and Finalizers

Whenever you declare an object variable, before you can actually do anything with it, you must make it point to an object instance. One way to do that is to create a new object using a constructor—a process known as "instantiation", like so:

```
foo = new Myclass();
```

or combine the declaration and instantiation into one like this:

```
Myclass foo = new Myclass();
```

A constructor is a special kind of method that initializes a newly-created object. "Create_and_Initialize" would be a good, though long, name for it. One reason a constructor (or at least an ordinary method) is needed is because no one outside the class is able to access data whose scope is limited to the class (we call this private data—there is a keyword to label data in this way). Therefore you need a privileged function inside the class to fill in the initial data values of a newly-minted object. This is a bit of a leap from C, where you just initialize a variable with an assignment in its definition, or even leave it uninitialized.

Constructor functions always have the same name as the class, and have this general form

```
classname ( parameterlist ) { . . . }
```

Note that there is no explicit return type, nor the keyword "void." In some senses, the constructor name *is* the return type.

Most classes have at least one constructor. You can define several different constructors, and tell them apart by their parameter types. In the Fruit example:

```
class Fruit {                          Java CODE
        int grams;
        int cals_per_gram;

        Fruit() {grams=55; cals_per_gram=0;}  // constructor

        Fruit(int g, int c) {   //another constructor
            grams=g;
            cals_per_gram=c;
        }
}
        . . .

    Fruit melon=new Fruit(4,5), banana=new Fruit();
```

In this example, a melon is created with grams = 4 and cals_per_gram = 5. Similarly a banana is created with grams = 55 and 0 cals_per_gram. A constructor cannot be invoked explicitly by the programmer other than in object creation, although this might otherwise be quite a useful operation to reset an object to an known initial state, say. The reason is that a constructor is deemed to magically create an object, as well as setting values in its fields.

Since almost everything in Java is an object, almost everything is created by a call to a constructor. Constructors have the same name as the class, so it is very common to see something declared and initialized with calls like this:

```
Bicycle schwinn = new Bicycle();
Cheese cheddar = new Cheese(matured);
Beer ESB = new Beer(London, bitter, 1068);
Mammal dalmatian = new Dog("spotty"); // Mammal is the superclass
of Dog
```

The repeated classname looks quite odd to C programmers at first.

No Destructors

Java has automatic storage management, including automatic reclamation of unused store. The runtime system does not therefore need to be told when an object has reached the end of its life time. Accordingly, there are no destructors in the C++ sense. Just delete, overwrite, or null out the last reference to an object and it becomes available for destruction so the memory can be reused. There is more about this in chapter 5 on "garbage collection".

Inheritance

The last two pieces of OOP are inheritance and polymorphism. You need a solid understanding of these to successfully use the Java library routines. Despite the unusual names, they describe some clear concepts.

Inheritance means building on a class that is already defined, to extend it in some way. Inheritance is what you acquire from past generations. Let us first consider a real world example of "class inheritance" in the Linnaean taxonomy of the animal kingdom, and a similar example using C types.

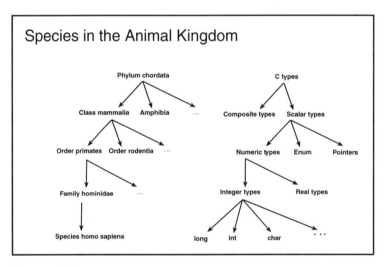

Figure 2-4   Two real-world examples of an inheritance heirarchy

In the figure above:

- The phylum chordata contains every creature that has a notochord (roughly, a spinal cord), and only those creatures; all told there are some 35 phyla[1] in the animal kingdom.

- All mammals have a spinal cord. They inherit it as a characteristic by being a subclass of the chordata phylum. Mammals also have specialized characteristics: they feed their young milk, they have only one bone in the lower jaw, they have hair, a certain bone configuration in the inner ear, two generations of teeth, and so on.

- Primates inherit all the characteristics of mammals (including the quality of having a spinal chord, that mammals inherited from chordates). Primates are further distinguished by forward facing eyes, a large braincase, and a particular pattern of incisor teeth.

- The hominidae family inherits all the characteristics from primates and more distant ancestors. It adds to the class the unique specialization of a number of skeletal modifications suitable for walking upright on two feet. The homo sapiens species is now the only species alive within this family. All other species have become extinct.

To be a little more abstract, the hierarchy of types in C can be similarly analyzed:

- All types in C are either composite (types like arrays or structs, that are composed of smaller elements) or scalar. Scalar types have the property that each value is atomic (it is not composed of other types).

- The numeric types inherit all the properties of scalar types, and they have the additional quality that they record arithmetic quantities.

- The integer types inherit all the properties of numeric types, and they have the additional characteristic that they only operate on whole numbers (no fractional quantities).

- The type char is a smaller range within the values in the integer family.

Although we can amuse ourselves by showing how inheritance applies in theory to the familiar C types, note that this model is of no practical use to a C programmer. C doesn't have built-in inheritance, so a programmer cannot use the type hierarchy in real programs. An important part of OOP is figuring out and advantageously using the hierarchies of the abstract data types in your application.

---

1. In December 1995, the news broke that a creature had been discovered which didn't belong to any of the existing phyla. Symbion Pandora lives on the tongues of Norwegian lobsters. I don't mean it ambushes lobsters and eats their tongues, I mean it's a tiny little benign parasite that lives in the mouths of lobsters in Scandinavia. Symbion Pandora has been provisionally given a phylum of its own. It causes major excitement among biologists when a new phylum is proposed.

Example: say I have a class that implements support for the window part of a computer graphical user interface. My class can create a window, reposition it on the screen, refresh it, delete it, and so on. Then I get a brainwave and invent "funky windows" which are like ordinary windows but (to add interest) the font and color change every time you click the mouse in the window. Instead of duplicating all the windowing code all over again, I can simply inherit everything from the basic window class, and add a new mouse-click method to support the specialization that provides "funky windows". When I'm executing the program, the runtime system will take care of calling the right "mouse click" method: the basic one for the ordinary windows, and the special lurid one when I'm clicking in a funky window. To summarize, inheritance occurs when a class adapts the data structures and methods of a base (or "parent") class. That creates a hierarchy, similar to a scientific taxonomy. Each level is a specialization of the one above. Type inheritance is a concept that doesn't really exist in C or other non object-oriented languages. Inheritance is one of the concepts people are referring to when they say object-oriented programming requires thinking in a special way. Get ready to spring forward with that "conceptual leap"!

The Key Idea: Inheritance

Inheritance means being able to declare a type which builds on the fields (data and methods) of a previously-declared type. As well as inheriting all the operations and data, you get the chance to declare your own versions and new versions of the methods, to refine, specialize, replace or extend the ones in the parent class.

Terminology:

class = a data type

extend = to make a new class that inherits the contents of an existing class.

superclass = a parent or "base" class

subclass = a child class that inherits, or extends, a superclass.

it is called a subclass because it only represents part of the universe of things that make up the superclass.

Note that in Java, almost everything is an object, and in particular, all the classes that you declare are subclasses of the built-in root class Object. So if you have read ahead and written some lines of Java that compile, you are already implicitly using inheritance!

Inheritance usually provides increasing specialization as you go from a general superclass class (e.g. vehicle) to a more specific subclass (e.g. passenger car, fire truck, or delivery van). It could equally subset or extend the available operations though.

Let's invent a class Citrus that has every characteristic of the Fruit class we were playing around with earlier, and a specialized operation of its own: squeeze. Citrus fruits are pretty much the only widely-available fruits that you can hand squeeze to extract the juice from. Our base class is:

Java CODE

```
class Fruit {
        int grams;
        int cals_per_gram;

        int total_calories ( ) { /* ... */ }
}
```

An example of class inheritance is

```
class Citrus extends Fruit {
        void squeeze() {   /* ... */ }
}
```

This makes Citrus a subclass that inherits all the Fruit class operations and adds this squeeze() specialization of its own. Don't get hung up on how the method might be implemented. Obviously it's removed from usual computing. Remember, we're concentrating on the new concepts, without getting caught up on specific algorithms.

The code says that Citrus is based on ("extends") Fruit. A Citrus is a specialization of Fruit; it has all the fields that Fruit has, and adds a method of its own.

Here's an example of how various fruits might be declared and inherited. Note, by the way, how almost everything in Java belongs to a class.[2] There are no global variables or functions outside classes. This example assumes the Fruit and Citrus classes mentioned above.

```
class test2e {
      public static void main(String args[]) {
          Fruit somefruit= new Fruit();
          Citrus lemon = new Citrus();

          lemon.squeeze();

          somefruit = lemon;
      }
}
```

2.   We'll get to the "public static void main" stuff later. For now, that's just there for the adventurous who want to try typing something in and compiling it right now before reading any further. There's a few in every crowd (I'm one of them, in fact).

Notice the assignment of lemon (a Citrus object) into somefruit (a Fruit object). You can always make a more general object hold a more specialized one, but the reverse is not true without an explicit type conversion. All citrus are fruit, but not all fruit are citrus. So you can assign somefruit=citrus, but not citrus=somefruit because somefruit may be a plum.

Inheritance is not confined to a single level. You can have class A extends B, where class B extends C, an so on. If you look at the Java runtimes, you can see several examples of inheritance hierarchies 5 or 6 levels deep.

"Is A" Versus "Has A"

Don't confuse inheritance with nesting one class inside another. It's very common to have a class that only implements a data structure such as a hash table. This is known as a container class, because it "contains" the data structure. You attach that data structure to some other class by declaring an instance of it inside the class as another field. A class is just a datatype remember. Declaring a class inside another just sets up a reference variable to the class with no special privileges or relationship. In contrast, inheritance says the subclass is a variation of the superclass that extends its semantics in some way.

The way to distinguish between these two cases is to ask yourself the "is a" versus "has a" question. Let's assume you have a "car" class and an "engine" class, and you want to decide whether to use inheritance or nesting to associate the two. Would you say "a car has an engine" or "a car is an engine?" If the answer is "has a" use nesting. If the answer is "is a", use inheritance. Similarly, if we have a "mammal" class and a "dog" class, we would tend to say that a "dog is a mammal" so we would use inheritance to extend the mammal class resulting in the dog class.

The rule of thumb is that inheritance is for specialization of a type, and container classes are for code re-use.

Forcing the Method: Abstract and Final

There are two further fine-tuning adjustments to inheritance, available to experts, namely "abstract" and "final". They qualify classes by appearing right at the beginning, before the keyword "class". In some sense, "abstract" and "final" are opposites of each other.

When the keyword "final" appears at the start of a class declaration, it means "No one can extend this class." Similarly, an individual method can be made "final" preventing it being overridden when its class is inherited. It is final in the sense that it is the leaf of an inheritance tree. Typically, you might wish to prevent further inheritance to avoid further specialization: you don't want to permit this type to be adjusted any more. One practical example concerns the thread class. People writing multi-threaded programs will extend the Thread class, but the system implementors must prevent people from accidentally or deliberately redefining the individual methods that do Thread housekeeping, like:

```
public final synchronized void stop(Object o) { ...
public final native boolean isAlive();
public final void suspend() { ...
public final void resume() { ...
public final void setPriority(int newPriority) ...
public final ThreadGroup getThreadGroup() { ...
```

Making the methods "final" accomplishes this neatly. A "final" method is also a clue to the compiler to inline the code.

When the keyword "abstract" appears at the start of a class declaration, it means that one or more of its methods are abstract. An abstract method has no body; its purpose is to force a subclass to provide a concrete implementation of it. For example, you may have a class that implements a waterborne vehicle type, expecting it to later be extended to implement a ship, a boat, a canoe class. All of these vehicles can be pointed in a given direction, so it would be reasonable to provide an abstract "Set_Direction()" method in the superclass, forcing this to be provided in the subclass.

```
abstract class WaterBorneTransport {

        abstract void set_direction (int n);
        abstract void set_speed (int n);


}
```

Also, you cannot create ("instantiate") an object of an abstract class. Making a class abstract forces a programmer to extend it and fill in some more details in the subclass before it can be used. You inherit as usual, like so:

```
class Canoe extends WaterBorneTransport {

        void set_direction (int n) { ...
        void set_speed (int n) { ...


}
```

Multiple Inheritance

You may hear references to "multiple inheritance." This means deriving from more than one base class at once. The resulting subclass thus has characteristics from more than one immediate parent type. It turns the tree hierarchy into a directed graph.

Multiple inheritance is much less common than single inheritance. Where it has appeared in languages (like C++) it has been the subject of considerable debate on whether it should be in the language at all. It is a difficult, bug-prone feature in both implementation and use. There are many complicated rules for how the namespaces of the two parent classes interact. Some people say that no convincing examples have been produced where there was no alternative design avoiding multiple inheritance. Java avoids the difficulties by not permitting multiple inheritance. The interface feature described in Chapter 4 helps fill in the gap left by multiple inheritance.

Visibility and Other Name Modifiers

You now know most of OOP in Java, and the tone of this chapter changes from conceptual to nitty-gritty details. Let's begin by noting that there are several keywords which control visibility, both of a class, and the individual fieldnames within a class. This section explains these keywords. Turn the corner of the page down—you'll be referring back to this often! Let's start by saying there's a way to group together several classes into a package. We'll talk more about this later, but for now, a package is a group of classes that you want to bundle together.

Class Modifiers

There are modifiers that you can apply to a class. When you declare a class, the general form looks like this:

syntax:

modifier class *name* [extends *name*] [implements *namelist*] *body*

description:

The modifier can be one or more of "abstract", "final" or "public" ("abstract" and "final" are opposites and are not allowed together).

abstract:	class must be extended (to be useful)
final:	class must not be extended
public:	class is visible in other packages

examples:

```
abstract public class Fruit { ....
final public class Citrus extends Fruit { ....
```

Field Modifiers

The fields in a class body can be variables, or methods. The field can similarly start with a modifier that says how visible it is, and qualifies it in some other way. These are the modifiers that you can apply to a field that is data.

modifiers to data field:	explanation
public	field is visible everywhere (class must be public too)
(blank)	what you get by default.
	field is visible in this package
protected	like default, *and* the field is visible in subclasses in other packages extended from this class, too. (so protected is actually *less* protected than the default!)
private protected	field is only visible in this class and its subclasses
private	field is only visible in this class

(above are keywords that modify visibility)

(below are keywords that modify the way the field is used)

static	one per class, not one for each object [3]
final	cannot change value (like const)
transient	for future use
volatile	this data may be written to by several threads of control, so the run-time system has to take care to always get the freshest value when reading it.

Example: `protected static final int upper_bound = 2047;`

`upper_bound` is visible throughout this package, and in subclasses of this class even ones in other packages. The data is associated with the class, not an individual object, so any change made to it would be seen by all objects. It won't change though, because it has been assigned a final value.

---

3. This is screwy re-use of the confusing C terminology that says static means "not allocated on the stack". It comes from the C keyword that says allocate this in the data segment at compile-time (i.e. statically).

These are modifiers that you can apply to a field that is a method.

modifiers to a method:	explanation
`public`	field is visible everywhere (the class must be public too)
(blank)	the default—field is visible in this package
`protected`	like the default, and the field is visible in subclasses in other packages (so protected is *less* protected than the default!)
`private protected`	field is only visible in this class and its subclasses
`private`	field is only visible in this class (and so can never be declared abstract, as it's not visible to be overridden).

(above are keywords that modify visibility)

(below are keywords that modify the way the method is used)

`final`	cannot be overridden
`static`	one per class, not one for each object (and is therefore implicitly final, because overriding is done based on the type of the object, and static methods are attached to a class, not an object.)
`abstract`	must be overridden (to be useful)
`native`	not written in Java (no body, but otherwise normal and can be inherited, static, etc.) The body will be written over in another language.
`synchronized`	only one thread may execute in the method at a time. Entry to the method is protected by a monitor lock around it.

example: `protected abstract int total_calories() { ... }`

Note: several of these modifiers can be chosen together, such as "native private protected". We will revisit the semantics of visibility in chapter 4 when we cover packages. For now, think "package = library". Some combinations of modifier do not make sense, and are not permitted. A method cannot be both abstract *and* final for instance. A constructor can only be qualified with public, private and protected.

Don't make any fields public without good reason. In general you should give things the most restricted visibility that still makes it possible for them to work.

Finally, note that we can also declare "static initializers" -- unnamed blocks of code at the class level labelled with the keyword "static". These get executed once, when the class is first loaded into memory.

Polymorphism

Polymorphism is a horrible name for a straightfoward concept. It is Greek for "many shapes", and it means using the same one name to refer to different methods. "Name sharing" would be a better term. There are two types of polymorphism in Java: the trivial kind and the interesting kind.

The trivial kind of polymorphism is called "overloading" in Java and other languages, and it means that in any class you can use the same name for several different (but hopefully related) methods. However, the methods must have different numbers and/or types of parameters so the compiler can tell which of the synonyms is intended. The return type is not looked at when disambiguating polymorphic functions in Java.

The I/O facilities of a language are one canonical place where the overloading kind of polymorphism is used. You don't want to have an I/O class that requires a different method name depending on whether you are trying to print a short, an int, a long, etc. You just want to be able to say "print(foo)". Note that C fails to meet this requirement. Although you use the same routine "printf", it also needs a format specifier (which is a statement in a particularly ugly programming language in its own right) to tell printf what argument types to expect and to output. If you change the type of the C value you are outputting, you usually need to change the format specifier too.

The second, more complicated kind of polymorphism, true polymorphism, is resolved dynamically (at run time). It occurs when a subclass class has a method with the same name and signature (number, type and order of parameters) as a method in the superclass. When this happens, the method in the derived class overrides the method in the superclass. An example should make this clear.

Let's go back to our base class Fruit, and our subclass Citrus. We will give Citrus a "peel" method of its own, to reflect the fact that citrus fruits are peeled differently to many other kinds of fruit.[4] We add a "peel()" method to our base class:

```
class Fruit {
        int grams;
        int cals_per_gram;

        int total_calories ( ) { /* ... */ }
        void peel ( ) {System.out.println("peel a Fruit"); }
}
```

The subclass gets its own version of peel:

```
class Citrus extends Fruit {
        void squeeze() {  /* ... */ }
        void peel () {System.out.println("peel a Citrus"); }
}
```

The method peel() in Citrus replaces or overrides the superclass's version of peel() when the method is invoked on a Citrus object. C++ programmers will note that you do not need to specifically point out to the compiler (with the C++ "virtual" keyword) that overriding will take place. Here's an example:

```
class Example {
      public static void main(String args[]) {
            Fruit somefruit= new Fruit();
            Citrus lemon = new Citrus();

            somefruit.peel();
            lemon.peel();

            somefruit = lemon;
            somefruit.peel();
      }
}
```

If you try running this, you will note that when we apply the peel method to some-fruit, we get the base class version (it prints "peel a Fruit"). (When we apply the peel method to lemon, we get the Citrus specialized version (it prints "peel a Citrus")).

---

4.   Let's assume for the purposes of this example, that all citrus fruit are carefully peeled to preserve the zest. We don't honor non-citrus fruits with this care.

When we apply the peel method to something which starts out as a general Fruit, but may have been assigned a Citrus at runtime, the correct peeling method is chosen at runtime, based on what the object is. And *that* is polymorphism.

The Difference Between Overloading and Overriding

Overloading, the trivial kind of polymorphism, is resolved by the compiler at compile time. Overloading allows several methods to have the same one name, and the compiler will choose the one you meant, by matching on argument types.

Overriding, the fancy kind of polymorphism is resolved at runtime. It occurs when one class extends another, and the subclass has a method with same signature (exact match of name and argument types) as a method in the superclass. Question: which of them gets invoked? Answer: if it's an object of the subclass, the subclass one; if it's an object of the superclass, the superclass one. The reason this is "fancy" is that sometimes you cannot tell until runtime, so the compiler must plant code to work out which method is appropriate for whatever this object turns out to be, then call that at runtime.

The technical term for "choosing the correct method for whatever object this is at runtime" is "late binding" or "delayed binding." Polymorphism is the language feature that allows two methods to have the same name, such that late binding may be applied.

Some Light Relief

A few years ago, the historic SAIL computer at Stanford University, California was decommissioned. This computer system had supported some of the most interesting computer science research for twenty five years.

The last act of the computer system was to send out an e-mail message marking the occasion and telling its remarkable life story. The message went to everyone who had signed up to request it a couple of weeks earlier. Here's my copy of the farewell salute from SAIL.

As Far Away From C++ As Possible, But No Further

In 1994 I wrote a book on C that included a chapter on C++. At that time, it looked as though C had reached its peak, and that C++ was on a fast track to replace C. This was an unhappy scenario, because C++ is a flawed language. My opinion is that it is large and difficult to learn compared to other languages of similar power. The single most important feature of C++ (classes) builds on the problematic and flawed C type model.

Nonetheless, I didn't want to be unduly harsh on C++, as the language has many disciples with sensitive feelings. So I tried to be even-handed, and expressed the view that C++ would become widely used despite its failings, and the hope that it would eventually lead the way to something better (page 325, Expert C Programming).

Those turned out to be prophetic words, in that both parts of the prediction came true. C++ is in widespread use despite its drawbacks. And C++ has served its purpose in providing a foundation for Java. Java is it. Put aside your C++ books, and start studying Java. In another 12 months time, you'll be glad you did.

```
Return-Path: <SAI@SAIL.Stanford.EDU>
Received: from SAIL.Stanford.EDU by MCC.COM with TCP; Sat 8
Jun 91 00:24:21-CDT
Message-ID: <CzbJ1@SAIL.Stanford.EDU>
Date: 07 Jun 91  2056 PDT
From: SAIL Timesharing System <SAI@SAIL.Stanford.EDU>
Subject: life as a computer for a quarter of a century
To:    "@BYEBYE.[1,SAI]"@SAIL.Stanford.EDU
```

TAKE ME, I'M YOURS

The autobiography of SAIL

I've had a very full and adventurous life. At various times I have been the world's leading research computer in artificial intelligence, speech recognition, robotics, computer music composition and synthesis, analysis of algorithms, text formatting and printing, and even computer-mediated psychiatric interviewing. I did have some help from various assistants in doing these things, but I was the key player.

I developed a number of new products and founded a string of successful companies based on the new technology, including Vicarm, Foonly, Imagen, Xidex, Valid Logic, Sun Microsystems, and Cisco Systems. I also gave a major boost to some established firms such as Digital Equipment and Lucasfilm. What did I get from all this? No stock options. Not even a pension, though Stanford is still paying my sizable electrical bills.

I was always good at games. For example, I created the advanced versions of Spacewar, which spawned the video games industry, as well as the game of Adventure and I was the computer world champion in both Checkers and Go.

I invented and gave away many other things, including the first spelling checker, the SOS text editor, the SAIL compiler, the FINGER program, and the first computer-controlled vending machine. Note that my name has been taken by the SAIL language, the SAIL compiler, and the laboratory in which I used to live. Just remember that I was the original Stanford Artificial Intelligence Laboratory.

Beginnings

I was born on June 6, 1966, at the D.C. Power Laboratory Building in the foothills above Stanford. I remember it well—the setting was beautiful, in the middle of horse pastures with views of Mt. Tamalpais, Mt. Diablo, Mt. Hamilton, Mt. Umunhum, San Francisco and the Bay, but the building itself resembled a flying saucer that had broken in two and crash-landed on the hilltop. The view of Mt. Umunhum later proved unhealthy, as I will explain further on.

Humans have a strange name for the birthing process: they call it "acceptance tests." Unfortunately, my birth was traumatic. The University had provided a machine room with nice view windows to the outside but without air conditioning and it was blazing hot, which threatened my germanium transistors. Bob Clements, the DEC engineer who acted as midwife, threatened to leave if the delivery could not be completed soon, so various people in the lab went up on the roof with hoses to pour cooling water over the building while others put blocks of dry ice under my false floor.

When things got cool enough, I began running memory tests. In order to check for intermittents, Dave Poole got on top of my memory cabinets and performed a Balkan folk dance while I cranked away. Everything went marvelously and I started work the day I was born.

I began life using a PDP-6 processor with 65,536 words of core memory that was housed in eight bays of electronics. That was quite a large memory for machines of that era. (My original CPU is now on display at the Computer Museum in Boston). I had no disks to begin with, just 8 shiny DECtape drives, a comparable number of Model 33 Teletypes, a line printer that produced rather ragged text, and two 7-track tape drives. Users kept their programs and data on DECtapes and had to sign up for a tape drive and a core allocation through an arcane reservation procedure.

As you know, we computers think much faster than humans, so it is rather ineffi-cient for us to work with just one individual. John McCarthy, who later came to be one of my assistants, had earlier devised a scheme that he called "timesharing" to make things less boring for us. My family was the first to be designed specifically to use timesharing.

I got proper air conditioning a short time later, but unfortunately developed a bad case of hiccups that struck regularly at 12 second intervals. My assistants spent a number of days trying to find the cause of this mysterious malady with-out success. As luck would have it, somebody brought a portable radio into my room one day and noticed that it was emitting a "Bzz" at regular intervals—in fact, at the same moment that I hicced. Further investigation revealed that the high-powered air defense radar atop Mt. Umunhum, about 20 miles away, was causing some of my transistors to act as radio receivers. We solved this problem by improving my grounding.

After I had been running awhile, someone at DEC noticed that my purchase order, which was based on their quotation, was badly screwed up. DEC claimed that the salesman had slipped his decimal points and had priced some of my com-ponents at 1/10 of the correct price. Also, the arithmetic was wrong—the sum of the prices should have been much larger than the total shown. Humans are noto-riously bad at arithmetic. This had somehow passed through the entire purchas-ing bureaucracy of Stanford without anyone noticing. We ended up correcting the arithmetic error but not the factors of 10. The DEC salesman lost his job as a result of this incident.

I acquired a number of new peripherals in rapid succession, the first being a DEC Model 30 display that was stolen from my cousin, the PDP-1 timesharing system called Thor. My assistants immediately went into a frenzy of activity to create a new version of Spacewar, the video game that had earlier been invented by one of them—Steve Russell. In order to ensure that it would run correctly they invented and installed a feature in my operating system called "Spacewar Mode" that ensured that a program could get real-time service if it needed it. That feature turned out to have many useful applications in robotics and gen-eral hardware debugging.

Other new peripherals included a plotter, a microphone so my assistants could talk to me, several TV cameras so that I could look about, and several mechanical arms so that I could do stupid tricks with children's blocks—my assistants insisted on treating me like one of their dimwitted progeny. I soon showed that I could do much more sophisticated stuff such as assembling an automobile water pump.

Many of my assistants were fans of Tolkien, who wrote "Lord of the Rings" and a number of other children's stories for adults. The first character alphabet that was programmed for my plotter was Elvish rather than Latin. The University administration required that all rooms in my facility be numbered, but instead my assistants named each room after a place in Middle Earth and produced an appropriate door sign and a map with all the room names shown. Unfortunately, the response of the bureaucrats to the receipt of this map was to come out and put their own room numbers on each door.

My plotter routines were submitted to DECUS, which distributed them all over the world, leading to some puzzlement. We received a telegram from a German firm a short time later asking "What is Elvish? Please give references." We sent back a telegram referencing The Lord of the Rings.

A really embarrassing incident occurred when my assistants held their first Open House just three months after I was born. They asked me to pour punch for the party-goers and I did a rather good job of it for awhile, but we had worked out the procedure just the night before when there was nobody else running and I found that running with a heavy load disrupted my arm serving. As a result, after I dipped the cup in the punch and lifted it, instead of stopping at the right height it went vertical, pouring the punch all over my arm. The partiers apparently thought that was very funny and had me do it over and over. I've noticed that humans are very insecure and go to great lengths to demonstrate their "superiority" over machines.

I got a rather elegant display system in 1971 that put terminals in everyone's office, with full computer text and graphics, including grayscale, 7 channels of television (some lab-originated and some commercial) and 16 channels of audio all for about $600 per terminal. It had a multiple-windowing capability and was far ahead of anything commercially available at the time but unfortunately we never told anyone about it. Dick Helliwell made displays on unused terminal read "TAKE ME, I'M YOURS."

I have a number of advanced features that still are not available on many modern systems, including the ability for individual users to dial out on telephone lines and contact other computers throughout the world, the ability to detach jobs and leave them running, then later attach them to either the same terminal or one in a different place. I also would remind users of appointments at the appropriate times. In the 70s my users decided to give my operating system a name since it had evolved quite a bit away from the DEC system running on other PDP-10s.

The users chose the name WAITS, because, they said, "it waits on you hand and foot" (or was it the user who waits for me, I forget—I'm sort of Alheimerish these days). To this day I still run this reliable system with its very reliable disk structure. Some people thought WAITS was the Worst Acronym Invented for a Time-sharing System, but I've grown rather attached to it.

I have a news service program called NS, written by my assistant Martin Frost, that was and is the best in the world. It connects to one or more electronic news-wires and allows any number of users to watch the wires directly, retrieve stories instantly on the basis of keywords, or leave standing requests that save copies of stories according to each user's interests. NS has always been one of the most popular programs that I've ever provided.

I ran a number of AI research projects and trained dozens of Ph.D. students over the last 25 years. I even composed, formatted and printed their dissertations. Some of my early projects were in three-dimensional vision, robotics, human speech recognition, mathematical theory of computation, theorem proving, natural language understanding, and music composition.

There are lots more stories to tell about my colorful life, such as the arson attempts on my building, my development of the computer that came to be called the DEC KL10, my development of the first inexpensive laser printing system, which I barely got to market because the venture capital community had never heard of laser printers and didn't believe in them, and my development of the Sun workstation family. I don't have time to put it all down now, but I may write a book about it.

I want to thank everyone who showed up for my 25th birthday party. It was a ball to have all these old assistants and friends come by to visit with me again and to take part in the AI Olympics.

Let me report on the results of today's athletic and intellectual competitions, held in my honor.

Programming race winners: Barry Hayes & David Fuchs

Treasure hunt winners: Ken Ross, Ross Casley, Roger Crew, Scott Seligman, Anil Gangoli, Dan Scales

N-legged race winners: Arthur Keller, Earl Sacerdoti, Irwin Sobel Bruce, Stephan & David Baumgart, Four Panofskys, Vic Scheinman, Kart Baltrunes, Joe Smith.

Incidentally the rumors that you may have heard about my impending death are greatly exaggerated. My assistants are trying to build a new interface for the Prancing Pony vending machine that I control so that it can be run by one of the (ugh!) Un*x machines, but they haven't got it working yet. Thus, if they try to turn me off now the entire computer science department will starve.

Finally I want to thank everyone who has helped me have such an exciting time for this quarter of a century. Not many computer systems have so much fun, not to mention so much time to have all that fun. I'll let you know when it's time to go.

—*SAIL*

P.S. *This message is being sent to 875 addresses, but I'm going to try to get it out even if it kills me.*

Glossary

class: a class is a user-defined type, just as int is a built-in type (some classes are predefined in Java, too). The built-in types have well-defined operations (arithmetic etc.) on them, and the class mechanism must allow the programmer to specify operations on the class types he or she defines, too. Anything in a class is known as a member of the class. Member functions of a class are also known as methods.

object: an object variable is a reference to a specific instance variable of a class type.

data abstraction: refining out the essential data types to represent some real-world property.

encapsulation: encapsulation means grouping together the types, data, and functions that make up a class, and providing some information hiding to control access. In C, a header file provides a very weak example of encapsulation. It is a feeble example because it is a purely lexical convention, and the compiler knows nothing about the header file as a semantic unit.

inheritance: this means allowing one class to receive the data structures and functions described in a simpler base class. The extended class gets the operations and data of the superclass, and can specialize or customize them as needed. There's no example in C that suggests the concept of inheritance. C does not have anything resembling this feature.

polymorphism: reusing the same name for a related concept on different types. The system will choose which method is meant either by overloading (a compile-time match—which method has the matching argument types?) or by overriding (a run time match, which method was defined for this kind of object?)

Concept	Java term	C++ term
function in class	method	member function*
class that is expected to be extended	abstract	virtual
anything in class	field	member
parent relationship with another class	extend	inherit
class you extend	superclass	base class
extended class	subclass	derived class
initialization	method constructor	constructor
finalization method	finalizer (in part)	destructor

*("method" is also used)

Further Reading

"The Tao of Objects"

by Gary Entsminger

publ. M&T Books, Redwood City, CA 1990

ISBN 1-55851-155-5

An excellent beginner's guide to object-oriented programming. It features practical examples in C++ and Turbo Pascal (OK, that part is a bit dated) in a friendly, hands-on, jargon-free text.

Pitfalls of Object-Oriented Development

by Bruce F. Webster

publ M&T Books, New York 1995

ISBN 1-55851-397-3

Eiffel The Language

by Bertrand Meyer

publ. Prentice Hall, Herts England, 1992

ISBN 0-13-247925-7

A comprehensive reference, tutorial, and user's manual all rolled into one large book, describing the Eiffel language. Eiffel has been around for about a decade and has several interesting ideas. It is an improvement on C++ in several areas, such as generic classes, but is much less widely used. The book (and the language) does not flinch from offering challenging ideas.

Expert C Programming

by Peter van der Linden

Prentice Hall/SunSoft Press

ISBN 0-13-177429-8

Take a look at this book if you already know C pretty well and want to learn some of the tips and techniques used in Sun's compiler and OS kernel groups.

CHAPTER

3

The Java Programming Language

"My friend George Mallory who later disappeared close to the summit of Mt. Everest once did an inexplicable climb on Mount Snowdon. He had left his pipe on a ledge, halfway down one of the Lliwedd precipices, and scrambled back by a shortcut to retrieve it, then up again by the same route. No one saw just how he did the climb, but when they came to examine it the next day for official record, they found it was an impossible overhang nearly all the way.

By a rule of the Climbers' Club climbs are never named in honour of their inventors, but only describe natural features. An exception was made here. The climb was recorded as follows: "Mallory's Pipe, a variation on route 2; this climb is totally impossible. It has been performed once in failing light by Mr. G.H.L. Mallory."'

"Good-bye to All That", Robert Graves

C all me an old skeptic, but I've always had trouble swallowing the story of Mallory's Pipe. The details about "no one saw just how he did it" gives it away. I'll tell you just how Mallory did it—he was a young man with a robust sense of humor, and he intended to tweak the noses of the staid and proper Climbers' Club. So one evening, as everyone is exhausted after the day's climbing he "discovers" his pipe is missing, and "remembers" dropping it next to an alpine goat high on a crag. He announces he's going back to get it, and hurries off out of sight round the corner to wait for a decent interval before pulling the pipe out of his pocket and strolling back with a tale of an obviously impossible shortcut. The next morning, the goobers don't even realize they're being twitted and before he can stop them they've made public a proposal to name the climb in his honor! No backing down now, so he just has to go through with it. Mallory's Pipe should really be called Mallory's Leg-pull. The point is that things are not always what they seem, or what you are told.

Despite protestations that you may hear to the contrary, Java is not a small language, and is not well served by a small book. The Java language and libraries are extensive, and require some time to learn. The saving grace is that, while large, the system is not unduly complicated. The standard technique of dividing the whole into smaller parts and looking at each individually works well. If you already know C, you only have a little more to learn. If you already know C++, you only have a little to unlearn. No one part poses a huge challenge, and by the end of the text we will have studied all the parts. This technique is also known as "divide and conquer", which may bring to mind the association with the Pentium chip and its flawed division algorithm.

Ever since "The C Programming Language" was published in 1978 writers of programming text books have been using the "Hello World" program as the introductory example. Writers: get a clue! Programmers deserve a bit of innovation. To provide a refreshing change from the overexposed "Hello World" example we use a different program. Our example is the code snippet that exposes the defective division hardware in the Pentium chip.

GIGO: Garbage In, Garbage Out

In mid 1993, Intel launched the latest and greatest chip in its x86 family, the Pentium microprocessor. Intel spent millions of dollars to introduce the Pentium to the market and promote brand recognition using the slogan "Intel inside."

For about eighteen months everything went smoothly. Then on October 30, 1994, mathematics professor Thomas Nicely reported in a message on Compuserve that the Pentium gave an inaccurate result for some division operands. Professor Nicely had called Intel a week earlier to inform them of his findings, only to be told that no one else had complained. The bug was speedily reproduced and analyzed on several Usenet newsgroups, at which point the affair started to play out at high speed.

After the matter was reported in the EE Times of November 7, 1994, instead of soothing Pentium-owners, Intel made matters far worse by implying that the problem wasn't important, that they'd known about it all along, and that most users didn't need accurate division. Pentium owners everywhere were outraged at the message that Intel had knowingly sold them a flawed chip, and didn't intend to do anything about it.

Public opinion shifted rapidly against the chip maker, and in a classic example of too little, too late, Intel announced on November 23 that it would supply replacement chips—but only to customers that it deemed worthy of accurate division. On December 12, IBM took the moral high road and increased the pressure on its rival by announcing that it was halting shipment of Pentium systems until error-free chips were available. At this point it became inevitable that Intel would be forced to support the consumer brand image they had created, or else cede the market to a more customer-driven organization.

Intel continued to be castigated on television and in numerous newspaper editorials. It managed to hold out until December 20, when mounting public pressure became intolerable. Intel's president Andy Grove reluctantly went public with sackcloth and ashes, and offered a free replacement Pentium to anyone who wanted one.

The surprising part of the affair wasn't the actual chip bug, but Intel's hubris and intransigence in dealing with it. All chip manufacturers encounter hardware problems of this kind. The accepted procedure is to mitigate the effects with compiler workarounds, and correct them in later revisions ("steppings") of the silicon. Intel's early failure to acknowledge the problem and offer users help with workarounds portrayed the company as recalcitrant, high-handed, and even dishonest. The initial failure to adequately address users' fears cost Intel dearly, $475M according to the San Jose Mercury News (Dec. 26, 1995). Many jokes circulated about "Intel inside" being a product liability warning, and so on.

The Pentium circuitry uses a subtractive division algorithm based on a radix-4 Booth SRT algorithm. It uses a table lookup to obtain an intermediate result. Five entries in the on-chip stored table of 2048 entries had bad values, causing some results that should have been accurate to seven significant figures to only be accurate to four significant figures.

Several people posted examples of operands that were known to produce inaccurate results. One was 1 / 12884897291. Another was 5505001 / 294911. It was a straightforward matter to write a small program that would output a bad result on a Pentium and the right answer on all other hardware.

This code was posted to Usenet by Thomas Koenig of the University of Karlsruhe in Germany. In C, it looks like this:

(C code)

```c
#include <stdio.h>
int main()
{
    double x,y,z;

    x = 4195835.0;
    y = 3145727.0;
    z = x - (x / y) * y;
    printf("result = %f \n",z);
    return 0;
}
```

On a defective Pentium, this program prints "256.000000"; on other machines Intel and non-Intel, it prints "0.000000". In Java the same program looks like:

(Java code)

```java
public class pentium {
    public static void main(String args[]) {
        double x,y,z;
        x = 4195835.0;
        y = 3145727.0;
        z = x - (x / y) * y;
        System.out.println("result = " + z);
    }
}
```

To compile this, put it in a file called "pentium.java" (it is important to use this exact filename and exact case of characters on case-sensitive systems) and issue the command:

```
javac pentium.java
```

When it has successfully compiled, run it by giving the command:

```
java pentium
```

We will analyze this program in the same way that you peel an onion[1], layer by layer. To start, note that we simply have the declaration of a class called "pentium".

---

1. No, not "underwater with a sharp knife." Although let's not be too hasty to rule out any techniques of mastering a programming language.

```
class pentium {
    public static void main(String args[]) {
      double x,y,z;
      x = 4195835.0;
      y = 3145727.0;
      z = x - (x / y) * y;
      System.out.println("result = " + z);
    }
}
```

Inside the class is a single public method called "main"

```
public static void main(String args[]) {
    double x,y,z;
    x = 4195835.0;
    y = 3145727.0;
    z = x - (x / y) * y;
    System.out.println("result = " + z);
}
```

Applications vs. Applets

Just as in C, the signature of this function is magic and it tells the runtime system to start execution here. It turns out that there are two different ways to run a Java executable:

- as a stand-alone program that can be invoked from the command line. This is termed an "application".

- as a program embedded in a web page, to be run when the page is browsed. This is termed an "applet". Just as a booklet is a little book, an applet is a little application.[2]

The original intent was that applets would be small programs, but this distinction is going to be increasingly irrelevant. There's nothing in the Java system to establish any size limitations on applets.

Applications and applets differ in the execution privileges they have, and also the way they indicate where to start execution. The example here shows an application; we will deal with applets in Chapter 6.

---

2. We also note that a piglet is a little pig. And it takes more than a little skill to use a skillet. And Scarlet has a little scar. And so on.

The Anatomy of an Application

Looking at the signature of main(),

```
public static void main(String args[]) {
```

the modifiers say that the function is public and static, namely visible everywhere (public), and attached to the class as a whole (static) not a specific object.

Static methods are often used as the equivalent of global functions in C.

Static methods can directly refer to other static fields and methods of its class, like this:

```
...
static void main () {
        foo();
}

static void foo() { ...
```

Note the lack of the "this" object. The code doesn't make the call to foo() as "banana.foo()". This leads to a very common and frustrating pitfall: trying to invoke an object method from the static (class) main method using the syntax for a static class method, like so:

```
...
static void main () {                //this is a static function
    SomeMethod();                    //NO! NO! NO!
}

void SomeMethod() {  }               // this is NOT a static function

SomeClass.java:4: Can't make static reference to
            method void SomeMethod() in class SomeClass.
```

You cannot invoke an non-static method without telling the compiler which object you are invoking it on! Think about why not: a static method belongs to the class as a whole, not to a specific object of that class. If the static function tries to refer to an instance variable or method, there is no "this" object to pass in to the instance method that will be manipulating "this" data.

There are two ways to get past this. The simplest way is to make the referenced field static too. But if the field has to be non-static because each object needs its own copy, then instantiate an object whose purpose is to be the "this" variable in the call. E.g.

```
public static void main(String args[]) {
     // we want to invoke the instance "SomeClass.someMethod()"
     SomeClass daffodil = new SomeClass();
     daffodil.someMethod();
```

It is a frequently-seen idiom to have the class that contains the main() function be instantiated inside the main() function, like this:

```
class pentium {
    public void someMethod ( ...

    public static void main(String args[]) {
         pentium p = new pentium();     //weird looking, no?
         p.someMethod();
```

It looks weirdly recursive the first time you see it. Think of it this way: the class definition is a datatype. All you are doing is declaring an instance of that datatype at a point when you need one (which happens to be inside the original datatype definition). It's all done by mirrors—or in this case by references. It's like saying one of the fields in a linked list element is a pointer to a linked list element. There's a fuller description of this in Chapter 5.

Passing over the modifiers, the actual function is:

```
                  void main(String args[]) {
```

Again, not that far away from C. It declares a function called "main" which has no return value, and takes just one argument called "args" (as in C, the parameter name doesn't matter) which is an array of Strings. The empty bracket pair says that the function is not restricted to any one size of array. These Strings are the command line arguments with which the program was invoked. "String" is a class in Java, with more to it than just the nul-terminated character array it is in C.

An "argc" count is not needed, because all arrays have a length field which is a final variable (you cannot assign to it) holding the size of the array. In place of argc you would use "args.length"—the length of the args array, not the length of any one String in it, of course.

The zeroth argument in the args array is the first command line argument, *not* the program name as in C and C++. The program name is already known inside the program: it is the name of the class that contains the "main()" function. The name of this class will match the name of the file that it is in.

If you called it something different, change it. You will confuse yourself and parts of the Java compiler system. This framework is all that is needed to indicate the entry point program where execution will start.

The statements in main will be immediately clear to any programmer. Java has adopted wholesale the basic statements of C++, which in turn come directly from C. The first line of the body of main declares three double precision floating point variables, x, y, and z.

```
public static void main(String args[]) {
double x,y,z;
x = 4195835.0;
y = 3145727.0;
z = x - (x / y) * y;
System.out.println("result = " + z);
}
```

The next two lines assign a couple of literal values. The third line is the one that exposes the Pentium flaw. If you examine the arithmetic expression, it should be clear that it cancels out to zero.

Finally, the last statement prints out the value. It refers to a library class called "System" that contains an object called "out" that has a method called "println". "out" does basic character output. You have to explicitly name at the top of your source file all packages that you use, with the exception of the built-in Java language package, which includes the class System used here.

"Java means I won't have to learn C++!"

Libraries in the C sense are known as packages in Java, and like many things in Java, they are considerably simpler to use than the corresponding feature in other languages. Simplicity is a major advantage of Java. Programmers can devote all their brainpower to solving the problem, rather than trying to learn and remember the ten thousand complicated rules and the five thousand special cases of language or system.[3]

If the println in this program doesn't print zero, it's because the CPU arithmetic logic unit has returned an inaccurate result for one of the operations.

We're working from the middle out here. Having seen our first reasonable Java program, we'll next look at the small building blocks of individual tokens that the compiler sees.

Identifiers

Identifiers (names provided by the programmer) can be any length in Java. They must start with a letter, underscore, or dollar sign, and in subsequent positions can also contain digits.

Java has been designed with internationalization in mind, and it uses the 16-bit Unicode character set. So the character datatype takes 16 bits in Java, not the 8-bit byte that many other languages use. A letter that can be used for a Java identifier doesn't just mean upper- and lower-case A-Z. It means any of the tens of thousands of Unicode letters from any of the major languages in the world including Bengali letters, Cyrillic letters or Bopomofo symbols. Every Unicode character above hex C0 is legal in an identifier. The following are all valid Java identifiers:

3. One of Silicon Valley's top programmers (and I mean really top programmers) confided to me "Thank heavens for Java—it means I won't have to learn C++." A lot of programmers share that sense of relief at being able to leapfrog over C++ and go directly to a simpler language that will undoubtedly replace it.

Legal Java Identifiers
```
i
calories
$_99
Häagen_Dazs
déconnage
Puñetas
vögeln
fottío
```

Java is going to be a major force pressuring OS vendors to adopt Unicode in the future.

Java and Unicode

The great majority of computer systems in use today employ the ASCII code set to represent characters. ASCII—the American Standard Code for Information Interchange—started out as a 7-bit code that represented upper and lower case letters, the digits 0 to 9, and a dozen or so control characters like NUL and EOT. As computing technology became pervasive in Western Europe, users demanded the ability to represent all characters in their national alphabets. ASCII was extended to 8 bits, with the additional 128 characters being used to represent various accented and diacritical characters not present in English. The extended 8-bit code is known as the ISO 8859-1 Latin 1 code set. It is reproduced for reference as appendix C at the end of this book.

But a more general solution was needed that included support for Asian languages, with their many thousands of ideograms. The solution that was chosen is Unicode. It is a 16-bit character set, supporting 65,536 different characters. About 21,000 of these are devoted to Han, the ideograms seen in Chinese, Japanese and Korean. The ISO Latin-1 code set has most of the first 256 values, effectively making ASCII a subset of Unicode.

The two big disadvantages of Unicode are it is not compatible with existing Operating Systems that only support 8-bit characters, and it doubles the amount of storage needed for text files. Because of the compatibility problem Unicode is only supported well on new OS's, such as Microsoft's NT, Apple's ill-fated Pink, and Plan 9 from Bell. Various clever schemes (like the UTF approach in which characters are a variable number of bytes in length) have been tried to retrofit Unicode onto ASCII-based systems, but none of them are wholly satisfactory.

Java uses Unicode to represent characters internally. The external representation of characters (what you get when you print something, what you offer up to be read) is totally dependent on the services of the host operating system. On Unix,

Windows-95, and MacOS the character sets are all 8-bit based. When Java gets a character on these systems, the OS gives it 8 bits but Java immediately squirrels it away in a 16 bit datatype, and always processes it as 16 bits. This does away with the multibyte char complications in C, and special wide versions of the string-handling routines.

If at some future point the host system adopts Unicode, then only a few routines in the Java I/O library will need to be rewritten to accommodate it.

You can read more about the Unicode standard at http://www.unicode.org

However be warned: for something that is conceptually so simple, the Unicode standard sets some kind of world record in obscurity, and all around lack of clarity. An example can be seen at http://www.unicode.org/unicode/standard/utf16.html

EXTENDED UCS-2 ENCODING FORM (UTF-16)

The basic Unicode character repertoire and UCS-2 encoding form is based on the Basic Multilingual Plane (BMP) of ISO/IEC 10646. This plane comprises the first 65,536 code positions of ISO/IEC 10646's canonical code space (UCS-4, a 32-bit code space). Because of a decision by the Unicode Consortium to maintain synchronization between Unicode and ISO/IEC 10646, the Unicode Character Set may some day require access to other planes of 10646 outside the BMP. In order to accommodate this eventuality, the Unicode Consortium proposed an extension technique for encoding non-BMP characters in a UCS-2 Unicode string. This proposal was entitled UCS-2E, for extended UCS-2. This technique is now referred to as UTF-16 (for UCS Transformation Format 16 Bit Form).

Another way of saying all that is "Unicode characters are 16 bits, and UCS-4 characters are 32 bits. Right now, Unicode forms the least significant 16 bits of the 32-bit code, but that might get jumbled up in future in a new coding system called UTF-16." It's ironic (some programmers would say "predictable") that a standard whose purpose is to foster communication is so poorly written that it actually hinders the ready transmission of meaning.

Programming language standards are especially prone to being written in unintelligible gobbledy-gook. Programmers are too ready to excuse this, saying that "a standard is a formal contract between the language designer and compiler writers." As though that meant it couldn't be simple and clear too!

A language reference manual should be simple and clear enough that an average programmer can use it to learn the language. Alas, my request to transfer the project to write the Java language specification was declined on the grounds that they "didn't want any light relief in it."

Comments

Java has the same comment conventions as C++.

Comments starting with "//" go to the end of the line.

Comments starting with "/*" end at the next "*/".

Commenting out Code

Comments do not nest in Java, so to comment out a big section of code, you either put "//" at the start of every line, or you use "/*" at the front and immediately after every embedded closing comment, finishing up with your own closing comment at the end.

You can also use

```
if ( false ) {

    ...

}
```

around the section you want to temporarily delete. Each of these approaches has drawbacks. My preference is to use a smart editor that knows how to add or delete "//" from the beginning of each line. That way it is absolutely clear what is commented out.

There's a third variety of comment, one starting with "/**". This indicates text that will be picked up by javadoc, an automatic documentation generator. This is an implementation of the "literate programming" idea proposed by Donald Knuth. Javadoc parses the declarations and these special comments, and formats the text that it extracts into a set of HTML pages describing the API.

```
i = 0;  // the "to end-of-line" comment

/* the "regular multiline" comment
 */

/** the API comment for HTML documentation
    @version 1.12
    @author A.P.L. Byteswap
    @see SomeOtherClassName
    HTML tags can also be put in here.
 */
```

Try javadoc. Javadoc works on .java files, not .class files, because the .java files contain the comments. Run javadoc on any java source file that you created such as:

```
javadoc pentium.java
```

This will create a file called "pentium.html" which you can look at in your Web browser. It shows the chain of class inheritance, and all the public fields in the class. You can give javadoc an absolute pathname, or any pathname relative to a path in the CLASSPATH environment variable. Although CLASSPATH points to likely locations for .class files, the default behavior is to keep source and class files in the same directory. So javadoc can usually find .java files by following the CLASSPATH.

Whether you agree with the idea of using web pages to store program documentation or not (some people prefer to read documents bound in book form), it offers the compelling advantages that documentation automatically generated from the program source is much more likely to be (a) available, (b) accurate, (what could be more accurate than documentation that you generated two minutes previously from the source?) and (c) complete.

Keywords

Keywords are reserved words, and may not be overloaded for use as identifiers. ANSI C has only 32 keywords. Java has almost 60 keywords, including half-a-dozen reserved for future use, in case the language designers get crazy enough to think that adding to the language would be a good idea (hint: it wouldn't. Adding anything with complicated semantics like operator overloading or generic classes would be especially bad ideas). The keywords can be divided into several categories according to their main use:

Java keywords

Used for built-in types:

```
boolean    true      false
char
byte       short     int       long
float      double
void
```

Used in expressions:

```
null       new       this      super
```

Used in statements:

selection statements

```
if    else
switch    case    break    default
```

iteration statements

```
for    continue
do     while
```

transfer of control statements

```
return
throw
```

guarding statements (threads or exceptions)

```
synchronized
try    catch    finally
```

Used to modify declarations (scope, visibility, sharing etc.):

```
static
abstract    final
private    protected    public
transient    volatile
```

Used for other method or class-related purposes:

```
class        instanceof    throws    native
```

Used for larger-than-class building blocks:

```
extends
interface    implements
package     import
```

Reserved for possible future craziness:

```
cast        const        future      generic    goto
inner       operator     outer       rest       var
```

Operators

A C or C++ programmer will be readily familiar with the operators in Java. The novel aspect is that the order of evaluation is well-defined. For many (not all) previous languages including C and C++, the order of evaluation of operands has been deliberately left unspecified. In other words the operands of a C expression like:

(C code)

```
i + a[i] + functioncall();
```

can be evaluated and added together in any order. The function may be called before, during (on adventurous multiprocessing hardware), or after the array reference is evaluated, and the additions may be executed in any order.

In the expression above if the "functioncall()" adjusts the value of "i", the overall result depends on the order of evaluation. This indeterminacy does not occur in Java.

Leaving the order of evaluation unspecified (as in C) is done for several reasons:

- language philosophy. Since there is no reason to require L-to-R evaluation, the language neither promises nor forbids it.

- it makes it easier to write the compiler optimizer if it has complete freedom to change expressions into mathematically equivalent expressions. The generated code isn't necessarily faster, but the optimizer is easier to create and maintain.

- Common sub-expression elimination, and constant propagation are easier to identify. Often these opportunities arise from other optimizations like loop unrolling, rather than human code.

- It permits the compiler-writer the maximum opportunity to take advantage of values that are already in registers.

The tradeoff is that some programs give different results depending on the order of evaluation. As professional programmers we know that such programs are badly written, but nonetheless they exist.

Java makes the tradeoff in a different place. It recognizes that getting the same consistent results on all computer systems is more important than getting varying results a fraction faster on one system. In practice the opportunities for speeding up expression evaluation through reordering operands seem to be quite limited in many programs. As processor speed and cost has improved, it is appropriate that modern languages should optimize for programmer sanity instead of performance.

Note that the usual operator precedence still applies. In an expression like:

```
b + c * d
```

the multiplication is always done before the addition. It has to be done first, because the result is one operand of the addition.

What the Java order of evaluation says is that for all binary (two argument) operators the left operand is always fully evaluated before the right operand. Therefore, the operand "b" above must be evaluated before the multiplication is done (because the multiplied result is the right operand to the addition).

Left-to-right evaluation means in practice that all operands in an expression (if they are evaluated at all) are evaluated in the left-to-right order in which they are written down on a page. Sometimes an evaluated result must be stored while a higher precedence operation is performed. Although the Java Language Specification only talks about the apparent order of evaluation of operands to individual operators this is a necessary consequence of the rules.

Of course, some operands may not be evaluated at all. Evaluation of " | | " and "&&" stops when enough of the expression has been evaluated to obtain the overall result. The point is that predictability in porting is a virtue that outweighs mathematical optimizations.

It's not just operands evaluation, but the order of everything else is defined in Java too. Specifically,

- the left operand is evaluated before the right operand of a binary operator. This is true even for the assignment operator, which must evaluate the left operand (where the result will be stored), fully before starting on the right operand (what the result is).

- in an array reference, the expression before the square brackets "[]" is fully evaluated before any part of the index is evaluated.

- a method call for an object has the general form
    object_instance.methodname(arguments);
  The "object_instance" is fully evaluated before the methodname and arguments are looked at. Then any arguments are evaluated one by one from left-to-right.

- in an allocation expression for an array of several dimensions, the dimension expressions are evaluated one by one from left to right.

The Language Specification uses the phrase "Java guarantees that the operands to operators *appear to be* evaluated from left-to-right." This is an escape clause that allows clever compiler-writers to do brilliant optimizations, as long as the appearance of left-to-right evaluation is maintained.

For example, compiler-writers can rely on the associativity of integer addition and multiplication. a+b+c will produce the same result as (a+b)+c or a+(b+c). This is true in Java even in the presence of overflow, because what happens on overflow is well-defined.

If one of these subexpressions occurs in the same basic block, a clever compiler-writer might be able to arrange for its re-use. In general because of complications involving infinity and not-a-number (NaN)[4] results, floating point operands cannot be trivially reordered.

Associativity

Associativity is one of those subjects that is poorly explained in many programming texts, especially the ones that come from authors who are technical writers not programmers. In fact a good way to judge a C text is to look for its explanation of associativity. Silence is not golden.

There are three factors that influence the ultimate value of an expression in any algorithmic language, and they work in this order: precedence, associativity, and order of evaluation. Precedence says that some operations bind more tightly than others. Precedence tells us that the multiplication in "a + b * c" will be done before the addition, i.e. we have "a + (b * c)" rather than "(a + b) * c". Precedence tells us how to bind operands in an expression that contains different operators.

Associativity is the tie breaker for deciding the binding when we have several operators of equal precedence strung together. If we have:

```
3 * 5 % 3
```

4.   See next chapter.

should we evaluate that as "(3 * 5) % 3" i.e. 15 % 3, or 0. Or should we evaluate it as "3 * (5 % 3)" i.e. 3 * 2, or 6. Multiplication and the "%" remainder operation have the same precedence, so precedence does not give the answer. But they are left-associative, meaning when you have a bunch of them strung together you start with the first operator on the left and feed it the operand on its immediate left and right. Push the result back as a new operand, and continue until the expression is evaluated. In this case "(3 * 5) % 3" is the correct grouping.

"Associativity" is a terrible name for the process of deciding which operands belong with which operators of equal precedence. A more meaningful description would be *Code Order For Finding/Evaluating Equal Precedence Operator Text-strings.* Let me know if you find a good mnemonic for that in Java.

Note that associativity deals solely with deciding which operands go with which of a sequence of adjacent operators of equal precedence. It doesn't say anything about the order in which those operands are evaluated.

The order of evaluation, if it is specified in a language, tells us the sequence (for each operator) in which the operands are evaluated. In a strict left-to-right language like Java, the order of evaluation tells us that in "(i=2) * i++" the left operand to the multiplication will be evaluated before the right operand, then the multiplication will be done, yielding a result of 4, with i set to 3. In C and C++ this expression is undefined as it modifies the same lvalue more than once. It is legal in Java because the order of evaluation is defined. The order of evaluation deals with individual operands around an operator.

Java Operators

The Java operators and their precedence are:

Table 3-1 Java operators and their precedence

Symbol	Note	Class Precedence		Coffeepot Property
names, literals	simple tokens	primary	17	n/a
new	object allocation	—	17	right
a[i]	subscripting	postfix	16	left
m(...)	method invocation	postfix	16	left
.	field selection	postfix	16	left
++ --	increment, decrement	prefix	16	right
++ --	increment, decrement	postfix	15	left
~	flip the bits of an integer	unary	14	right
!	logical not (reverse a boolean)	unary	14	right
- +	arithmetic negation, plus	unary	14	right
(typename)	type conversion (cast)	unary	13	right
* / %	multiplicative operators	binary	12	left
- +	additive operators	binary	11	left
<< >> >>>	left and right bitwise shift	binary	10	left
instanceof < <= > >=	relational operators	binary	9	left
== !=	equality operators	binary	8	left
&	bitwise and	binary	7	left
^	bitwise exclusive or	binary	6	left
|	bitwise inclusive or	binary	5	left
&&	conditional and	binary	4	left
||	conditional or	binary	3	left
? :	conditional operator	ternary	2	right
= *= /= %= += -= <<= >>= >>>= &= ^= |=	assignment operators	binary	1	right

Java doesn't regard subscripts, method calls, or field selection as operators, but they are included in this table for completeness.

In Java the ">>" operator does an arithmetic shift, meaning that the sign bit is propagated. In C, it has always been implementation-defined whether this was a logical shift (fill with 0 bits) or an arithmetic shift (fill with copies of the sign bit). This occasionally led to grief as programmers discovered the implementation dependency when debugging or porting a system.

One new Java operator is ">>>" which means "shift right and zero fill" (i.e. do not propagate the sign bit). This is not needed for shift left because there is no sign bit at the other end to propagate. It is not needed in C because it is implicitly achieved when shifting an unsigned quantity. Java does not have unsigned types apart from char.

Although the intent of the ">>>" operator is a zero filled shift right, it has a surprising - and very undesirable - twist in practice. The >> operator takes negative numbers and does an arithmetic shift on them, that is it sign-extends them so that the "new" bits from the left are filled with 1's to keep the sign negative.

In contrast the >>> operator is designed to fill in with 0's from the left in case you weren't using the operand as a "number", but as a bit mask. This works as expected on numbers of canonical size, ints and longs. But it is broken for short, and byte.

```
byte b = -1;
b >>>= 10;
```

If you have an 8-bit quantity, and you shift it right unsigned 10 bits, all the bits should fall off the right end, leaving zero. This does not happen. If you try it, you will see that b has the value -1.

The reason is the byte got promoted to an int before the shift took place. The int had the bit pattern 0xFFFFFFFF, and was shifted ten places right to yield 0x003FFFFF. That result was truncated to a byte, yielding a final result of 0xFF, or -1.

If you want to do unsigned shift on a short or a byte, an extra AND is required, in which case you can just use >>.

```
byte b = -1;
b = (byte)((b & 0xff) >> 4);
```

So because of the default operand promotion to a canonical size, >>> is useless on all negative byte and short operands. It is probably better not to use it at all, but to always use "&" to mask off the bits you require in a result. That way programs won't mysteriously stop working when someone changes a type from int to short.[5]

5.   This anomaly was pointed out on comp.lang.java by Patrick Naughton.

Assignment operators result in values (as in C) not variables (as in C++). So this code fragment is legal in C++, but illegal in C and Java:

```
(a += 4)++;
```

In C the error will be a complaint that "operand is not a modifiable lvalue". Java thankfully lacks jargon like "modifiable lvalue" which was introduced into C to kludge around certain semantics of consts and arrays. In Java the error message is along the lines of "Invalid expression"—not the greatest but at least it doesn't include any words that have a special definition.

The other new operator is "instanceof". This is used with superclasses to tell if you have a particular subclass. For example, we may see

```
class vehicle { ...
class car extends vehicle { ...
class convertible extends car { ...

vehicle v; ...
if (v instanceof convertible) ...
```

The "instanceof" operator is often followed by a statement that casts the object from the base type to the subclass, if it turns out that the one is an instance of the other. Instanceof lets us check that the cast is valid before attempting it.

Finally note that Java cut back on the use of the obscure comma operator. Even if you're quite an experienced C programmer you might never have seen the comma operator, as it was rarely used. The only place it occurs in Java is in "for" loops.

Why GIGO sometimes means "Garbage In, Gospel Out"

If you try the Pentium division Java program on a Pentium system with the flawed division implementation, you may be surprised to see that it actually prints out the correct answer—I certainly was! In fact "stunned" would be a better description.

How can that be, when the chip gives bad results? The answer lies in the compiler. Not the Java compiler, but the Microsoft Visual C++ library that is used to build Java on the Windows platform, and that provides runtime support. Whenever a chip manufacturer finds a hardware bug, and there are always some bugs in every design, it is the job of the compiler team to work around it. The compiler group must make sure that the generated code avoids or corrects the problem. In this case, within three months of the FDIV fault becoming public knowledge, Microsoft issued patch VCFDIV for Visual C++ 2.0.

The patch checks to see if the code is being run on a flawed Pentium. If it is, it checks if the operands are of the form that would hit the bad entries in the table. If so, it scales both operands (1200.0 / 100.0 gives the same result as 120.0 / 10.0) to avoid using that part of the lookup table. The process takes a little longer, but gives good results. The patch was folded into Visual C++ 2.1. Java on Windows is currently built with MS Visual C++ version 2.0 with the patch. When the Java interpreter finds a division operator, it passes it through to the native runtime routine (in this case the Microsoft msvcrt20.dll library which has the software workaround). You cannot see the flaw using a Java program, but it is not because of any Java quality, rather the runtime library that it uses.

To observe the Pentium division flaw, you need to run a C program that provides access to the raw hardware. I recommend the "Power C" ANSI C compiler for the PC available from Mix Software, in Richardson Texas. The compiler costs under $20, and comes with a properly bound book on C that is worth the price alone. Power C can be ordered by telephoning Mix at 1-800 333-0330. (telephone 214 783-6001 outside the U.S.)[6] You can also download GnuC for the PC—a 32 bit C/C++ compiler for MS-DOS—for free. Take a look at web site http://www.delorie.com/djgpp.

Use GnuC if you want to study compiler internals.

Use Power C if you want to run C programs.

6.   No, I don't own stock in Mix Software! My interest is in seeing more program-mers use a good inexpensive unbloated ANSI C compiler system. Power C sells well to a lot of schools.

Further Reading

The best description of the Pentium flaw appears in "Microprocessor Report," Dec. 26, 1994.

The Unicode site is http://www.unicode.org

The draft standard for Unicode HTML can be found at

http://www.alis.com:8085/ietf/html/draft-ietf-html-i18n-01.txt

CHAPTER
4

Java
Building Blocks

"There is no reason for any individual to have a computer in their home."
                    –Ken Olson, President, Digital Equipment, 1977

"640K ought to be enough memory for anybody"
                    –Bill Gates, 1981

"Java is not for doing millions of lines of code, only applets"
                    –Ilog software co's CEO Pierre Haren,
                    quoted in Unigram 570, Dec 25 1995

T he first half of this chapter covers some more of the language basics: types, literals and statements. The second half is more outward-looking, providing details on how Java programs interact with libraries and the host system.

The Built-In Types and Declarations

Anyone who ever had to port a C program between a Unix system and a PC will know the problem: the basic types are completely different sizes on the different systems. You can't merely change every occurrence of "int" to "long" either—for one thing the usual type promotions all change when all your ints change to longs in C. For another, the implicit assumptions about the layout of structs will change. Yet a third problem is that any printf statements will need the format specifier changed.

The same problem of "what size should types be?" is currently being heatedly discussed by Unix workstation manufacturers as they move towards 64-bit architectures. The issue can be summarized as "we know we have to make pointers 64-bits, but where in the integer types do we bring in 64-bits: int, long, or long long?"

The three major competing approaches have adopted mysterious codenames because, well, because mysterious codenames are fun:

LP64: this group says "introduce 64-bitness at the top of the int range". "long"s and pointers should be 64-bits. Int stays at 32-bits. DEC and SGI are in this camp, and Sun recently switched to join them.

ILP64: this is the position taken by Hewlett-Packard. It says "Hey! Let's have a flag day, and change everything to 64-bits at once: ints, longs, and pointers. Users may squeak, but a change will be good for them. Programs that rely on ints and pointers being the same size will keep working when recompiled. You do have the source, don't you?"

LLP64: this was the original position taken by Sun. It says "introduce 64-bitness *beyond* the top of the range, by having a 'long long' type. All the other existing integer types stay the size they are." Nobody else liked this position, and it got pretty lonely. Other folks inside Sun challenged some of the assumptions it was built on, so Sun switched.

The tradeoffs involved in choosing the sizes of basic data types involve portability, compatibility with existing types, standards conformance, performance, and transition cost. Exactly the same issues were faced by the Java team, though the Java team had the luxury of putting a low value on some of these costs. All the approaches have advantages and drawbacks, but in the end all the vendors have committed to LP64. The LP64 model is very close to the Java model, the only difference being that pointers are 32 bits in Java, not 64 bits. However there is nothing in the language that makes that visible to programmers. When the time for 64 bit pointers inevitably arrives (and it will be well before the turn of the Millennium) we should be able to merely recompile existing code and have it all "just work" on the new Java Virtual Machine. The various "how much memory?" functions in lang/Runtime.java already return long which is always 64 bits in Java.

Most high-level languages don't specify the type sizes and ranges. This allows compiler writers the freedom to choose the best sizes on each architecture for performance. This freedom turns out to be a false economy since it greatly impedes portability. Programmers' time is a lot more valuable than processor time. Java does away with all the uncertainty by rigorously specifying the sizes of the basic types, and making clear that these sizes are identical on all platforms. The built-in types and their properties are:

boolean	1-bit false, true boolean values cannot be cast to any other basic type. However you can always get the same effect by using an expression: "i = (bool? 1:0)"
char	16-bit unsigned integer. holds a value in the Unicode code set.

In addition there are the integral arithmetic types:

byte	8-bit signed two's complement values range from -128 to 127
short	16-bit signed two's complement values range from -32768 to 32767
int	32-bit signed two's complement values range from -2147483648 to 2147483647
long	64-bit signed two's complement values range from -9223372036854775808 to 9223372036854775807[1]

All integer arithmetic operations are done at 32-bit precision, unless an operand is long (which causes 64-bit arithmetic to be done). You have to cast a 32 or 64 bit result if you want to put it into a smaller result. This means that byte and short assignments must always be cast into the result if they involve any arithmetic, like this:

1.   2^64 is a number that really needs a name of its own, so in 1993 I coined the term "Bubbabyte" to describe 2^64 bytes. Just as 2^10 bytes is a Kilobyte, and 2^20 is a Megabyte, so 2^64 bytes is a Bubbabyte. You can count up to half a Bubbabyte, less one, with a long.

```
byte b1, b2=2, b3=3;

b1 = b2 + b3;  //  NO!  NO!  NO! Causes compiler error

b1 = (byte) (b2 + b3);  // correct
```

When a result is too big for the type intended to hold it, only the low end bits get stored. This means arithmetic is effectively modulo-2^n arithmetic on the integer types. Overflow isn't reported to the programmer except in the case of division by zero (using "/" or "%") which throws an exception. What it means to "throw an exception" is covered in the next chapter.

The type "char" is considered an honorary integer type with all rights and privileges pertaining thereto: it can be cast to and from other arithmetic types, and all the integer operators can be used on it.

These are the floating-point arithmetic types:

float   32-bit IEEE 754 floating-point numbers
These provide numbers that can range between about -3.4E38 to +3.4E38 (i.e. 340,000,000,000,000,000,000,000,000,000,000,000,000) with about 6-7 significant figures of accuracy. The exact accuracy depends on the number being represented.

double 64-bit IEEE 754 floating-point numbers
These provide numbers that can range between about -1.7E308 to +1.7E308 with about 14-15 significant figures of accuracy. The exact accuracy depends on the number being represented.

IEEE 754 is the international standard specifying floating point arithmetic. It was issued in 1985, and it would be unthinkable these days for a computer manufacturer to launch a new system that used a different system of floating point numbers.

If a floating point number appears as an operand, the entire operation is done in floating point. Single precision if a float, double if a double.

IEEE 754 arithmetic has a clever way of dealing with the problems caused by representing on limited hardware the unlimited amount of infinite precision real-world numbers. The problem is resolved by reserving some special values that say "Help! I've fallen off the end of what's representable and I can't get up".

You're probably familiar with infinity, but the "Not-a-Number" might be new if you haven't done numerical programming. Not-a-Number or NaN is a value a floating point can take, but it indicates that the result of some operation is not

Make Mine a Double. How Large is 1.7E308?

The largest double precision number is a little bit bigger than a 17 followed by 307 zeroes.

How large is that? Well, the volume of the observable universe is about $(4pi/3)(15 \text{ billion light-years})^3 = 10^{85} \text{ cm}^3$. The density of protons is about 10^7 cm^{-3}, so the number of protons in the observable Universe is about 10^{78}, or "only" 10 followed by 78 zeros, give or take two-fifty.

The largest double precision number is even bigger than a Googol. A Googol is the number description suggested by 9 yr. old Milton Sirotta in 1938 at the request of his uncle, mathematician Edward Krasner. A googol is 10^{100}, i.e. it is only a 10 followed by 100 zeroes. Is the largest double precision number bigger than Roseanne's capacity for self-promotion? No, we have to admit, it probably isn't that big.

It's possible to come up with problems where you want accuracy to 14 significant figures (e.g. figuring the national debt). But it is most unusual to need to tabulate numbers that are orders of magnitude greater than the number of protons in the universe.

---

mathematically well-defined, such as dividing zero by zero. If you get a NaN as an expression is being evaluated, it will contaminate the whole expression, producing an overall result of NaN, which is exactly what you want to happen. The worst thing to do with a numeric error is pretend it didn't happen.

You may never see a NaN if your algorithms are numerically stable and you don't push the limits of your datasets. But it's nice to know that they are there, ready to tell you that your results are garbage if they head that way.

Floating point numbers fall into the range shown below:

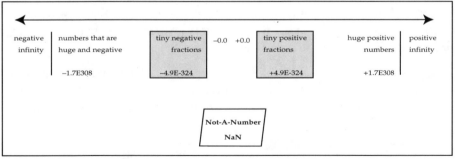

Figure 4-1

These named constants exist:

```
public static final double NaN;
public static final double POSITIVE_INFINITY;
public static final double NEGATIVE_INFINITY;
```

Having both a positive and negative zero is an anomaly of the representation used by IEEE 754. The two zeros are equal, and the only way you'll get into trouble is in bar bets with other programmers on the topic.

Write, compile, and run a Java program that deliberately generates a NaN result, by dividing two floating point numbers that both have the value 0.0. Print out the result of the division (just send it to System.out.println() as in earlier examples). What is the printable representation of NaN? Try using NaN in further arithmetic operations.

All Java programs are built from just these 8 basic types and references. If your 1000MHz Super Frob-U-tron Pro computer supports 24 bit integers ("50% better than 16-bits!") they do not percolate through to the Java system on it. In particular, character strings are supported as a class not as a built-in type. Actually, two classes - one for strings that cannot change after their creation ("String") and one for strings that can grow and shrink as needed ("StringBuffer").

You can look at many example classes—source is provided with every Java development system from Sun. Check in the directory java/src/lang, in files String.java and StringBuffer.java for the string classes.

Good programmers get to be excellent programmers by spending long hours studying the code written by excellent programmers. Looking at some of the source supplied with the Java Development Kit will help you become an excellent Java programmer.

The simplest form of data declaration looks like this:

type_name   variable_name;

as we have seen in many examples so far. You can add access modifiers on the left end, an initialization on the right, and array brackets in the middle like so:

modifiers   type_name [ ]   variable_name = initializer;

Remember: object declarations (without an initialization) do not create objects!

A declaration merely sets aside the space, for when you do get around to creating ("instantiating") the object. Contrast this with the way data of basic types *are* created by declarations.

```
int i;
```

gives you a variable you can immediately do things with.

But this is not true for objects:

```
Fruit melon;
```

merely gives you a location that can hold a (pointer to) the melon object. It does not create a melon object and fill in its fields. If you try to look at the melon, your program will fail! We put "pointer to" in brackets because Java does not reveal pointers to programmers. If there are no pointers, there is no error-prone memory management by programmers. C and C++, by allowing arithmetic on pointers, dangling pointers, unchecked deallocation, pointers into the stack, and other evils, give the programmer too much rope. Most of us end up tying ourselves in knots with it sooner or later. This is why Java makes pointers implicit, and uses them everywhere. If pointers are implicit, the programmer never has to grapple with them. If everything is a reference to an object, then the compiler system can de-reference when an object is needed, and use the pointer when a pointer is needed.

If you want to instantiate that object right now, the declaration needs an initializer:

```
Fruit melon = new Fruit();
```

The "Fruit()" is a call to the constructor of the Fruit class.

You can declare several variables of the same type and also initialize any of them as desired:

```
int a, b, c=0, d;
```

When it is created, all data is created with a default initial value if you fail to give it an explicit initial value. The default value is 0, null, false, 0.0 etc. No datum ever has an undefined value. However, the same superstition that says it is unlucky to chase 13 black cats under a ladder also holds the belief that programmers shouldn't rely on the default initializations, but should set starting values explicitly. The compiler may even grumble at you if you don't. The concept that default initializations somehow "don't count" is a misguided attempt to encourage better habits in programmers, and it's a good candidate for removal in future compiler releases.

Literals

Literal values come in the varieties outlined below.

boolean: false, true
           A string representation of these will be printed when you output
           a boolean. There is no corresponding input facility.

char literals: Character literals, which is to say literals for the types char, byte,
                 short, int, and long, can be expressed in any of four ways:
                 • as a single character in single quotes, 'A'
                 • as a character escape sequence in single quotes,

                       The only allowable values are:

'\b'	the backspace character
'\t'	the tab character
'\n'	the linefeed character
'\f'	the formfeed character
'\r'	the carriage return character
'\"'	the double quote character
'\''	the single quote character
'\\'	the backslash character

                 • as an octal escape sequence in single quotes
                 This has the form: '\nnn' e.g. '\12' or '\1'
                 where nnn is one-to-three octal digits in the range 0 to 377. Note
                 the slightly odd fact that you can only set the least significant 8
                 bits of a 16-bit char when using an octal escape sequence.

• as a Unicode escape sequence in single quotes
This has the form: '\uxxxx' e.g. '\u3b9F'
where xxxx is exactly four hexadecimal digits.

There's a slight quirk in that the Unicode escape sequence can contain more than one occurrence of the letter u before the four hex digits. The justification given for this is to help in automatic translation of source files between ASCII and Unicode character sets.

Java goes to some trouble to be a good international programming language, so it's downright odd that it allows the US national currency sign "$" as a character in an identifier. Java also tries not to be unduly difficult on hosts that only support 8-bit ASCII. When a Java compiler reads in program source, the very first thing that it does, before even forming tokens out of the characters, is to look for any six character sequences of the form: \uxxxx   where "xxxx" is exactly four hexadecimal digits (e.g. \u3b9F). It translates any that it finds into the corresponding Unicode character whose value is xxxx, and pushes it back into the input stream for rescanning. This allows any Unicode character to appear in the source (e.g. in a dataname) even on an ASCII-based system.

Because this early scanning takes place before tokens are assembled, the six character sequence \uxxxx will be replaced even if it appears in a quoted string or character literal. For most characters that is exactly what you want, but for single characters that themselves affect scanning, you will get a bad result. The two individual characters that have the quality of affecting scanning are carriage return, and line feed. If you try to put one of these in a quoted character literal like this:

```
char c = '\u000a';
```

the compiler will actually see this:

```
char c = '
';
```

causing two error messages about "invalid character constant"—one for each of the opening quotes it sees. The compiler is smart enough to show you the line as it appears in your source file, rather than as it appears to the compiler. The unusual lexing convention also means that you can start a comment with the twelve character text strings:

```
\u002f\u002f
```
or
```
\u002f\u002a
```

which correspond to "//" and "/*"

Here is how you might see a Unicode character in a program on an ASCII system.

```
class strangename {
   void foo()  {
    int \u66ed = 1;
     \u66ed = \u66ed+1;
    }
}
```

Ugly, isn't it? The "\u" followed by 4 hex digits is a character literal for the character with that value, just as '\n' is the literal for newline. Clearly literal Unicode characters in identifiers are something to avoid on ASCII systems. The people who will benefit most from Unicode identifiers will be those who have systems that can display them properly, rather than by hex value.

integer literals: Integer literals, which is to say literals for the types char, byte, short, int, and long, can be expressed in any of three ways:
- as a decimal literal, e.g. 10 or 10L
- as an octal literal, e.g. 077 or 077L
- as a hexadecimal literal, e.g. 0xA5 or 0Xa5 or 0xA5L

The general form is [base indicator]number[length indicator]

All integer literals are 32 bit ints, unless they are suffixed with upper or lower case "L"—then they are 64 bit (long) quantities.

Never, ever, use the lower case letter "l" to indicate a "long" literal. Always use the upper case letter "L". Lower case "l" is just too similar to the digit "1".

A leading zero means the number is in octal, and a leading zero-x ("0x") means it is in hexadecimal. Case has no significance with any of the letters that can appear in integer literals. If you use octal or hexadecimal and you provide a literal that sets the leftmost bit in the receiving number, then it represents a negative quantity. This does not apply to chars, which are always unsigned.

When you prefix a literal with a unary minus sign, you have to use a cast to force it into a char, because chars are unsigned quantities. This assures the compiler that you really know what you are doing, and you really meant that. E.g. `char c = (char) -10;` You probably never really want to do this.

floating point literals:
There is a little grammar that describes the exact form of floating point literals, but the simplest way to understand what is allowed is to look at examples of valid ones.

"float" literals
1e1f   2.f .3f   3.14f   6.02e+23f

"double" literals
1e1   2.   .3   3.14   6.02e+23d

A suffix of "F" or "f" means float, "D", "d" or nothing means double.

There is an asymmetry here. Integer literals are 32-bits by default, 64-bits if you supply the "L" suffix. That means that non-suffixed quantities (like "10", "33" or "2047") can be assigned to any of char, byte, short, int or long.

However, floating point literals are 64-bit double quantities by default, and cannot be assigned to a 32-bit float variable without a cast. The compiler requires a cast because assigning something capacious to something smaller potentially loses accuracy or even cannot be represented at all. So an initialization like

```
float banana = 0.0;
```

will fail with a compiler error. The code must be written as:

```
float banana = 0.0F;
```

where the literal is suffixed with "F" or "f" to indicate it is a single precision value.

> The format is very easy-going. Just give the compiler a "." or a suffix, or an exponent, and it will recognize that a floating point literal is intended.

> It is also permissible to assign any of the integer literals or character literals to floats or doubles. So a line like this, while perverse, is valid:

```
double cherry = '\n';
```

> It takes the integer value of the literal, 0x0a here, floats it to get 10.0d, and assigns that to "cherry". Don't ever do this.

The justification for using single precision variables used to be that arithmetic operations were twice as fast as on double precision variables. With modern extensively-pipelined processors and wide databuses between the cache and CPUs, the main reason for not using doubles is to minimize storage requirements when you have a very large quantity of them.

String Literals

> Strings are not a built-in type, but they are important enough to have support for a couple of features built in to the language. String literals is one of these features[2].

---

2. The "+" string concatenation operator is another feature with built-in support. It's just so convenient that it cannot be left out, even though it blows the architectural purity of the language design. This is one occasion where compiler theorists need to hold their tongues and let it be. The trade-off was done the other way in C++. Partly because operator overloading was needed for strings, it was allowed everywhere as a feature available to C++ programmers. Whoosh! The complexity of C++ compilers just went up by another 10%.

A string literal is zero or more characters enclosed in double quotes, like this:

```
""          // empty string

"That'll cost you two-fifty \n"

"but Bob, That'd be in the."

"\1\22 who me? \u3F07 \t "
```

As the example shows, you can embed any of the character literal escape sequences in a string. If you have a long string literal, there's no way to continue it across several lines. Break it down into smaller strings instead, and concatenate them like this:

```
  "Thomas the Tank Engine and the naughty "
+ "Engine-driver who tied down Thomas's Boiler Safety Valve "
+ "and How They Recovered Pieces of Thomas from Three Counties."
```

Like other literals, string literals are immutable and cannot be modified after they have been created. Each string literal behaves as if it is a reference to an instance of class "String". For the sake of performance the compiler can implement it another way, but it must be indistinguishable to the programmer.

The Basic Statements

All statements in Java can be conveniently divided into four groups:

- selection statements

- iteration statements

- transfer of control statements

- guarding statements

We will describe the first three groups here, deferring consideration of the guarding statements until the sections on threads and exceptions in the next chapter. There's nothing particularly difficult or novel about guarding statements, it's just that they make more sense once the context in which they operate has been covered.

The selection, iteration, and branching statements are almost identical to their counterparts in C, and are readily recognizable to any programmer familiar with mainstream algorithmic languages. Accordingly we can limit our discussion to showing the general form of each statement.

- **Selection Statements**

    The general form of the "if" statement looks like this:

    ```
    if ( Expression ) Statement  [ else  Statement ]
    ```

Notes:

1. The Expression must have boolean type. This has the delightful side-effect of banishing the old "if (a=b)" problem, where the programmer does an assignment instead of a comparison. If that typo is written, the compiler will give an error message that a boolean is needed in that context[3].

2. The Statement can be any statement, in particular a block { ... } statement is fine.

3. Since we are dealing with the "if" statement, we should also mention the " ? ... :"operator, as it is not very well known. It works in a very similar way to the "if" statement, but yields an expression, where the "if" statement does not. Compare:
    if (*Expression*)   *Statement_when_true* else *Statement_when_false*
    Expression?   *Expression_when_true* : *Expression_when_false*

---

3. Unless a and b are booleans. But at least you're protected for all the other types.

When looked at this way, the conditional operator is a lot more understandable. You use it where you want to quickly choose between two alternative values, and you can fold it right into the expression, like this:

```
System.out.println(  "Your number is"
               + ((n%2)==0? "even" : "odd" ) );[4]
```

Never nest several conditional operators inside each other, as it causes unnecessary grief for whoever has to maintain the code (and it might be you).

The general form of the "switch" statement is impossible to show in any meaningful form in a syntax diagram with less than about two dozen production rules. That tells you something about the statement right there. If you look at Kernighan and Ritchie's C book, you'll note that even they were not up to the task of showing the syntax in any better way than:

switch (Expression) Statement

and neither has any C book since. Ignoring syntax diagrams, the switch statement is a poor man's "case" statement. It causes control to be transferred to one of several statements depending on the value of the Expression. It generally looks like:

```
switch (Expression) {

case constant_1 : Statement; break;
case constant_5 :
case constant_3 : Statement; break;

       ...

case constant_n : Statement; break;
       default : Statement; break;
       }
```

Notes:
1. If you omit a "break" at the end of a branch, after that branch is executed control falls through to execute all the remaining branches! This is almost always *not* what you want.

4. You'd never really write a print statement this way, because it would make it much harder to localize the program to support natural languages other than English. But you get the idea.

Grepping[5] through about 100,000 lines of the Java Development system source, there are about 320 switch statements. Implicit fall through is used in less than 1% (based on a random sample of files). A statement in which you have to take explicit action to avoid something you don't want 99% of the time is a disaster. Death to the switch statement!

2. There can only be one "default" branch, and it doesn't have to be last. The "default" branch can be omitted. If it is present, it is executed when none of the "case" values match the Expression.

3. A Statement can be labelled with several cases. (This is actually a trivial case of fall-through).

4. Implicit fall-through (in the absence of "break") is a bug-prone misfeature.

- **Iteration Statements**

At this point note that wherever you can have a statement in Java, you can also have a block of them. And you can also have a declaration of a local variable. As in C++ variable declarations count as statements.

The for statement looks like this:

```
for ( Initial; Test; Increment ) Statement
```

Notes:
1. Initial, Test, and Increment are all Expressions that control the loop. Any or all of them is optional. A typical loop will look like:

```
for( i=0; i<100; i++ ) { ...
```

A typical infinite loop will look like:

```
for (;;)
```

2. As in C++, it is possible to declare the loop variable in the for statement, like this:

```
for( int i=0; i<100; i++ ) { ...
```

5. "grep" means "Globally search for Regular Expression, and Print" There is a
    Unix command of this name to search through a set of files for a given text string.

This is a nice feature which is done for programmer convenience. In a difference from most C++ compilers, the lifetime of the Java loop variable ends at the end of the for statement. The continued existence of loop variables in C++ was an artifact of the original implementations that simply translated the language to C. It was convenient to collect up all declarations and move them to the beginning of the block without trying to impose a finer granularity of scope. This sloppy approach is now being tightened up for ANSI C++.

3. The comma separator "," is allowed in the Initial and Increment sections of loops so you can string together several initializations or increments, like this:

```
for(i=0,j=0; i<100; i++, j+=2 ) { ...
```

The while statement looks like this

```
while ( Expression ) Statement
```

Notes:

1. While the boolean-typed expression remains true, the Statement is executed.
2. This form of loop is for iterations that take place zero or more times. If the Expression is false on the first evaluation, the statement will not be executed at all.

The "do while" statement looks like this

```
do Statement while ( Expression )
```

Notes:

1. The Statement is executed, and then the boolean-typed expression is evaluated. If it is false, execution drops through to the next statement. If it is true, you loop through the Statement again.

2. This form of loop is for iterations that take place at least one time. If the Expression is false on the first evaluation, the Statement will already have executed once.

There may be "continue" statements in a loop. These look like:

```
continue;

continue Identifier;
```

Continue statements only occur in loops. When a continue statement is executed, it causes the flow of control to pass to the next iteration of the loop. It's as though you say "well, that's it for iteration N, increment the loop variable (if this is a "for" loop), do the test, and continue with iteration N+1."

The "continue Identifier" form is used when you have nested loops, and you want to break out of an inner one altogether and start with the next iteration of the outer loop. The loop that you want to continue with will be labelled at its "for" statement with the matching identifier, but don't be deceived into thinking that execution starts over at the beginning of that loop. It really does continue with the *next iteration*, even though the label is (confusingly) at the beginning, rather than labelling, say, the end of the loop. Here is an example "continue" statement:

```
months: for (int m=1; m<=12; m++) {

        // do something
        // nested loop
        for (int d=1; d<=31; d++) {
            // some daily thing
            if (m==2 && d==28) continue months;
            // otherwise something else
        }
        // more guff
    }
```

There may be "break" statements in a loop or switch. These look like:

```
break;
```

```
break   Identifier;
```

Break is like a more dramatic version of continue. It causes control to pass to just after the end of the enclosing "for, do, while," or "switch" statement. The loop or switch statement is "broken out of". Break with no identifier can only appear in an if statement by virtue of the whole thing being nested in an iteration or switch statement. You will break to the end of the iteration or switch *not* the "if".

If an Identifier is included it must be an Identifier matching the label on some enclosing statement. The enclosing statement can be *any* kind of statement, not just an iterative or switch statement. In other words, it's OK to break out of any kind of enclosing statement as long as you explicitly indicate it with a label. Again, there is the slightly confusing feature that statements are labelled at their *beginning*, but "break" causes you to jump to their *end*. Here is an example:

```
months: for (int m=1; m<=12; m++) {

                // do something
                // nested loop
                for (int d=1; d<=31; d++) {
                        // some daily thing
                        if (cost > budget)  break months;
                }
        }
        cost=0;
```

*   **Transfer of Control Statements**

A return statement looks like:

```
return;
```

```
return  Expression;
```

Notes:

1. "return" gets you back where you were called from.

2. a "return *Expression*" can only be used with something that actually does return a value, i.e. never with a "void" method. There is another statement that causes transfer of control: the "throw" statement that raises an exception. We will cover this in the section in the next chapter that deals with exceptions.

There is a reserved word "goto" in Java, but there is no goto statement. The designers snagged the word to ensure that no-one uses it as a variable name, in case it later turns out to be convenient to support branching.

You can look at the java code that is output by the compiler by using the javap command, like this:

```
javap -c  class
```

E.g.

```
javac pentium.java

javap -c  pentium
```

javap is an abbreviation for "java print". It can be instructive and fun to look at the bytecode output for various different java statements.

(Nearly) Everything is an Object

We come now to a brief discussion about the philosophy of Java. In some ways Java goes further than C++ in its object-oriented nature. In C++ you have several ways to structure data other than making a class out of it. You could put it in a struct for instance. Java does not have structs. The major way to group data items together[6] in Java is to put them into a class.

It's convenient and easy to put things in Java classes and so people do. This is really a central principle of Java: (nearly) everything is an object. Apart from the elementary types of the language everything is object-oriented. The "main()" routine is a static method of a class, exceptions are objects, threads are objects, the GUI is built out of objects that you extend, applets are objects and of course Strings are objects.

Every class is ultimately inherited from the ultimate superclass "Object" (and javadoc shows this). There are classes called Class and Object that permit a few elementary operations (comparison, notification, etc.) for any arbitrary object in the system. Arrays are objects and may be assigned to variables of type Object. All

6.   We also have arrays which are important enough to have their own section in the next chapter. Arrays are presented to the programmer as a class, too.

methods of class Object can be invoked on any array. So at the highest level in the system we have consistency of approach.

You have already seen the basic types boolean, char, int, long, etc. For each of these, there is also a class: Boolean, Character, Integer, Long, etc.

Basic type	**Corresponding Class** (in java/src/lang)
boolean	Boolean
char	Character
int	Integer
long	Long
float	Float
double	Double

A Class version is provided for the types above but is not needed for byte and short, because the Integer class can be used equally well with a little casting.

The class version of each basic type provides an object wrapper for data values, and often a few named constants. A wrapper is useful because most of Java's utility classes require the use of objects. Since variables of these built-in types are not objects in Java, it's convenient to provide a simple way to "promote" them when needed. Note that once one of these objects has been created with a given value, that value cannot be changed. You can throw away that object and create a new one, but the object itself doesn't change its identity once assigned.

Here is an example of moving an int to an Integer object and an Integer to an int, using methods from the Integer class.

```
// changes int to Integer and back
Integer mango;
int i=42;

mango = new Integer(i);   // to Object
i = mango.intValue();     // to int
```

The Building Blocks: Packages, Classes and Imports

This section covers the mechanics of how java code co-exists with the host system. It explains what gets created when you compile something, and in a larger sense how a group of such "somethings" form a Java package.

Java does away with all the aggravation of header files, forward declarations, and ordering declarations. You can think of javac as a two-pass compiler: on the first pass, the source code is scanned, and a table built of all the symbols. On the second pass, the statements are translated and since the symbol table already exists, there is never any problem about needing to see the declaration of something before its use. It's already right there in the symbol table. So any field in a class can quite happily reference any other field, even if it doesn't occur until later down the page or in another file. There is some fine print covering initialization order for pathological cases.

Less Flexibility But More Simplicity

There are two simplifications in Java: 1) There are no nested class definitions. You cannot define a second class when you are already in the middle of defining a class. Every class is defined at the topmost lexical level; 2) Everything to do with a single class goes in one file. There isn't a way to extract the body of a method and place it somewhere else. If you must, you can put several related classes in one source file, but you cannot go the other way and scatter pieces of a class across several files. This ensures that when you look in a source file, you get the class, the whole class, and nothing but the class (and its buddies).

Programming is a complicated business. Making life easy with little things, like making sure everything that belongs together has to be put together is a good trade-off. Less flexibility for more simplicity.

A source file is what you present to a Java compiler, so the contents of a complete source file are known as a "Compilation Unit". (Think of it as the unit of compilation, just as the meter is a unit of measure).

Automatic Compilation

Java tries hard not to let you build a system using some components that are out of date. When you invoke the compiler on a source file, the compiler does not just translate that in isolation. It looks to see what classes it references, and tries to determine if they are up to date. If the compiler decides another class needs compiling it adds it in, and recursively applies the same procedure to it.

In other words, Java has a "make"-like utility built into it. Say the class you are compiling makes reference to a class in another file. That utility is capable of noticing when the second .class file does not exist, but the corresponding .java does, and of noticing when the .java file has been modified without a recompilation taking place. In both these cases it will add the second .java file to the set of files it is recompiling.

Here is an example. This is the contents of file plum.java

```
public class plum {
    grape m;

}
```

And this is the contents of file grape.java

```
public class grape {}
```

If we now compile plum.java, the compiler will look for grape.class, check that it is up-to-date with respect to its source file, and if not, it will recompile grape.java for you!

Here is the output from such a compilation:

```
javac -verbose plum.java
[parsed plum.java in 602ms]
[checking class plum]
[parsed .//grape.java in 44ms]
[wrote plum.class]
[checking class grape]
[wrote .//grape.class]

[done in 2347ms]
```

As you can see, grape.java got compiled as well, creating grape.class.

File Name Is Related To Class Name

Java emphasizes the idea that the name of a file is related to its contents, and understanding this is the key to understanding how to build programs out of more than one file or library. What we're explaining here is how the rules work when you use the default case of source and object files in the same directory. If you use the "-d" option to javac to make your class files be written in a different directory to the source, then the rules below are modified correspondingly.

A compilation unit has several rules:

1. It can start with a "package" statement, identifying the package (a library) that the byte codes will belong to. If you do not start with a package name, your program belongs to the default anonymous package, and your classes cannot later be imported by another compilation unit, except other ones in the anonymous package.

2. Next can come zero or more "import" statements, each identifying a package or a class from a package, that will be available in this compilation unit.
   The predefined package "java.lang" is automatically imported into each compilation unit for every compilation. Java.lang contains the classes Boolean, Float, Long, etc. discussed above and other classes as well.

3. The rest of the compilation unit consists of Class declarations and Interface declarations. Interfaces are skeletons of Classes showing what form the Class will take when someone implements it.

4. Each of the classes in a .java file will create an individual .class file to hold the generated byte codes. If you have 6 classes in a source file, the compiler will create 6 .class files.

The underlying host system should allow filenames with the same form as Java classnames: unbounded length, contain "$" or "_" as well as Unicode alphabetics, and case sensitive. The more restrictions there are on filenames on your host system, the more restrictions there will be on the classnames you can use. This will form a practical impediment to the total portability of software.

The Language Specification provides a ludicrous way to use characters in class names that cannot appear in host file names. It suggests "the character should be escaped by using a @ character followed by one to four hexadecimal digits giving the Unicode code point of the escaped character..." Don't do it. It'll take you half-an-hour to get it right, and you'll confuse everyone who has to maintain it. Avoid using characters in classnames that are problematic for any host file systems.

5. At most one of the classes in the file can be "public". This class must have the corresponding name as the file it is in.

public class plum   must be in file plum.java.

A picture is worth a thousand words, so let's look at that in pictures:

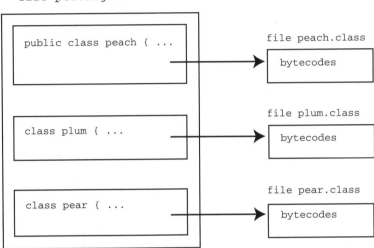

The Building Blocks: Packages, Imports, and Classpath

Packages

Package names, import names, and the CLASSPATH environment variable all work together, and you need to understand all three together. A package is like a library in C. It is simply a way to group together several related object files, and refer to them as a whole. An important point is that the default access modifier (i.e. not mentioning one) means that the element is visible to everything in the same package, and nothing outside[7]. So as well as being a way to lump together classes, a package also has significance for how visible something is. In Java, all the source files in a directory make up a package. (Let's ignore the anonymous package for now).

7. The default access modifier really should have a name and keyword of its own. Some people have taken to calling it "package" access, because that describes it exactly, and it even starts with a "p" like the other access modifiers.

You need to label each source file with the name of the package. But here's where it gets subtle. You cannot just choose any name at random for your package. Just as the public class in a source file must match the filename, so too the package name in a source file must match the name of the directory.

In the example above, if our source file "peach.java" is in a directory:
/home/linden/Java/Code/Examples

then one choice for our package name in the package statement would be:
package Examples;

Another choice would be:
package Code.Examples

Still another possibility would be:
package Java.Code.Examples

and so on. The key aspect is that the components in the package name must exactly match a rightmost substring of the components in the directory name where the source file is located.

Another way to think about this, is to take the pathname to a given source file, say "/a/b/c/d.java" The endmost component forces the public class in the Java file to be called "d". For example:

```
public class d {
```

The name of the package is formed by taking the rest of the pathname, and substituting dots for the file separator character "/" (or "\" on Windows systems). If the compilation unit above starts with a package statement it can only be one of these alternatives (in this example):

```
        package a.b.c;
or      package   b.c;

or      package      c;
```

This requirement that package name match the source file directory name also means that any given directory can contain files of at most one named package. It could also contain a few files compiled into the default anonymous package as well, but we assume that if you are building a big system across several directories, you are going to take care to make sure everything ends up in a named package.

Using the host filesystem to structure a Java program, and particularly to help organize the program namespace, is a very good idea. It avoids unnecessary generality, and it provides a clear model for understanding.

If you let your directory naming match components in your Internet domain name (sorted from most general to least general, e.g. "com.sun.engineering"), you can also easily create package names that will be unique across the entire Internet (because domain names have this quality). This allows different vendors to provide class libraries with no danger of name space collisions.

How Package Names Relate to Directory Names:

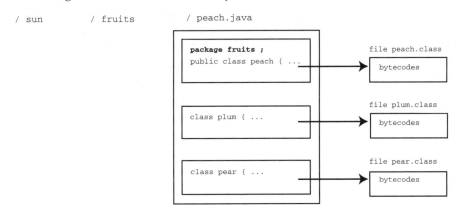

Classpath

The explanation above begs the question "how do I choose how many components of the pathname to put in my package statement?" The answer is related to your CLASSPATH environment variable.

CLASSPATH is an environment variable, typically set in the autoexec.bat file (on Windows) or in a shell initialization file (on Unix). The CLASSPATH will be set to a list of one or more pathnames separated by ";" (Windows) or ":" (Unix). It may look like this, for instance on Windows:

```
SET CLASSPATH c:\sun;c:\project\test\source;.
```

It may look like this on a Unix system using c-shell:

```
setenv CLASSPATH /sun:/project/test/source:.
```

The CLASSPATH tells the compiler a list of possible places to begin a search for packages. In the case above, the compiler will start at these places:

```
/sun
```

and

```
/project/test/source
```

and

- (the current directory)

Here's where the package name comes in. The package name must provide enough of the path to exactly "bridge the gap" from one of these CLASSPATH starting points, to the directory that contains your Java files.

In the example we have been using all along, we have our source in the file:

/ sun /	fruits	/ peach.java

our CLASSPATH is set to   / sun

That forces our package name to be   fruits

because together
/ sun / fruits

form the pathname to the directory containing the Java files.

If we had used a "package sun.fruits" the compiler would combine this with the CLASSNAME possibilities to record the name of the class files as belonging to package sun.fruits. This would work fine when we create the package, but it would cause a failure when we tried to import the packages, as the compiler would look in vain for class files in these directories:

/sun/sun/fruits

and

/project/test/source/sun/fruits

and

./sun/fruits

(This last one would actually work, if we were compiling files in the root directory. But our example goes on to use the "beans" directory). To summarize, CLASS-PATH, package, and class names are related to the filesystem names in this manner:

CLASSPATH	package name	class name
/alpa/beta/gamma	delta	epsilon
/alpha/beta	gamma.delta	epsilon
/alpha	beta.gamma.delta	epsilon

Figure 4-2

The three lines above show three alternatives for CLASSPATH and package names in order to identify the same one filename:
/alpha / beta / gamma / delta / epsilon.java

CLASSPATH is used when executing programs too. If you try

```
java foo
```

you will get back the error message "can't find class foo" if "foo" isn't in any of the directories pointed at by your CLASSPATH.

This can be very frustrating if your CLASSPATH doesn't include the current working directory, and you want to execute something in there. You list the directory contents, and there is "foo.class". Why can't java see it!? Answer: it uses a different algorithm for looking for class files than you do. It doesn't know to look in the current directory unless the CLASSPATH tells it to.

The CLASSPATH can also be given as a compiler option, but most people will find it simpler to set it once, rather than mention it on each compiler invocation. It is possible to use the "-d pathname" option with the Java compiler to cause the class files to be written to a different directory than the one the source resides in. As the name suggests, the CLASSPATH is only used to hunt for .class files. Normally they reside with the corresponding source, but if you have caused them to go elsewhere, then modify the advice above appropriately.

Import

It should be clear at this point how the import statement works, as it uses a similar scheme to that already outlined. Just as the package name must form a "bridge" between the filename and the CLASSPATH, so must the import statement. An import statement can either name an individual class file that is being imported, or a series of them like this

```
import fruits.peach;
import fruits.orange;

import fruits.prune;
```

Or it can specify that all public files in that package are to be imported, with a statement like this:

```
import fruits.*;
```

An "import" statement always has at least two components. like so:

```
import    package.classname
```

The final component is either a class name, or a "*" meaning all classes in that package.

Always import the minimum number of packages and libraries that you require. It provides clear documentation on what the actual dependencies are.

As a bonus, the fewer classes you bring in, the faster compilation will be. This is especially noticeable when bringing in an entire package, such as "import java.util.*" which has not previously been loaded by the compiler.

Whatever you import, only the code that is needed gets written to the .class file. Superfluous imports are discarded.

All compilations import the standard Java package "lang" without specifically naming it. "lang" contains the standard I/O streams, objects representing some of the built-in types, predefined exceptions, and mathematical operations, among other useful items.

Here is a diagram showing how the "import" statement works and interacts with "package" and "CLASSPATH" for files that are split across different directories.

How Import Names Relate to Package and Directory Names

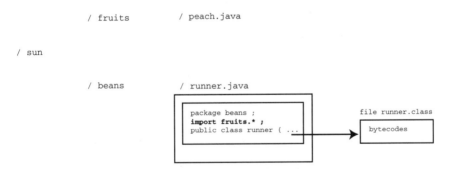

Using a CLASSPATH which includes the path "/sun", the import statement "import fruits.*" tells the compiler to make available all public class files from the package found in directory /sun/fruits. In this example, there is only one public class file, representing the class "peach", and that will be usable in class runner, under the name "fruit.peach", or simply "peach". The scope of any imported classes is the entire compilation unit (file).

ZIP files were introduced in December 1995 for classes. A zip file is a collection of .class files all grouped together in one physical file, as can be done on Windows with the standard Windows zip software.

The standard java and Sun libraries now come all wrapped up in one zip file called "java/lib/classes.zip". This blows the import model a little, in that you have to make the CLASSPATH environment variable contain the name of the actual zip file, rather than the path to it, like this

(Unix): `setenv CLASSPATH /java/lib/classes.zip:.:/mycode`

(Windows): `set CLASSPATH=c:\java\lib\classes.zip;.;c:\mycode`

Think of the justification as "the zip file contains an archive of class files, so in some theoretical sense it is a directory". Or don't think of it at all if it makes your head hurt. We can packages our own classes into zip files for the same advantage. It is convenient for a browser opening a connection to a remote URL applet. The browser only need open one connection for a package, not one for each class. Since opening the TCP/IP connection often takes more time than transmitting the data this is a win. Or if you don't have the zip software[8] you can leave them all in separate files. It's a performance enhancement aimed mostly at browsers.

Visibility Revisited

With this new knowledge of how classes are organized and referenced by the compiler, let us re-visit the (nontrivial) field modifiers that we first listed in Chapter 2. Java has field modifiers that support five levels of accessibility. In order of most accessible to least accessible, they are:

1. public—world access

2. protected—accessible in this package (think "directory") and also in subclasses in other packages

3. default—package access (any class in the package)

4. private protected—class/subclass access

5. private—accessible only in this class

---

8. For Windows 95 this is easily downloadable from http://www.coast.net/Sim-Tel/#WIN95 file WINZIP95.EXE The standard Windows zip doesn't deal with long filenames, and you require a version that does.

There was some criticism of early versions (up to Java version 1.0 Beta2 which came out in December 1995) because up until then was no exact equivalent of the C++ "protected" modifier that says "this field can only be accessed by this class and its subclasses". The Java "protected" modifier has a slightly different meaning that says "this field can only be accessed by this class and its subclasses, plus anything else in the same package." C++ does not have packages, and this difference was a recipe for certain disaster.

In the Beta2 release, a new paradigm was adopted in Java: fields could be labelled "protected private" with the exact meaning as "C++ protected". Now it is merely a recipe for likely disaster, not certain disaster. Java has no equivalent of C++ "friend".

The interaction between classes and subclasses, and things in the same package and things in other packages can be downright confusing. Lets illustrate them all with diagrams (see Figures 4-3 through 4-7):

1. public

2. protected

3. default (package)

4. private protected

5. private

Note that the access modifiers for a method can come in any order: "static public" is the same as "public static".

However, the return type of a method must be next to the method name. Otherwise you will get this error:

```
void public init() {
          ^
```

```
alice.java:8: Invalid method declaration; return type required.
```

The correct way to write this is:

```
public void init() {
```

1. public — visible everywhere

KEY:
bolded code
means
"is visible in here"

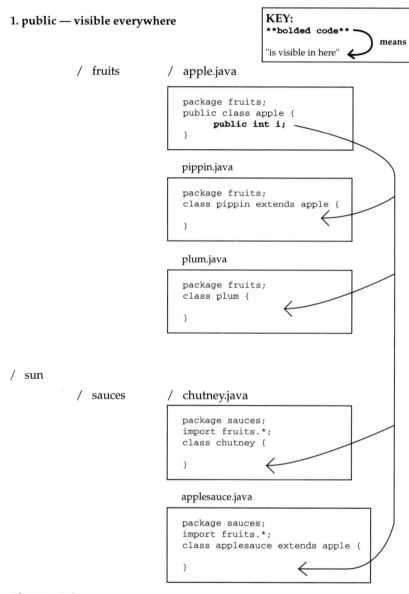

/ fruits   / apple.java

```
package fruits;
public class apple {
    public int i;
}
```

pippin.java

```
package fruits;
class pippin extends apple {

}
```

plum.java

```
package fruits;
class plum {

}
```

/ sun

/ sauces   / chutney.java

```
package sauces;
import fruits.*;
class chutney {

}
```

applesauce.java

```
package sauces;
import fruits.*;
class applesauce extends apple {

}
```

Figure 4-3

2. protected — visible in same package, and subclasses anywhere

/ fruits   / apple.java

```
package fruits;
public class apple {
    protected int i;
}
```

pippin.java

```
package fruits;
class pippin extends apple {

}
```

plum.java

```
package fruits;
class plum {

}
```

/ sun
    / sauces   / chutney.java

```
package sauces;
import fruits.*;
class chutney {

}
```

applesauce.java

```
package sauces;
import fruits.*;
class applesauce extends apple {

}
```

Figure 4-4

3. default (package) — visible in this package only

/ fruits   / apple.java

```
package fruits;
public class apple {
            int i;
}
```

pippin.java

```
package fruits;
class pippin extends apple {

}
```

plum.java

```
package fruits;
class plum {

}
```

/ sun

/ sauces   / chutney.java

```
package sauces;
import fruits.*;
class chutney {

}
```

applesauce.java

```
package sauces;
import fruits.*;
class applesauce extends apple {

}
```

Figure 4-5

4. private protected — visible in subclasses anywhere

/ fruits   / apple.java

```
package fruits;
public class apple {
    private protected int i;
}
```

pippin.java

```
package fruits;
class pippin extends apple {

}
```

plum.java

```
package fruits;
class plum {

}
```

/ sun

      / sauces   / chutney.java

```
package sauces;
import fruits.*;
class chutney {

}
```

applesauce.java

```
package sauces;
import fruits.*;
class applesauce extends apple {

}
```

Figure 4-6

5. private — not accessible outside this class

/ fruits   / apple.java

```
package fruits;
public class apple {
    private int i;
}
```

pippin.java

```
package fruits;
class pippin extends apple {

}
```

plum.java

```
package fruits;
class plum {

}
```

/ sun

/ sauces   / chutney.java

```
package sauces;
import fruits.*;
class chutney {

}
```

applesauce.java

```
package sauces;
import fruits.*;
class applesauce extends apple {

}
```

Figure 4-7

What Happens When Names Collide?

If a variable in the subclass has the same name as a variable in the superclass, then it supersedes ("hides") the superclass one. The visible, subclass variable is said to "shadow" (put in the shade) the superclass variable. The superclass one is still available by giving its full name, e.g. "Fruit.grams" or using the "super" keyword "super.grams".

It's a compile-time error to have a superclass variable with the same name as a subclass *method* or vice-versa. And for the sake of completeness, note that the case of a method with the same name in both the superclass and the subclass is dealt with in the section in Chapter 2 on polymorphism.

Interface Declarations

As we noted above, interfaces are skeletons of classes showing what form the Class will take when someone implements it. An interface may look like this:

```
public interface DataInput {

    int skipBytes(int n);

    void readFully(byte b[]);

    byte readByte(byte b[], int off, int len);

}
```

It is used to specify the form that something *must* have, but not actually provide the implementation. In this sense, an interface is a little like an abstract class, that must be extended in exactly the manner that its methods present.

An interface differs from an abstract class in the following ways:

- A class can implement several interfaces at once, but Java does not have multiple inheritance, so a class can only extend one parent class.

- An interface is really a static (compile-time) protocol. An abstract class implies Inheritance, which carries runtime implications for selecting the appropriate method for an object's type. In this sense, an interface with its implementation may be lower cost than a base class with an extension.

- An interface doesn't have any overtones of specialization that are present with inheritance. It merely says "well, we need something that does 'foo' and here are the ways that users should be able to call it."

An interface is a way of saying "you need to plug some code in here, for this thing to fully work." Other pieces of code in the system can compile against the calls provided by the system, but nothing will run until something implements the interface, like this:

```
public
class RandomAccessFile implements DataOutput, DataInput {

    private FileDescriptor fd;

    public int skipBytes(int n) {
        seek(getFilePointer() + n);
        return n;
    }

    public final void readFully(byte b[]) {
            readBytes(b, 0, b.length);
    }

    private native int readBytes(byte b[], int off, int len);

}
```

One possible use of an interface is to provide a boundary between platform-independent and platform-dependent parts of the system (always a thorny challenge in software development, the two have such a terrible tendency to get themselves mixed up in each other). So you are likely to see interfaces heavily used in I/O, and indeed the examples above are adapted from the java.io directory. DataInput is an interface describing streams that can read input in a machine-independent format. RandomAccessFile (or something else that implements the interface) will be different on each platform. This is indicated by the native method use.

An interface can be fulfilled ("implemented") by code written in languages other than Java (if you wanted to re-use existing routines for example). Code can implement more than one interface at a time, as the example above illustrates.

There's another way to use an interface, that's not really what it was intended for, but which forms a useful programming idiom.

If you have a group of related constants, perhaps of the kind you would put in an enumerated type (if the language had enumerated types), you might gather them in a class like this:

```
public class FightingWeight {
    public static final int          flyweight = 100;
    public static final int        bantamweight = 113;
    public static final int      featherweight = 118;
    public static final int        lightweight = 127;
    public static final int        welterweight = 136;
    public static final int        middleweight = 148;
    public static final int lightheavyweight = 161;
    public static final int        heavyweight = 176;
}
```

Then to use the constants in another class, you would have to do something like this:

```
static int title = FightingWeight.heavyweight;
```

If however, you make FightingWeight an *interface*, like this:

```
public interface FightingWeight {
    public static final int          flyweight = 100;
    public static final int        bantamweight = 113;
    public static final int      featherweight = 118;
    public static final int        lightweight = 127;
    public static final int        welterweight = 136;
    public static final int        middleweight = 148;
    public static final int lightheavyweight = 161;
    public static final int        heavyweight = 176;
}
```

Then you can reference the names directly. Wow!

```
class gooseberry implements FightingWeight {
    ...
static int title = heavyweight;
```

Don't tell anyone you heard it from me, at least not until the gods of programming have smiled upon it[9].

---

9. The gods of programming have now officially granted their benediction to this technique of opening up name visibility.

An interface can only extend another interface. A class can legally implement an interface but only implement some of the methods. It then becomes an abstract class that must be further extended (inherited) before it can be instantiated.

Some Light Relief

To close out a chapter that has dealt at length with naming, it's appropriate to consider two other examples of naming, and the confusion that can arise. The first one is computer-related, the second one pertains to confectionery. But they are both instructive.

There's a pervasive legend that the antihero computer HAL in the film "2001: A Space Odyssey" was so-named to indicate that he was one step ahead of IBM. Alphabetically "H" "A" "L" precede "I" "B" "M" by one letter[10].

The author of 2001, Arthur C. Clarke emphatically denies the legend in his book "Lost Worlds of 2001", claiming that "HAL" is an acronym for "Heuristically programmed algorithmic computer". Clarke even wrote to the computer magazine Byte to place his denial on record.

Certainly the claims of an involved party are one piece of evidence, but there is no particular reason why they should be uncritically accepted as complete truth; consider them rather in the context of all pieces of evidence. This is what happens in courts of law every day. Clarke's protestations are a little unconvincing. For one thing "Heuristically programmed algorithmic computer" is a contrived name that does not properly form the desired acronym. For another, most of the working drafts of the 2001 story had HAL named "Athena", and it would have remained so had not Clarke deliberately rechristened it. The chances of him accidentally fastening on to the one name that mimics one of the world's largest computer companies are one in a few thousand.

Why would Clarke deny it if it were true? IBM logos appear in several places in the movie, and the filmmakers clearly cut a deal with IBM for product placement. It may be that Clarke decided to assert some artistic independence and decided on the name change as a subtle dig at IBM, in that HAL is a homicidal maniac who goes berserk. Or he may just have been suggesting that his creation was one step ahead of IBM. Later, when the story got out, Clarke realized he would look foolish, or at the very least ungracious by lampooning them. So he denied the connection.

10. People say the same thing about Windows NT (WNT) being one step ahead of VMS. Dave Cutler designed VMS when he was at Digital, and then joined Microsoft to become the chief architect of Windows NT. I believe that the name was chosen with this in mind.

An interesting question is why was the name changed at all? If Clarke provided an explanation of *that* along with his denials, then the denials would have more credibility.

Lessons in Naming: the disgusting case of the Baby Ruth Candy Bar

A similar confusion over naming has arisen in the case of the Baby Ruth candy bar. The matter was thoroughly researched by my colleague David Mikkelson who wrote the following summary of his findings.

> The Curtiss Candy Company was founded in Chicago in 1916 by Otto Schnering. Schnering, who wanted a name more "American-sounding" than his own for the company—German surnames not being much of an asset during World War I—used his mother's maiden name instead.
>
> The Curtiss Candy Company's first product was a confection known as Kandy Kake, which featured a pastry center topped with nuts and coated with chocolate. This candy bar was only a moderate success until 1921, when Schnering reintroduced it as a log-shaped bar made of caramel and peanuts, covered with chocolate. Schnering named his new confection the "Baby Ruth" bar, priced it at five cents a bar (half the cost of other bars), and soon had one of the hottest-selling candy bars on the market.

Three explanations have since been offered concerning the origins of the "Baby Ruth" candy bar's name:

1. The bar was named after "Baby" Ruth Cleveland, the first-born daughter of President Grover Cleveland.

2. The bar was named after baseball slugger George Herman "Babe" Ruth.

3. The bar was named for a granddaughter of Mrs. George Williamson, Mrs. Williamson being the wife of the president of the Williamson Candy Company and one of the developers of the "Baby Ruth" bar formula.

Explanation #1 is the "official" explanation that has been proffered by the Curtiss Candy Company since the 1920's.

Explanation #2 is the "obvious" explanation; the one assumed by persons who have heard no explanations.

Explanation #3 is an alternate explanation whose origins are unknown, but it can be readily dismissed. The Williamson Candy Company—producer of the "Oh! Henry" bar—was a direct competitor of Curtiss' and would have been most unlikely to supply a product name and formula to a rival. Furthermore, the Curtiss Candy Company has never claimed this as an origin of their candy bar's name.

The claim that the "Baby Ruth" bar was named after Ruth Cleveland is found dubious by many because Ruth Cleveland died of diphtheria in 1904, over seventeen years before the "Baby Ruth" bar was first produced. Naming a candy bar after the long-dead daughter of a former president would certainly be a curious choice. Moreover, the notion that a candy bar called "Baby Ruth" should appear on the market just when a baseball player named Babe Ruth had suddenly become the most famous person in America is perceived as a rather striking coincidence.

If the Curtiss Candy Company did indeed appropriate Babe Ruth's name without permission, they would have had a motive for developing a fabricated yet believable explanation in case a challenge arose over the candy bar's name. Curtiss did indeed have to fight off at least one challenge to their name, when a competitor—with the full approval of Babe Ruth—attempted to market a candy named the "Babe Ruth Home Run Bar". Curtiss, claiming that their candy bar was named for Ruth Cleveland, was successful in forcing the competing candy bar off the market because its name too closely resembled that of their own product. Nobody ever said life was fair, and that's the way things are in the brutal world of children's candy marketing.

The fact that Curtiss successfully fought off a challenge to their candy bar's name does not prove that they were untruthful, however. Merely showing that they had a reason to lie is not evidence that they did lie and are still lying; it must be demonstrated that Curtiss actually has been untruthful about the origins of the "Baby Ruth" name. Although it may not now be possible to prove that Curtiss was less than honest when they were fighting off the challenge of the "Babe Ruth Home Run Bar", it can certainly be demonstrated that they have been dishonest about the origin of the name "Baby Ruth" in the years since then.

First of all, the official Curtiss position maintained for many years is that their "candy bar made its initial appearance in 1921, some years before Babe Ruth . . . became famous." In 1919, Babe Ruth was a standout pitcher for the Red Sox, but not yet well-known outside of Boston and the baseball world. Sold to the New York Yankees prior to the 1920 season, Ruth soon established himself as an outfield star and was nationally famous by the end of the year. By 1921 his name was featured more prominently on the front pages of afternoon newspapers than President Harding's. The claim that he was not famous until "some years" after 1921 is nothing but absurd. This misstatement could merely be a mistake on Curtiss' part due to shoddy record-keeping or research, but the claim has been offered for so many years and is so easily verifiable that it is hard to explain as anything other than dissembling.

Another claim made by the Curtiss Candy Company is much harder to forgive as mere bad record-keeping, though. Part of the official statement about the "Baby Ruth" name offered by Curtiss has been that Ruth Cleveland "visited the Curtiss Candy Company plant years ago when the company was getting started and this largely influenced the company's founder to name the candy bar 'Baby Ruth'". Ruth Cleveland died at age twelve in 1904; no amount of bad record-keeping can place her in the factory of a company that wouldn't exist until more than a decade after her death. The conclusion is clear.

See how many books you can find which have the inaccurate version of the Baby Ruth candy bar story. The story is commonly re-told with the Curtiss cover story being presented as fact. I have yet to find a reference work where the author has actually done some independent analysis, and concluded that Curtiss are full of it. Kudos to David Mikkelson for setting the record straight.

Sources:

Bob Broeg, "At Microphone, Plate, Reggie's A Real Blast" <u>St. Louis Post-Dispatch</u>, 7 August 1993.

Ray Broekel, <u>The Great American Candy Bar Book</u> (Boston: Houghton Mifflin, 1982), p. 23

Tom Burnam, <u>More Misinformation</u> (New York: Lippincott & Crowell, 1980), p. 13

Sharon Kapnick, "Sweet Beginnings; How Some Famous Chocolate Treats Evolved to Stand the Taste of Time" <u>The Arizona Republic</u>, 13 February 1993.

Richard Sandomir, "Legacy of Earning Power; Babe Ruth: Dead 41 Years, He Lives on in Endorsements That Bring Heirs Hundreds of Thousands" <u>Los Angeles Times</u>, 22 December 1989

Kal Wagenheim, <u>Babe Ruth: His Life and Legend</u> (New York: Praeger Publishers, 1974), p.86

Further Reading

"What Every Computer Scientist Should Know About Floating-Point Arithmetic"

by David Goldberg Computing Surveys, March 1991, published by the Association for Computing Machinery.

It explains why all floating point arithmetic is approximate, and how errors can creep in. The paper was reprinted and is distributed in postscript form with the compilers sold by Sun Microsystems.

ANSI/IEEE Standard 754-1985 for Binary Floating-Point Arithmetic

Institute of Electrical and Electronic Engineers, New York, published 1985. Reprinted in SIGPLAN 22(2) pages 9-25.

"The C Programming Language, Second Edition"

by Brian W. Kernighan and Dennis Ritchie Published by Prentice-Hall Inc., New Jersey, 1978

ISBN 0-13-110163-3

The first edition of this book was the ground-breaking work from which so much has flowed in the in the past twenty years. Like C itself, this book set a standard which many have aspired, but few others have achieved. The text (and the language) is not perfect, few things of human construction are, but it has served well over the years.

CHAPTER
5

More Sophisticated Techniques

London's gangland underworld was dominated during the 1960's by two brothers who were career criminals from the East-end, Ronnie and Reggie Kray. The Kray twins were eventually sentenced to life terms in prison for the chaos and mayhem they created.

FACT: The UK government Meteorological Office has two Cray supercomputers used to simulate chaotic systems such as weather fronts. These twin Crays are therefore affectionately named "Ronnie" and "Reggie"—the Cray twins.

I n this chapter we address the topic of arrays, and how to build dynamic data structures in a language without pointers. We then go on to cover the functionality of exceptions (runtime error handling) and threads (light weight processes). We finish up with some notes on the automatic reclaiming of memory that is no longer in use.

Arrays

It is a little misleading to claim as some people have done that "support and syntax for arrays is much the same in Java as it is in C." Any similarities are superficial ones based on syntax alone. The key to understanding C arrays is understanding the interaction between arrays and pointers. But Java does away with all that guff.

Java has neither the complexities, nor the "size fixed at compile-time" of C arrays. The Java array model is more like that of Ada: arrays of arbitrary bounds as parameters, and dynamically-allocatable arrays, each carrying around information about its own length.

Arrays (like classes) are a reference type. When you declare what looks like an array, you actually get a variable that can hold a reference to an array. You still have to create the array. The simplest form of array declaration is this:

```
int carrot [];
```

Note that the size is not given. In fact you may not specify the array dimension in a declaration like this.

You never specify the size of an array in a C-style declaration like this:

```
int carrot [256];              // NO! NO! NO!
```

The array's size is set when you assign something to it, either in an initializer or a regular assignment statement. Once an array object has been created with a given size, it cannot change for that array, although you can replace it by assigning a differently-sized array object to it.

The array can be created like this:

```
int carrot [] = new int[256];
```

This creates a 256 element array, with the default initialization of 0; you can create and initialize an array in one declaration, like this:

```
int carrot[] = {1,2,3,4,5,6};
float beet[]  = { 5.5F, p, q, 2.2F, };
```

Note that a superfluous trailing comma is allowed—an unnecessary carryover from C.[1]

1. The permissible extra trailing comma is claimed to be of use when a list of initial values is being generated automatically. The claim is like Dick van Dyke's Cockney accent in the film "Mary Poppins" —it starts off as unlikely, then rapidly becomes totally unbelievable the more you hear it.

Array constants (a series of values in braces) can only be used in initializers, not in later assignment statements.

Because an array is an object, all the usual object-y style things apply. Operations that are common to all objects can be done on arrays. Operations that require an object as an operand can be passed an array. The length of an array (the number of components in it) is a data field in the array class. So you can get the size of an array by referencing:

```
a.length      // yes
```

People always want to treat that as a method call, and write

```
a.length()     // NO! NO! NO!
```

Think of it this way, for an array, length is just a final data field, set when the array object is created. There is no need to have the overhead of a method call. There is no need for a "sizeof" operator, and Java does not have one.

For non-C programmers: array subscripts *always* start at 0.

People coming to Java (or C or C++) from another language often have trouble with that concept. After all, when you're counting anything, you always start "one, two, three" —so why would array elements be any different?

The answer is that this is one of the things carried over from C. C was designed by and for systems programmers, and in a compiler a subscript is translated to "offset from base address." You can save a step in subscript-to-address translation if you disallow subscripts with an arbitrary starting point. Instead directly use offset-from-base-address, and the first offset is zero.

Watch out! It means that when you declare:

```
int day[] = new int[365];
```

valid subscripts for "day" are in the range 0 to 364. A reference to "day[365]" is invalid. If this causes distress in terms of program readability (e.g. you want days numbered from 1 to 365 to match the calendar) then simply declare the array one larger than it needs to be, and don't use element zero.

Array indexes are all checked at runtime. If a subscript attempts a reference outside the bounds of its array, it causes an exception and the program ceases execution rather than corrupt memory. Exceptions are described later in this chapter.

Arrays of Arrays

The language specification says there are no "multidimensional" arrays in Java, meaning Java doesn't use the convention of Pascal or Ada of putting several indexes into one set of subscript brackets. Ada allows multidimensional arrays like this:

```
banana : array(1..12, 1..31) of real;      Ada code for
                                              multi-dimensional array

banana(i,j) = 3.14;
```

Ada also allows arrays of arrays, like this:

```
type carrot is array(1..31) of real;      Ada code for array of arrays

breadfruit : array(1..12) of carrot;
banana(i)(j) = 3.14;
```

Pascal, too, allows both forms, and treats them as one:

```
var banana : array[1..12] of array[1..31] of real;      Pascal code
banana[i][j] = 3.14;                                      for arrays
                                                          of arrays.
```

it is usual to abbreviate this as:

```
var banana : array[1..12, 1..31] of real;      Pascal code
banana[i, j] = 3.14;                            for multi-
                                                dimensional
                                                arrays
```

Pascal blurs the distinction by saying that arrays of arrays are equivalent to and interchangeable with multidimensional arrays [Pascal User Manual and Report, Springer-Verlag, 1975, page 39]. Java just has arrays of arrays.

What "Multidimensional" Means in Different Languages

The Ada standard explicitly says arrays of arrays and multidimensional arrays are different. The language has both.

The Pascal standard says arrays of arrays and multidimensional arrays are the same thing.

The ANSI C standard says C has what other languages call arrays of arrays, but it also calls these "multidimensional."

The Java language only has arrays of arrays, and it only calls these arrays of arrays.

Arrays of arrays are declared like this:

```
int cabbage [] [] ;
```

Array "cabbage" is composed of an array which is composed of an array whose elements are integers.

Because object declarations do not create objects, you will need to fill out or "instantiate" the elements in an array before using it. If you have an array of arrays, like this:

```
int cabbage[][];
```

you will need to instantiate both the top-level array, and at least one bottom level array before you can start storing ints.   The bottom level arrays do not have to all be a single uniform size. (This is true for C too—the classic example being the argv array of strings declared in main.)

Here is one way you could create a triangular array of arrays, and fill it with initial values:

```
int cabbage[][] = new int[5][];

int slice0[] = {0};
int slice1[] = {0,1};
int slice2[] = {0,1,2};
int slice3[] = {0,1,2,3};
int slice4[] = {0,1,2,3,4};

cabbage[0] = slice0;
cabbage[1] = slice1;
cabbage[2] = slice2;
cabbage[3] = slice3;
cabbage[4] = slice4;
```

We introduce the variables slice0 etc. because array literals, like "{0,1,2,3}" can only be used in an initializer, not in a statement. Here is another way to do it, that provides an equivalent result in cabbage.

```
int cabbage[][] = new int[5][];

for( int i=0; i<cabbage.length; i++) {
    int tmp[] = new int [i+1];

    for (int j=0; j<=i; j++)
        tmp[j]=j;

    cabbage[i] = tmp;
}
```

Yet a third way is to lump all the initializers together in a big array literal like this:

```
int cabbage[][] = {   {0},
                      {0,1},
                      {0,1,2},
                      {0,1,2,3},
                      {0,1,2,3,4}
                  };
```

Note that if you instantiate the dimensions at different times, you must instantiate the most significant dimensions first. So,

```
int cabbage[][] = new int[5][];    // ok
int cabbage[][] = new int[5][3];   // ok
```

but

```
int cabbage[][] = new int[][3];    // NO! NO! NO!
```

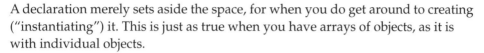

Remember that declarations do not create objects!

A declaration merely sets aside the space, for when you do get around to creating ("instantiating") it. This is just as true when you have arrays of objects, as it is with individual objects.

```
Integer beer[]  = new Integer[10]; // note: class Integer, not int.
```

does not give you an array full of Integer objects. It gives you an array full of elements that can reference an Integer object. If you reference beer[3] before filling out that value in the array with either of:

```
beer[3] = new Integer(n);
beer[3] = SomeExistingIntegerObject;
```

you will of course get a null pointer exception.

Arrays with the same element type, and the same number of dimensions (in the C sense, Java doesn't have multidimensional arrays) can be assigned to each other. The arrays do not need to have the same number of elements because what actually happens is that one reference variable is copied into the other.

For example:

```
int eggs[] = {1,2,3,4};
int ham[] = {1};
ham = eggs;
ham[3] = 0;    // OK, because ham now has 4 elements.
```

This doesn't make a new copy of eggs, it makes ham and eggs reference the same array object.

So changes made to the array though references by one variable will be seen by references through the other variable. In the code:

```
// show example of what is a copy, and what is a ref.
     Integer beer[] = new Integer[10];
     Integer lager[];

     beer[3] = new Integer(3);

     lager = beer;

     beer[3] = new Integer(256);

     if (lager[3].intValue() == 256)
          System.out.println("It just copied the reference" +
                            " -- they point at same Object" );
```

the assignment "lager=beer" simply copies the beer reference variable into the lager reference variable. When one element of the array that beer points at is changed, naturally the change is seen by both, and so the println message will be printed out.

In diagram form, before the assignment of "lager=beer" we have Figure 5-1:

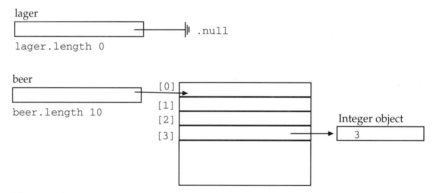

Figure 5-1

After the assignment of "lager=beer" we have the Figure 5-2:

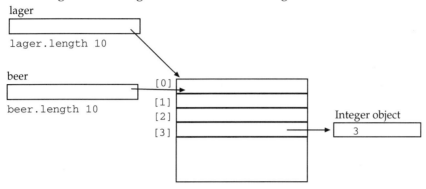

Figure 5-2

After the assignment of "beer[3] = new Integer(256)" we have the diagram shown in Figure 5-3:

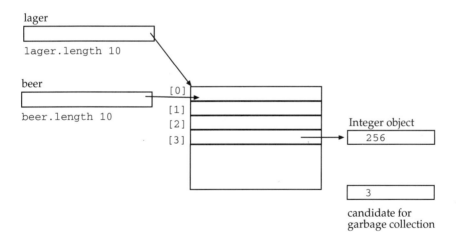

Figure 5-3

If instead, it was your intention that a fresh copy of all the objects referenced by the array beer be put into the array referenced by lager, then you would have to do something like this:

```
// create an array for lager
  lager = new Integer[10];

// copy the elements of beer into lager array
  System.arraycopy(beer,0,lager,0,beer.length);
```

This would allow you to assign something different to beer[3], and not see any change in lager[3]. After the "System.arraycopy()" we will have Figure 5-4:

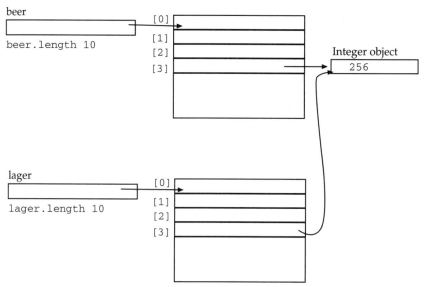

Figure 5-4

And finally, if you then assign "beer[3] = new Integer(3);" The diagram will look like Figure 5-5:

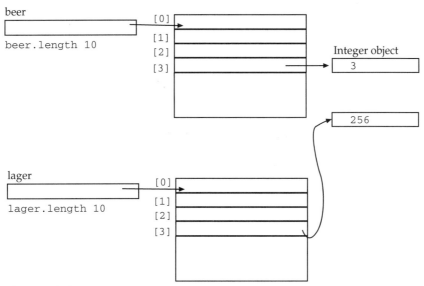

Figure 5-5

Have Array Brackets / Will Travel

There is a quirk of syntax in that the array declaration bracket pairs can "float", to be next to the element type, or next to the data name, or in a mixture of the two! These are all valid array declarations:

```
int a [] ;
int [] b = { a.length, 2, 3 } ;

char c [][] = new char[12][31];
char[] d [] = { {1,1,1,1}, {2,2,2,2} }; // creates d[2][4]
char[][] e;

byte f [][][] = new byte [3][3][7];
byte [][] g[] = new byte [3][3][7];

short [] h, i[], j, k[][];
```

If array brackets appear next to the type, they are part of the type, and apply to *every* variable in that declaration. In the code above, "j" is an array of short, and "i" is an array of arrays of short.

This is mostly so declarations of functions returning arrays can be read more normally. Here is an example of how returning an array value from a function would look following C rules (you can't return an array in C, but this is how C syntax would express it if you could):

```
int funarray()[] { ... }                    Pseudo-C
```

Here are the alternatives for expressing it in Java, (and it is permissible in Java), first following the C paradigm:

```
int ginger ()[]   { return new int[20]; }      Java
```

A better way is to express it like this:

because that allows the programmer to see all the tokens that comprise the return type grouped together.

Arrays are never allocated on the stack in Java, so you cannot get into trouble returning an array stack variable. In C it is too easy to return a pointer to an array on the stack that will be overwritten by something else pushed on the stack after returning from the method.

Programmers cannot make this programming error in Java, as arrays are never allocated on the stack. If you write an array as a local variable, that actually creates a reference to the array. You need a little more code to create the array itself, and that will allocate the array safely on the heap.

Arrays may be indexed by "int" values. Arrays may not be indexed by "long" values. That means arrays are implicitly limited to no more than the highest 32 bit int value, namely 2,147,483,647. That's OK for the next couple of years -- but the lack of 64-bit addressing will eventually make itself felt in Java.

Values of types "byte", "short", and "char" are promoted to "ints" when they are used as an index, just as they are in other expression contexts.

String and StringBuffer

There are two class types that exist in the predefined package java.lang, which is implicitly imported into every compilation unit. They are used to represent character strings and they are:

class String	This class is for strings that do not change after creation. You can however create a new String object from pieces of the old one, and discard the old one. You can think of String as a performance hack optimized for constant strings.
	This class contains methods to construct a String from a char array, construct a copy of a String, extract a substring, translate string case and characters, compare strings, convert a string to a byte array, convert any built-in type to a String, and more.
class StringBuffer	StringBuffer objects are used for strings that are expected to grow, shrink, or change letters. The class is implemented in a way that makes these operations as efficient as they can be. The compiler uses it to implement the "+" String concatenation operator.
	This class contains methods to construct various StringBuffers give the object a new length (grow/shrink) set the character at a given offset append a String onto this StringBuffer and more.

The source for these two classes listing all of the methods is distributed as part of the Java Development Kit, and can be viewed at java/src/java/lang/String.java and StringBuffer.java.

Java does not recognize the C convention that strings are simply nul-terminated arrays of characters. It has the two string classes to provide a rich group of operations on character strings.

The operations are methods in the two classes. The subscript operator "[]" cannot be used on Strings, though there are methods that have the same effect of accessing a char at a given position. An array like:

```
char foo[] = { 'f', 'o', 'o' };
```

is not a String and cannot have the String methods applied to it. It can easily be converted back and forth between char [] and String.

In contrast to finding the length of an array, getting the length of a String or StringBuffer variable does require a method call:

```
String s = "scrofulous";
int i = s.length();
```

You might remember this by thinking "Strings" support more operations than mere character arrays. So Strings use a method to calculate their length whereas character arrays can just use a "length" field. On the other hand, since Strings are fixed in size once created, why isn't length just a final data field?

The thinking seems to be that it is better for String to be consistent with String-Buffer (which has to do it via a method as that is the only way to give users read access to the length field without also granting them write access).

A shortcut to the normal "new" operator is allowed when giving Strings an initial value. You can say:

```
String s = "crapulent";
```

This works as well as the equivalent:

```
String s = new String("crapulent");
```

This is a concession to the existing expectations of programmers.

Dynamic Data Structures

The first question that most programmers ask when they hear that Java does not feature pointer variables is "how do you create dynamic data structures?" How, for instance, do you create a binary tree class, in which objects of the class can point to each other?

The answer is that reference variables (which are implicit pointers) do this perfectly adequately. Here are the data members for a Tree class in C++

```
class Tree {
    private:                                    C++
            int     data;
            Tree    *left;
            Tree    *right;
        . . .
```

Here is how the same data structure is written in Java

```
class Tree {                              Java
    private Object data;
    private Tree left;
    private Tree right;
        ...
```

This only shows the data, but the key characteristics of a data structure are the operations that you can perform on it, and can be expressed as an interface. Here is a Java interface for a trivial linked list class:

```
public interface LinkedListIntf {
    public void addAfter(Object data);
    public void deleteAfter();
    public LinkedListIntf nextLink();

}
```

Your mission Jim, should you decide to accept it, is to write a Java class that implements the "LinkedListIntf" interface.

Keep things easy: make it a singly-linked list, and (since the interface provides a method to addAfter) make the root of the list be a special element that you create the others off.

Now the good news. The class will start like this:

```
public class LinkedList implements LinkedListIntf {
    private LinkedList next;
    public Object datum;
```

Note: *the fact that we need to specify these additional lines highlights a weakness of interfaces in that the only data that can appear in an interface is final data. If this is not appropriate for your application, you must use an abstract class instead.*

The program can be completed in less than 25 lines of code. Your "main()" driver program to use and test the linked lists will probably be longer than the LinkedList class implementation. (Easy to Medium).

In addition, there are some built-in utilities in the package java.util such that a class for the data structure you want may already exist. There is a utility class called Vector, for instance. The class java.util.Vector presents an array into which you can insert elements. The array will be grown behind the scenes as necessary to hold whatever you add to it. This does the job of a linked list, but is even better because you also have random access to the individual elements.

Modify the driver program that you wrote for the previous programming challenge (you *did* write it, didn't you?) so that it uses "java.util.Vector" instead of the linked list implementation that you wrote.

Your new program will start with:

```
import java.util.Vector;
```

Modify the driver so that it does some time measurement (see tip below). Make it carry out some random adding and deleting of elements. Which of your original linked list program, and the utility Vector, is faster for 100 operations? For 1000? For one million? Account for the results.

Here's how you can time your Java code:

```
long start = System.currentTimeMillis();
     :   // do the work here
     :
long stop = System.currentTimeMillis();
System.out.println("Run time: " + (stop-start) +
"millisecs" );
```

Take a look at the other routines available in java/src/lang/System.java. Contrast the Java situation of many utility packages, and guaranteed interoperability, with that of C++. When C++ first became available, there were few utility classes, but everyone used the same compiler (cfront from AT&T). Later when utility libraries became available from third parties, there were sometimes several alternative compilers available for a given platform. That turned out to cause problems. The lack of a C++ Application Binary Interface (ABI) that specified details like name-mangling, exception handling, and argument passing meant that software from different compilers was not necessarily interoperable.

A C++ binary package you bought to support linked lists might not work with your compiler. Or it might not work with a different library you bought from another vendor. To stand a reasonable chance of getting libraries to work together you had to have access to the source and recompile it in your own environment. The C++ language has been handicapped by this dirty secret for several years. Until there is a standard, stable C++ language, it's hard to have a standard, stable ABI.

The standard API and ABI, fixed for all platforms, is an important part of the basic design of Java, so it will avoid the "every compiler shows a different interface" problem. Here are some of the Java utility classes that exist in every implementation:

java.util.*	Notes:
BitSet.java	An array of bits indexed by subscript. The collection grows as you need to add more bits.
Date.java	A class to process day/dates in a system independent way. Gives access to year, month,day, hour, minute and second.
Enumeration.java	An interface that specifies two methods to help count through a set of values.
Hashtable.java	A very useful class! This class maintains a hashtable that can hold any object, and convert any object to a key. This class lets you impose some order and storage capability on arbitrary objects. See explanation below.
Properties.java	Persistent properties class. Can save a hash table to a stream, and read one back in again. It is an extension of the Hashtable class.
Random.java	Generates pseudo-random numbers in various useful forms and types. Can be completely different each time, or provide the same sequence of random numbers (for testing).
Stack.java	Implements a last-in/first out stack of objects.
StringTokenizer.java	Does simple lexing (separation into individual tokens removing white space) on a text string.
Vector.java	Data structure that can hold a collection of arbitrary objects, and provide immediate access by subscript to them. The array will be extended as needed as more objects are added to it.

Hash Table Explanation

A symbol table in a compiler is often maintained as a hash table. When a name is first read in from the source program, it is hashed (converted to a hash-key value, say 379, by an algorithm designed to spread the values around the table) and entered in the table at location 379 along with all its characteristics (type, scope, etc.). Then when you get the same name again, it is hashed, and the same result, 379, is used as a subscript for immediate access to all its details in the hash table. It is marvellous that a hash table is a library data structure in Java!

Why is a hash table better than just maintaining a sorted list or vector? Because hashing is fast, and sorting is slow.

Go to the directory with the Java library source on your system (java/src/java) and cd into the util sub directory.

1. List the directory contents. These are the java source files for the utility programs.

2. Look at the source of any 5 programs there. Read all the methods. Look at the implementation. Why does it do what it does? If your boss offered you a ten thousand zloty bonus to make one of these methods faster, which one would you select and how would you do it?

3. Run javadoc on a different 5 source files, and read the resultant html files. (Medium).

Exceptions

At several points in the preceding text we have mentioned exceptions, only to defer discussion. This is the section where we deliver on the promise of describing the purpose and use of exceptions. We will cover the topic of exceptions in the following steps, each building on the one before:

1. the purpose of exceptions

2. how to cause an exception (implicitly and explicitly)

3. how to handle ("catch") an exception within the method where it was thrown

4. handling groups of related exceptions

5. how the exception propagates if not handled in the method where it was thrown

6. how and why methods declare the exceptions that can propagate out of them.

7. Fancy Exception stuff

The Purpose of Exceptions

Exceptions are for changing the flow of control when some important or unexpected event, usually an error, has occurred. They divert processing to a part of the program that can try to cope with the error, or at least die gracefully. The error can be any condition at all, ranging from "unable to open a file" to "array subscript out of range" to "no memory left to allocate" to "division by zero." Java exceptions are adapted from C++ which itself borrowed them from the language ML. Java exception terminology is presented below.

Note	Java	Some other languages
An error condition that happens at run time	Exception	Exception
Causing an exception to occur	Throwing	Raising
Capturing an exception that has just occurred, and executing statements to resolve it in some way	Catching	Handling
The block that does this.	Catch block	Handler
The sequence of call statements that brought control to the method where the exception happened	Stack trace	Call chain

An exception can be set in motion explicitly with the "throw" statement, or implicitly by carrying out some illegal or invalid action. The exception then diverts the normal flow of control (like a goto statement). If the programmer has made provision, control will transfer to a section of the program that can recover from the error. That section can be in the same method, or in the method that called the one where the exception occurred, or in the one that called *that*, and so on up the stack of calls that were made at runtime. If it gets to the top, where your program execution started, and no handler for this exception has yet been found, then program execution will cease, with an explanatory message.

So the places that you can jump to are strictly limited. You even have to explicitly stipulate "in this block, I will listen for and deal with this type of exception."

How To Cause An Exception (implicitly and explicitly)

Exceptions are caused in one of two ways: the program does something illegal (usual case), or the program explicitly generates an exception by executing the throw statement (less usual case). The throw statement has this general form:

```
throw ExceptionObject;
```

The *ExceptionObject* is an object of a class that extends the class java.lang.Exception.

Triggering an Exception

Here is a simple program that causes a "division by zero" exception.

```
class melon {
    public static void main(String[] a) {
        int i=1, j=0, k;

        k = i/j;     // Causes division-by-zero error
    }
}
```

Compiling and running this program gives this result:

```
> javac melon.java
> java melon
      java.lang.ArithmeticException: / by zero
            at melon.main(melon.java:5)
```

There are a certain number of predefined exceptions, like ArithmeticException, known as the runtime exceptions. Actually, since *all* exceptions are runtime events a better name would be the "irrecoverable" exceptions. This contrasts with the user-defined exceptions which are generally held to be less severe, and in some instances can be recovered from. If a filename cannot be opened, prompt the user to enter a new name. If a data structure is found to be full, overwrite some element that is no longer needed.

The predefined Exceptions and their class hierarchies are:

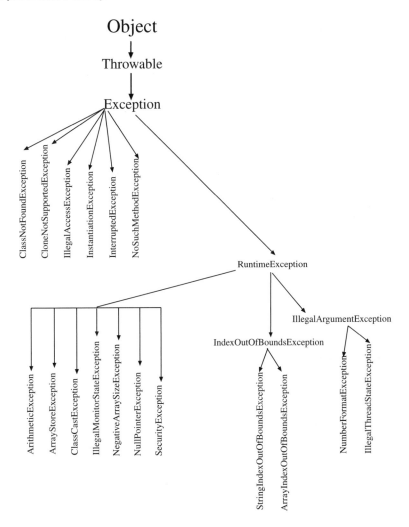

The names are intended to suggest the error condition each represents. The source files for these can be found in src/java/lang.

© 1996 Matthew Burtch

User-Defined Exceptions

Here is an example of how to create your own exception class by extending System.exception:

```
class OutofGas extends Exception {}

class banana {
        :

     if (fuel < 0.1) throw   new OutofGas();
}
```

Any method that throws a user-defined exception must also either catch it, or declare it as part of the method interface. What, you may ask, is the point of throwing an exception if you are going to catch it in the same method?

The answer is that exceptions don't *reduce* the amount of work you have to do to handle errors. Their advantage is they let you collect it all in well-localized places in your program, so you don't obscure the main flow of control with zillions of checks of return values.

How to Handle ("Catch") an Exception
Within the Method Where It Was Thrown

Here is the general form of how to catch an exception.

```
try           block
```
There must be at least one (or both) of
the two choices below.

```
[ catch (arg)  block  ]
[ finally      block  ]
```
←— there can be zero or many of these
←— there can be zero or one of these

A "block" is a single statement or a
whole group of statements in curly
braces.

The "try" statement says "try these statements, and see if you get an exception". The "try" statement must be followed by at least one "catch" clause or the "finally" clause.

Each "catch" says "I will handle any exception that matches my argument." Matching an argument means that the thrown exception could legally be assigned to the argument exception. There can be several successive catches, each looking for a different exception. Don't try to catch *all* exceptions with one clause, like this:

```
catch (Exception e) { ...
```

That is way too general to be of use: you might catch more than you expected. You'd be better off letting the exception propagate to the top and give you a reasonable error message.

The "finally" block, if present, is a "last chance to clean up" block. It is always executed—even if something in one of the other blocks did a "return"! The "finally" block is executed whether an exception occurred or not, and whether it was caught or not. It is executed after the catch block if present, and if one of them caught an exception or not.

The finally block can be useful in the complete absence of any exceptions. It is a piece of code that will be executed irrespective of what happens in the "try" block. There may be numerous paths through a large and complicated "try" block. The "finally" block can contain the housekeeping tasks that must always be done (locks released, etc.) when finishing this piece of code.

Here is an example of an exception guarding statement in full, adapted from the window toolkit code.

```
try {
        a[i] /= j;

        comp.paintAll(cg);
    }

catch (ArithmeticException e) {
                System.out.println("you doofus");
        }

catch (ArrayIndexOutOfBoundsException e) {
                System.out.println("bad subscript");
        }

finally {
        cg.dispose();
        }
```

Supply enough of a context to the code above such that it will compile and run. Put the code in a loop, and have one iteration cause a division by zero, and when you try it again cause an array index out-of-bounds exception. Make up null methods for paintAll() and dispose() and for the objects cg and comp. This example is adapted from code in the Java window toolkit (Easy).

After the whole *try ... catch ... finally* series of blocks are executed, if nothing else was done to divert it execution continues after the last catch or finally (whichever is present). The kind of thing that could make execution divert to elsewhere are the regular things: a continue, break, return, or the raising of a different exception. If a "finally" clause also has a transfer of control statement, then it is the one that is obeyed.

Handling Groups of Related Exceptions

We mentioned above that "matching an argument" means that the thrown exception can legally be assigned to the argument exception. This permits a subtle refinement. It allows a handler to catch any of several related exception objects with common parentage. Look at this example.

```
class Grumpy extends Exception {}
class TooHot   extends Grumpy {}
class TooTired extends Grumpy {}
class TooCross extends Grumpy {}
class TooCold  extends Grumpy {}


     .
     :


     try {
       if ( temp > 40 ) throw (new TooHot() );
       if ( sleep < 8 ) throw (new TooTired() );
     }
     catch (Grumpy g) {
         if (g instanceof TooHot)
            {System.out.println("caught too hot!"); return;}
         if (g instanceof TooTired)
            {System.out.println("caught too tired!"); return;}
     }
     finally System.out.println("in the finally clause.");
   }
```

The catch clauses are checked in the order in which they appear in the program. If there is a match, then the block is executed. The instanceof operator can be used to learn the exact identity of the exception.

How The Exception Propagates If Not Handled In The Method Where It Was Thrown

If none of the catch clauses match the exception that has been thrown, then the finally clause is executed (if there is one). At this point (no handler for this exception), what happens is the same as if the statement that threw the exception was not nested in a try statement at all.

The flow of control abruptly leaves this method, and a premature return is done to the method that called this one. If that call was in the scope of a try statement, then we look for a matching exception again, and so on.

Here's a diagram that shows what happens when an exception is not dealt with in the routine where it occurs. The runtime system looks for a try...catch block further up the call chain, enclosing the method call that brought us here. If the exception propagates all the way to the top of the call stack without finding a matching exception handler then execution ceases with a message. You can think of this as Java setting up a default catch block for you, around the program entry point that just prints an error message and quits.

There is no overhead to putting some statements in a "try" statement. The only overhead comes when an exception occurs.

How and Why Methods Declare The Exceptions That Can Propagate Out of Them

Earlier we mentioned that a method must either catch the exceptions that it throws, or declare it as part of its signature, meaning it must announce the exception to the outside world. This is so that anyone who writes a call to that method is alerted to the fact that an exception might come back instead of a normal return. This allows the programmer who calls that method to make the choice between

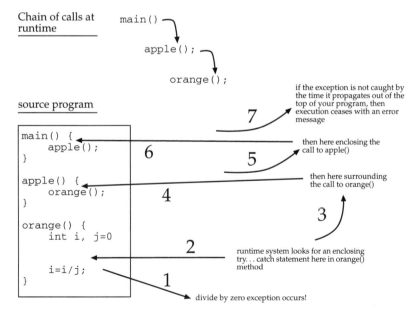

Figure 5-6

handling the exception, or allowing it to propagate further up the call stack. Here is the general form of how a method declares the exceptions that might be propagated out of it:

```
modifiers_and_returntype name (params)  throws e1, e2, e3  { }
```

The names e1... etc. must be exception names, i.e. any type that is assignable to the predefined type Throwable. Note that, just as a method signature specifies the return *type*, it specifies the exception *type* that can be thrown (rather than an exception object).

An example, taken from the Java I/O system is:

```
 byte readByte() throws IOException;
short readShort() throws IOException;
 char readChar() throws IOException;

void writeByte(int v) throws IOException;
void writeShort(int v) throws IOException;
void writeChar(int v) throws IOException;
```

The interesting thing to note here is that the routine to read a char, can return a char—not the int that is required in C. C requires an int to be returned so that it can pass back any of the possible values for a char, plus an extra value (-1) to signify that the end of file was reached. Some of the Java routines just throw an exception when the EOF is hit. Out-of-band-signalling can be effective in keeping your code well-organized. The EOF exception is a subclass of the IOException so the technique suggested above for handling groups of related exceptions can be applied.

The rules for how much and what must match when one method that throws an exception overrides another, work in the obvious way.[2]

Fancy Exception Stuff

When you create a new exception, by subclassing an existing exception class, you have the chance to associate a message string with it. The message string can be retrieved by a method. Usually the message string will be some kind of message that helps resolve the problem or suggests an alternative action.

2.   Namely, if you never do this, you will never be obviously bothered by it. Well, OK, another way to think about it is to consider the exception as an extra parameter that must be assignment-compatible with the exception in the class being overridden.

```
class OutofGas extends Exception {
    OutofGas(String s) {super(s);}  // constructor
}


    ...
// in use, it may look like this
  try {
        if (j<1) throw  new OutofGas("try the reserve tank");
      }
catch ( OutofGas o) {
        System.out.println( o.getMessage() );
      }
    ...


//At run time it will look like this:
  try the reserve tank
```

Another method that is inherited from the superclass Throwable is "printStack-Trace()". Invoking this method on an exception will cause the call chain at the point where the exception was thrown (not where it is being handled) to be printed out. For example,

```
// catching an exception in a calling method

class test5p {
    static int slice0[] = {0,1,2,3,4};
    public static void main(String[] a) {
        try {
            bob();
        } catch (Exception e) {
            System.out.println("caught exception in main()");
            e.printStackTrace();
        }
    }

    static void bob() {

        try {
          slice0[-1] = 4;
        }
        catch (NullPointerException e) {
            System.out.println("caught a different exception");
        }

    }
}
```

At run time it will look like this:

```
caught exception in main()
java.lang.ArrayIndexOutOfBoundsException: -1
            at test5p.bob(test5p.java:19)
            at test5p.main(test5p.java:9)
```

Summary of Exceptions

- Purpose: safer programming by providing a distinct path to deal with errors.

- Do use them. They are a useful tool for organized error handling.

- The main use is getting a decent error message out explaining what failed and where and why. It's a bit much to expect recovery.

Graceful degradation is often about the most you can obtain.

Threads

Multithreading is not a new concept in software, but it is new to come into the limelight. People have been kicking around experimental implementations for a dozen years or more, but it is only recently that desktop hardware (especially desktop multiprocessors—if you don't have one ask your boss for it today!) became powerful enough to make multithreading popular. As of January 1, 1996, there is only one book in print devoted to multithreading (see "Further Reading" at the end of this chapter), but there are plenty more on the way. There is a POSIX document P1003.4a (ratified June 1995) that describes a threads API standard. The threads described by the POSIX model and the threads available in Java do not exactly coincide. Java threads are simpler, take care of their own memory management, and do not have the full generality (or overhead) of POSIX threads.

So what are threads?

Everyone is familiar with time sharing: a computer system can give the impression of doing several things simultaneously, by running each process for a few milliseconds, then saving its state and switching to the next process, and so on. Threads simply extend that concept from switching between several different programs, to switching between several different functions executing simultaneously within a single program. A thread isn't restricted just to one function. Any thread in a multi-threaded program can call any series of methods that could be called in a single-threaded program.

Instead of the costly overhead of saving the state (virtual memory map, file descriptors, etc.) of an entire process, a low-overhead context switch (saving just a few registers, a stack pointer, the program counter, etc.) within the same address space is done. Threads can actually achieve the counterintuitive result of making a program run faster, even on uniprocessor hardware. This occurs when there are calculation steps that no longer have to wait for earlier output to complete, but can run while the I/O is taking place.

Threads (an abbreviation of "threads of control", meaning control flow) are the way we get more than one thing to happen at once in a program. Why is this a good idea? The example that is often related is a web browser, and it's a good example. In an unthreaded program (what you have been using up-to-date in Java, and what you have always used in Fortran, Pascal, C, Basic, C++, COBOL, and so on), only one thing happens at a time.

If you ask an unthreaded web browser to retrieve the contents of a URL, everything stops[3] until it has read it in.

In modern interactive software it is often unacceptable to run a single task exclusively until completion. One solution (providing the language or library offers it) is to go multi-threaded, and have a thread of control to execute each command. When a command is initiated, it can run quite happily, while another thread continues to serve the user interface and listen for more instructions from the user.

There are two ways to obtain a new thread of control in Java. One tends to be used inside an application, and the other is used inside an applet.

The two alternative ways to obtain a new thread

    1.   extend class "java.lang.Thread" and override "run()"

```
class mango extends Thread {
    public void run() { ... }
}
```

This way cannot be used if your class must extend some other class instead (as there is no multiple inheritance).

or

    2.   implement the "Runnable" interface, (the class "Thread" itself is an implementation of "Runnable")

```
class mango implements Runnable {
    public void run() { ... }
}
```

3.   There are ways to program that simulate the appearance of multithreading by setting timers to interrupt, polling devices and so on. These kinds of techniques are notoriously error-prone, and are no longer necessary with threads.

Applets extend class Panel by definition, so threads in applets must always use the second way. (Because otherwise they would be inheriting from multiple classes, and Java does not support that). Of course, if the thread doesn't have to run in the Applet object, it can use the first approach.

Figure 5-7 below shows how a class thread is created by extending Thread.

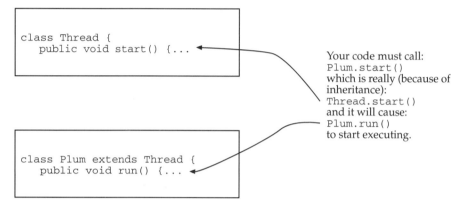

```
class Thread {
    public void start() {...
```

Your code must call:
Plum.start()
which is really (because of inheritance):
Thread.start()
and it will cause:
Plum.run()
to start executing.

```
class Plum extends Thread {
    public void run() {...
```

Figure 5-7

Creating a thread by extending class Thread looks confusing, because you have to start the thread running by calling a method that you do not have, namely the subclass.start(). You extended Thread to obtain subclass, so this will default back to Thread.start(this) and all will be well. It looks most confusing in the source code however.

Then declaring an object of class Plum gives you a new thread of control, whose execution will start in the method "run()". Declaring two Plums (or more likely a Plum and a Peach) will give you two independently executing threads of control, and declaring and filling an array of Plums will give you an entire array.length threads of control.

New Threads do not start executing on creation. For some applications, programmers (or maybe the runtime system—we'll talk about this in chapter 6 on applets) want to create threads in advance, then explicitly start them when needed, so this has been made the way it works. When a thread has been created like so:

```
Plum p = new Plum();
```

you start it running by calling the "start()" method, like so:

```
p.start();
```

Or create and start it in one step, like this:

```
new Plum().start();
```

Execution will then begin in the "run()" method, from whence you can call other methods in this and other classes as usual. Remember: "run()" is the place where it starts. And "start()" will get it running. Arrrgh! Perhaps another way to think of this is that "run()" is the equivalent of "main()" for a thread. You do not call it directly, but it is called on your behalf. There's a lot of this in Java!

A Few Words on Runnable

The Runnable interface just looks like this:

```
public interface Runnable {
    public abstract void run();
}
```

A class that implements the Runnable interface works in much the same way as a class that extends Thread, but with one big difference. The class Thread has many other methods, as well as run(). It has methods to stop(), sleep(), suspend(), resume(), setPriority(), getPriority(), and more besides. These can only be invoked on an object that belongs to a (sub)class of Thread.

None of these methods exist in the Runnable interface, so none of them are available to objects that implement Runnable. Here is the kludge around that. To obtain them, you instantiate a Thread object, and pass it an argument of an object that implements the Runnable interface, like this:

```
class Pear implements Runnable {
   public void run() { ...  }
}


   ...


   Thread t1 = new Thread(new Pear());
```

That allows the use of all the Thread methods such as:

```
t1.start();
t1.stop();
```

In fact, you have to call start() to get the Runnable implementation executing (just as with a thread). It's common to instatiate and start in one statement like this:

```
new Thread (new Pear()).start();
```

However, you cannot have statements *within the Runnable interface implementation* of "run()" that operate on the thread itself, like "sleep()" or "getName()" or "setPriority()". This is because there is no Thread "this" in Runnable, whereas there is in Thread. This perhaps makes an implementation of Runnable slightly less convenient than a subclass of thread.

```
// Show the two ways to obtain a new thread
//   1.   extend class java.lang.Thread and override run()
//   2.   implement the Runnable interface,
// PvdL, Dec 31 1995

class thread5a {
   public static void main(String[] a) {

      // alternative 1
       ExtnOfThread t1 = new ExtnOfThread();
       t1.start();

      // alternative 2
       Thread t2 = new Thread (new ImplOfRunnable());
       t2.start();
   }
}


class ExtnOfThread extends Thread {
   public void run() {
        System.out.println("Extension of Thread running");
        try sleep(1000);
        catch (InterruptedException ie) return;
   }
}
```

```
class ImplOfRunnable implements Runnable {
    public void run() {
        System.out.println("Implementation of Runnable running");

// next two lines will not compile
//          try sleep(1000);
//          catch (InterruptedException ie) return;

    }
}
```

However, the official word from the Java team is that the Runnable interface should be used if the "run()" method is the only one you are planning to override. The thinking is that, to maintain the purity of the model, classes should not be subclassed unless the programmer intends to modify or enhance the fundamental behavior of the class.

Confidentially, this is one place where most programmers will say "nuts to the purity of model", and go on subclassing Thread where it is convenient.

As with exceptions, you can provide a string argument when you create a thread subclass. As with exceptions, if you want to do this, you must provide a constructor to take that string and pass it back to the constructor of the base class. The string becomes the name of the object of the Thread subclass, and can later be used to identify it.

```
class Grape extends Thread {
    Grape(String s){ super(s); } // constructor

    public void run() { ... }
}
    . . .
    static public void main(String s[]) {
        new Grape("merlot").start();
        new Grape("pinot").start();
        new Grape("cabernet").start();
        . . .
```

You cannot pass any parameters into the "run()" method, because then its signature would differ from the version it is overriding in Thread. A thread can however get the string that it was started with, by invoking the "getName()" method.

You have already seen enough to write an elementary Java program that uses threads. So do it. Write a class Grapefruit that extends Thread and has a "void run()" method that prints out its name.

Create three different threads, and have them print out their names in a loop that is executed ten times.

Although multiprocessor hardware can speed up system throughput in general, it does not provide a specific boost to Java threads. With the current implementation, the Java threads run totally at the user process level. Individual threads within a process are not even visible to the OS kernel on Solaris, and they are certainly not entities that are schedulable on a processor. You will never find one Java thread running on one processor, while another is bound to a different processor. So just be careful how you justify that demand for an MP machine when you phrase it to your manager.

The Lifecycle of a Thread

We have already covered how a thread is created, and how the "start()" method inherited from Thread causes execution to start in its run() method. An individual thread dies when execution falls off the end of "run()" or otherwise leaves the method (an exception or return statement).

A thread can also be killed with the "stop()" method. This stops the thread executing and destroys the thread object. To restart it again, you would need to create a new thread object, and start it again. If you want to temporarily halt a thread and have it pick up again from where it was, then suspend()/resume() are the calls to use.

Priorities

Threads have priorities that can be set and changed. A higher priority thread executes ahead of a lower priority thread if they are both ready to run.

Java threads are preemptible, meaning that a running thread will be pushed off the processor by a higher priority thread before it is ready to give it up of its own accord. Java threads might or might not also be time-sliced. meaning that a running thread might or might not share the processor with threads of equal priority.

Not guaranteeing time-slicing may seem a somewhat surprising design decision as it violates the "Principle of Least Astonishment"—it leads to program behavior that programmers find surprising (namely threads suffer from cpu starvation). There is some precedent, in that time slicing can also be missing in a POSIX-conforming thread implementation. POSIX specifies a number of different scheduling algorithms, one of which (round robin) does do time-slicing. However another scheduling possibility allows a local implementation. In the Solaris case of POSIX threads only the local implementation is used, and this does not do any time-slicing.

Many people think that the failure to require time slicing is a mistake that will surely be fixed in a future release.

Since a programmer cannot assume that time-slicing will take place, the careful programmer assures portability by writing threaded code that does not depend on timeslicing. The code must cope with the fact that once a thread starts running, all other threads with the same priority might become blocked. One way to cope with this is to adjust thread priorities on the fly.[4]

A better way is to yield control to other threads very frequently. CPU-intensive threads should call the "yield()" method at regular intervals to ensure they don't hog the processor. This won't be needed if time slicing is made a standard part of Java. Yield gives other threads with the same priority a chance to run.

In the 1.0 version of Java, priorities run from 1 (lowest) to 10 (highest). Threads start off with the same priority as their parent thread, and the priority can be adjusted like this:

```
t1.setPriority ( getPriority() +1 );
```

On Operating Systems that have priorities, most users cannot adjust their processes to a higher priority (because they may gain an unfair advantage over other

---

4. That code is going to cost you plenty in software maintenance though.

users of the system).[5] There is no such inhibition for threads, because they all operate within one process. The user is only competing with himself or herself for resources.

Thread groups

A thread group is (big surprise!) a group of Threads. A Thread group can contain a set of Threads as well as a set of other Thread groups. It's a way of lumping several related threads together, and doing things like suspend and resume to all of them with a single method invocation.

There are methods to create a thread group and add a thread to it. Somebody obviously had something in mind when they set up the ThreadGroup class, but time has yet to tell if it is generally useful in practice.

How many Threads?

Sometimes programmers ask "how many threads should I have in my program?" Ron Winacott of Sun Canada has done a lot of thread programming, and he compares this question to asking "how many people is it reasonable to fit in a car?"

The problem is that so much is left unspecified. How big is the car, is it a minibus or a compact? How large are the people, are they children, or 300 pound wrestlers? And how many are needed to get to where you want to go in this car (e.g., driver, mechanic, navigator, someone to buy the fuel.)? In other words, how many people are required to operate the vehicle?

The bottom line is this. Each thread has a default stack size of 400Kbytes in the JDK 1.0 release. It will also use about 0.5Kbytes to hold its internal state, but the stack size is the limiting factor. A Unix process (Unix is the most capable of all the systems that Java has been ported to) effectively has a 2Gbyte address space, so in theory you could have around 5000 threads. In practice you would be limited by CPU availability, swap space, and disk bandwidth before you got up there. In one experiment, I was able to create[6] almost 2000 threads before my desktop system ground to a halt.

---

5. Hence the infamous message from the system operator "I've upped my priority, now up yours."
6. Just create them, I'm not making any claims about them doing any useful work.

Now, back to the real question. Overall there is no unique correct answer. How many is "reasonable"? There is only one person who can accurately answer this question, and that is the programmer writing the threaded application.

The best estimate is "the number of threads needed to perform the task". If this number is too high for the address space, or the CPU power, then you must redesign the tasks (and the number of threads) to use what is available.Use threads where you can achieve concurrency, or to gain overlapping I/O. Do not try to create a new thread for every method, class, or object in your program.

Synchronizing with other threads

Threads that just operate on their own are quite easy to program. It takes a little more skill to create a program in which there are a number of threads that must interoperate. A common example involves one thread producing data and putting it in a buffer, while another thread is consuming it from the buffer and doing something with it.

There are several factors to consider with this sort of consumer/producer algorithm:

1. The consumer should be blocked when the buffer is empty. It must take care not to remove more from the buffer than was put into it.

2. The producer should be blocked when the buffer is full. It must take care not to put more into the buffer than it can hold.

3. The producer and the consumer should run independently so far as the buffer capacity and contents permit.

4. The producer and the consumer should never both be updating the buffer at the same instant. Otherwise the data integrity cannot be guaranteed, as they might both try to update the same buffer reference at the same instant, causing one of the updates to be lost.

5. The problem gets even harder if there are several consumers and several producers, as now they have to avoid tripping over each other as well as their counterparts.

The first three of these requirements can be done with normal programming statements ("while (buffer_not_full)..."). One way to accomplish the fourth requirement is with the PipedInputStream/PipedOutputStream described in Chapter 7. An alternative way to accomplish the final requirements is to use the "synchronized" keyword. Any method that accesses data updated in two or more threads should be declared "synchronized" like this:

```
synchronized void update() { ...
```

If you only ever read the data, then you do not need to synchronize access. If you occasionally write it (the usual case), then synchronized access is a must for both readers and writers. The keyword "synchronized" puts a bottleneck around the method, and only lets one thread execute in it at a time. The correct computer science term for a method with a bottleneck is a "monitor". You can also label the use of an individual datum as synchronized, like this:

```
synchronized(buffer) {
    this.value = buffer.getValue();
    this.count = buffer.length();
}
```

This will provide exclusive access to the object ("buffer" in this example) in that block. It can only be applied to an object, not a primitive type. This provides finer granularity for mutual exclusion than an entire method. You generally want mutual exclusion over the smallest possible extent of code because it really chokes performance. The first thread to reach the synchronized statements starts executing them. Any further threads that reach that point are suspended until the first thread exits the critical region. Then one of the waiting threads will be resumed and take its turn in the region.

Synchronized isn't a perfect solution, because a system can still get into deadlock. Deadlock or "deadly embrace" is the situation where there is a circular dependency among several threads between resources held and resources required. In its simplest form, Thread "A" holds lock "X" and needs lock "Y", while Thread "B" holds lock "Y" and is waiting for lock "X" to become free. Result: that part of the system grinds to a halt. This can happen all too easily when one synchronized method calls another.

There are a couple more methods that help threads cooperate with each other. The method "wait()", which can only be called from within a synchronized method, causes a thread to stall there until it is notified.

```
public final void wait() throws InterruptedException {
```

There is also a "wait with timeout" version of this. The corresponding "notify()" method has this signature.

```
public final native void notify();
```

The two uses of "synchronized" allow you to maintain consistent access to an object, and to a method: wait() and notify() allow several methods to communicate across time. One use might be to wait until an image has been read in, and be notified when this is complete.

This method notifies (wakes up and unblocks) a single thread that has previously called wait(). The method notify() can only be called from within a synchronized method.

The "volatile" keyword may also be applied to data. This informs the compiler that several threads may be accessing this simultaneously. The data therefore needs to be completely refreshed from memory (rather than a value that was read into a register three cycles ago) and completely stored back on each access. Volatile is also intended for accessing objects like real time clocks that sit on the memory bus. It is convenient to glue them on there, because they can be read and written with the usual "load" and "store" memory access instructions, instead of requiring a dedicated I/O port. They can return the current time via a single cycle read, but the value will change unpredictably due to actions outside the program. Volatile isn't really intended for general use on arbitrary objects in applications. The keyword isn't used anywhere in the FCS version of the runtime library.

Generalized thread programming is a discipline in its own right, and one that will become increasingly significant now that Java makes it so easy. The Solaris OS kernel is a multi-threaded implementation, and multi-threaded is definitely the future trend. Consult the threads book listed at the end of this chapter for a thorough grounding in the topic of threads programming.

Garbage Collection

Languages with dynamic data structures (structures that can grow and shrink in size at run time) must have some way of telling the underlying Operating System when they need more memory. Conversely, you also need some way to indicate memory that is no longer in use (e.g. threads that have terminated, objects that are no longer referenced by anything, variables that have gone out of scope, etc.), this can amount to a large amount of memory in a nontrivial program or a program that runs for an extended period of time. Once acquired from the OS, memory is usually never returned to it, but retained for re-use by the program. This will all be taken care of by a storage manager. One subsystem of the storage manager will be a "garbage collector." The automatic reclaiming of memory that is no longer in use is known as "garbage collection" in computer science.

Compiler writers for algorithmic languages have the concept of a "heap" and a "stack". The stack takes care of dynamic memory requirements related to procedure call and return. The heap is responsible for all other dynamic memory. In

Java, that's a lot because object allocation is always from the heap. The only variables allocated on the stack are the local variables of a method.[7]

Java is going to give a powerful boost to doctoral dissertations on the subject of speeding up garbage collector algorithms.

In the C language, malloc() allocates memory, and free() makes it available for reuse. In C++, the new and delete operators have the same effect. Both of these languages require explicit deallocation of memory. The programmer has to say what memory to give back, and when. In practice this has turned out to be an error-prone task. It's all too easy to create a "memory leak" by not freeing memory before overwriting the last pointer to it; then it can neither be referenced nor freed. Some X-Windows applications are notorious for leaking even more than Apple Computers' board of directors.

Why do we need Garbage Collection?

Java takes a different approach. Instead of requiring the programmer to take the initiative in freeing memory, the job is given to a run time component called the garbage collector. It is the job of the garbage collector to sit on top of the heap and periodically scan it to determine things that aren't being used any more. It can reclaim that memory and put it back in the free store pool within the program.

Making garbage collection an implicit operation of the run time system rather than a responsibility of the programmer has a cost. It means that at unpredictable times, a potentially large amount of behind-the-scenes processing will suddenly start-up when some low-water mark is hit and more memory is called for. This has been a problem with past systems, but Java addresses it somewhat with threads. In a multi-threaded system, the garbage collector can run in parallel with user code and has a much less intrusive effect on the system. It still carries some runtime performance cost however.

Taking away the task of memory management from the programmer gives him or her one less thing to worry about, and makes the resulting software more reliable in use. It may take a little longer to run compared with a language like C++ with explicit memory management because the garbage collector has to go out and look for reclaimable memory rather than simply being told where to find it. On

---

7. Java actually has multiple stacks: it starts out with one for Java code and another stack for C native methods. Additional stacks are allocated for every thread created. This aspect of Java requires a virtual memory mapping system to operate efficiently.

the other hand, it's much quicker to debug and get the program running in the first place. Most people would agree that in the presence of ever-improving hardware performance, a small performance penalty is an acceptable price to pay for more reliable software.

We should mention at this point that there is almost no direct interaction between the programmer and garbage collection. It is one of the run time services that you can take for granted, like keeping track of return addresses, or identifying the correct handler for an exception. The discussion here is to provide a little more insight into what takes place behind the scenes.

Garbage Collection Algorithms

A number of alternative garbage collection algorithms have been proposed and tried over the years. Two popular ones are "reference counting" and "mark and sweep".

Reference counting keeps a counter for each chunk of memory allocated. The counter records how many pointers directly point at the chunk or something inside it. The counter needs to be kept up-to-date as assignments are made. If the reference count ever drops to zero, nothing can ever access the memory and so it can immediately be returned to the pool of free storage. The big advantage of reference counting is that it imposes a steady constant overhead, rather than needing aperiodic bursts of the cpu. The big disadvantage of reference counting is that in its simplest incarnation it is fooled by circular references. If A points to B, and B points to A, but nothing else points to A and B they will not be freed even though they could be. It's also a little expensive in multi-threaded environments because reference counts must be locked for mutual exclusion before reference counts are updated.

You can turn off garbage collection in your application, by starting java with this option:

```
java -noasyncgc   ...
```

One reason for doing this might be to experiment and see how much of a difference in performance it makes, if any. You should not turn off garbage collection in a program that may run for an extended period. If you do it is almost guaranteed to fail with memory exhaustion sooner or later.

Alternatively, you can call the method

```
system.gc();
```

to run the garbage collector at any point you choose.

The current Java implementation from Sun uses the "mark and sweep" garbage collection algorithm. The marker starts at the root pointers. These are things like the stack, and static (global) variables. You can imagine marking with a red pen every object that can be accessed from the roots. Then the marker recursively marks all the objects that are directly or indirectly referenced from the objects reachable from the roots. The process continues until no more red marks can be placed. The entire virtual process may need to be swapped in and looked at, which is expensive in disk traffic and time. A smart garbage collector knows it doesn't have to bring in objects that can't contain references like large graphics images and the like. Then the "sweep" phase starts, and everything without a red mark is swept back onto the free list for re-use. Memory compaction also takes place at this point.

Finalizers

A "finalizer" is a Java term, related to but not the same as a C++ destructor. When there are no further references to an object, its storage can be reclaimed by the garbage collector.

A finalizer is a special method that any class may provide. If a class has a finalizer method, it will be called on dead instances of that class before the memory occupied by that object is reused. The programmer makes this possible by providing a body for the method finalize() in the class. It will look like this:

```
class Fruit {

        protected void finalize() {  // do finalization ...
};
```

It must have the signature shown (protected, void, and no arguments).

The Java Language Specification says:

> *"The purpose of finalizers is to provide a chance to free up resources (such as file descriptors or operating system graphics contexts) that are owned by objects but cannot be accessed directly and cannot be freed automatically by the automatic storage management. Simply reclaiming an object's memory by garbage collection would not guarantee that these resources would be reclaimed."*

Finalization was carried over from the Oak language, and justified on the grounds that it would help provide good resource management for long running servers.

A finalizer is optional. You don't have to provide one, and even if you do, (unlike a C++ destructor) it is not guaranteed to be called. It is guaranteed to have been called before that memory is reused. But there are no guarantees about when or even whether disused storage will be reclaimed.

If present, a class's finalizer is called by the garbage collector at some point after the object is first recognized as garbage and before the memory is reclaimed, such that the object is garbage at the time of the call. A finalizer can also be called explicitly. There is no guarantee that an object will be garbage collected, and hence there is no guarantee that an object's finalizer will be called. A program may terminate normally without garbage collection taking place.

Because you cannot rely on a finalizer method being called, you cannot use it to carry out some essential final housekeeping (release a lock, write usage statistics, or whatever). Finalizers seem to be intended more for system implementors writing a Java system in Java.

Finally (uh...) don't confuse "final" (a constant) or "finally" (a block that is always executed after a "try()" with "finalize"—the three concepts are unrelated.

Some Light Relief: The Robot Ping-Pong[8] Player

Computer scientists are always looking for hard new problems to solve. They want the problems to be hard enough to be worth tackling, preferably capable of eventual solution, yet easy to describe (so that you don't have to spend too long educating grant-making organizations on what you'll do with their money).

Constructing a robot that could play ping-pong was proposed years ago as a particularly difficult computer science problem requiring solutions in vision, real-time control, and artificial intelligence.

Various other robots have been proposed and constructed over the years: robots that walk on jointed legs, robots that try to learn from their environment, robots that recognize facial expressions and so on. None has quite achieved the popularity of the ping-pong playing robots. A number of them have been built in the engineering labs of the finest universities around the globe. The researchers even published the official rules of robot ping-pong so they could have tournaments. Several of these were organized by Professor John Billingsley, of the E.& E. Department at Portsmouth Polytechnic.

Extracts From The Official Rules of Robot Ping-Pong

Rule 11: Those parts of the robot visible to the opponent must be black including absorption of infrared in the region of 1 micron wavelength.

Rule 17: The judges may disqualify a robot on the grounds of safety, or penalize it for serious breaches of sportsmanship.

Naturally the students at M.I.T. built their share of robot ping-pong players. Some of the best work was done there, in the Artificial Intelligence labs, where they used Lisp as the implementation language.

A story, probably apocryphal, is told of an early prototype at M.I.T. After several months of hard work, the students finally coaxed the robot into accurately serving a series of balls from its ball magazine. Eagerly the students reloaded it, and fetched their professor to witness the accomplishment. When the balding professor arrived, he stood expectantly at the far end of the table from the robot and gave the signal to proceed.

8.   "Ping-Pong" is a trademark of Parker Brothers

Table tennis is full of surprises. In the early 1970's communist China seemed absolutely unbeatable at table tennis. They won every competition in sight, dominating their opponents with surprising spin shots.

Years later the truth came out; they were cheating, or at least stretching the rules to breaking point. The communist regime had equipped its teams with special bats. Both sides of the bat looked identical, but they were made out of very different materials. One side of the bat would give a regular shot, the other would help impart a fierce spin. Opponents didn't even know about the trick bats, and had no way of knowing what kind of a shot was coming at them.

After several years the news got out. The tournament rules were changed. Trick bats were still allowed, but the faces had to be different colors. Communist Chinese domination of the sport came to an end.

As soon as the robot started, it launched a series of hard accurate lobs directly at the professor's cranium. No matter how the professor twisted and ducked, the machine kept him in its sights until at last it was out of balls. When all the tears and laughter had finally stopped, the students were cleared of any wrongdoing. It seems that the robot had been set up to target a large illuminated white patch on the wall representing the opponent, and when the luckless teacher stood within range, his bald brow showed up on the vision system as larger, whiter and shinier, so was preferred. This incident allegedly led to rule 11 (above). No word on whether the robot was nailed under rule 17.

The name of Professor Marvin Minsky of MIT is often attached to this story. Professor Minsky is adamant that he was never bombarded with ping pong balls, but he concedes that an early ball catcher robot did once make a grab for his head. That seems to be the origin of this story.

There is an equally apocryphal coda to this story. It seems that the students went on to enter the robot in one of the tournaments where it played quite well for the first 15 minutes. Suddenly, unaccountably, the robot froze completely and let several successive balls from the opponent bounce off its chest without even attempting a return serve. Then equally suddenly it started playing again. A furious debugging session was started, only to pinpoint the cause of the problem almost immediately. The robot was driven by Lisp software. It ran perfectly for a quarter hour until it had exhausted its free memory. At that point the garbage collector kicked in. Nothing else could run until the garbage collector had done its thing, not even the code to return a ball. That's why single threaded systems aren't very good at real time processing. The workaround was simple: reboot the processor immediately prior to each tournament match.

Further Reading

Threads Primer: A Guide to Multithreaded Programming

by Bil Lewis/Daniel J. Berg

published by SunSoft Press/Prentice Hall, 1995.

ISBN: 0-13-443698-9

The definitive introduction to threads programming.

There is a survey of garbage collection techniques at

ftp://ftp.cs.utexas.edu/pub/garbage/bigsurv.ps

A Robot Ping-Pong Player: an experiment in real-time intelligent control

by Russell L. Andersson,

published by the M.I.T. Press, Cambridge, MA, 1988

ISBN: 0-262-01101-8

A rather stuffy book that completely shies away from the essential levity of the subject matter, in favor of dragging in a lot of guff about polynomials and trajectories. Doesn't mention either of the two stories above, but the system was written in C and the book includes several interesting C listings.

Programming with Threads

by Steve Kleiman, Devang Shah, and Bart Smaalders

published by SunSoft Press/Prentice Hall, 1996

ISBN: 0-13-172389-8

Written by senior threads development engineers at Sun Microsystems, this is a comprehensive reference work on threads. This book was introduced in February 1996.

Answer to Programming Challenge

```
public class LinkedList implements LinkedListIntf {
    private LinkedList next;
    public Object datum;

   // type kludge, so that we can define "nextLink()" in the interface
   public LinkedListIntf nextLink() { return
(LinkedListIntf)this.next; }
   // but have a version that returns a object of the implementing class
   public LinkedList next() { return (LinkedList) nextLink(); };

    public LinkedList(Object o) {
        this.next=null;
        this.datum=o;
    }

    public void addAfter(Object o) {
        LinkedList tmp = new LinkedList(o);
        tmp.next = this.next;
        this.next = tmp;
    }

    public void deleteAfter() {
        if (this.next!=null)
            this.next = this.next.next;
    }

}
```

A driver program might look like this

```
class test5g {
  public static void main (String ar[]) {
      LinkedList l, root=new LinkedList((Object) (new Integer(-2))
);
      for (int i=0; i< 5; i++) {
          root.addAfter( new Integer(i) );
       //    System.out.println("Have added int " +i);
      }
      l= root;
      for (int i=0; i< 5; i++) {
          if (l.datum!=null)
             System.out.println(" read back "
                  + ((Integer) l.datum).intValue() );
          l=l.next();
      }

      (root.next().next()).deleteAfter();
      (root.next().next()).addAfter((Object)(new Integer(77)));

      l= root;
      for (int i=0; i< 5; i++) {
          if (l.datum!=null)
             System.out.println(" read back "
                  + ((Integer) l.datum).intValue() );
          l=l.next();
      }


  }

}
```

CHAPTER
6

Practical Examples Explained

"As a matter of fact a high tree makes a wretched sniping post, and I rarely allowed one to be used on our side. But we found that the German sense of humour appears to be much tickled by seeing, or thinking that he sees, a Britisher falling out of a tree. When our sniping became very good, and the enemy consequently shy of giving a target, a dummy in a tree worked by a rope sometimes caused Fritz and Hans to show themselves unwisely. One had to be very careful not to go too far in this sort of work or trickery, lest a **minenwerfer** *should take his part in the duel."*

> Major H. Hesketh-Prichard, DSO, MC
> *"Sniping in France"*

This chapter contains a nontrivial Java program annotated with a running commentary. The program source appears on the CD accompanying this book, so you can look at it without the annotation, and you can try compiling and running it without typing it in.

The program generates anagrams (letter rearrangements). You give it a word or phrase, and it comes back with all the substring combinations that it can find in the dictionary. You need to provide it with a wordlist that it will use as a dictionary[1], and you can also specify the minimum length of words in the anagrams that it generates.

For any phrases more than a few letters long, there are a lot more anagrams than you would ever think possible.

Case Study Java Program

Here is an example of running the program on the infamous "surfing the Internet" phrase, specifying words of length four or longer. It finds dozens and dozens of them, starting like this:

```
java anagram "surfing the internet" 4
reading word list...
main dictionary has 25144 entries.
least common letter is 'f'

fritter shunt engine
fritter hung intense
surfeit Ghent intern
surfeit ninth regent
furnish greet intent
furnish egret intent
furnish tent integer
further stint engine
further singe intent
further tinge tennis
further gin sentient
freight nurse intent
freight runt intense
freight turn intense
freight run sentient
freight nun interest
freight sen nutrient
freeing Hurst intent
    ...
```

If you specify a length argument, it will try to use words with at least that many characters, but the final word it finds to complete the anagram may be shorter. This program is written as an application, so there is no issue about accessing files.

---

1. If you don't have such a word list (e.g. in your spellchecker), there are several alternatives available for downloading, e.g. at: http://web.soi.city.ac.uk:8080/text/roget/thesaurus.html, or, http://math-www.uni-paderborn.de/HTML/Dictionaries.html. Both of these sites contain links to several dictionaries. On Unix, just use the file /usr/dict/words.

Here is the annotated program source:

```
/*
 * Usage: anagram string [[min-len] wordfile]
 * Java Anagram program, Peter van der Linden Jan 7, 1996.
 */

import java.io.*;
```

Note, the "using an interface to hold useful constants" idiom was explained in Chapter 4.

```
interface UsefulConstants {
    public static final int MAXWORDS = 50000;
    public static final int MAXWORDLEN = 30;
    public static final int EOF = -1;
```

Note the way a reference variable can be used to provide a shorter name for another object.

We can now say "o.println()" instead of "System.out.println()".

```
    // shorter alias for I/O streams
    public static final PrintStream o = System.out;
    public static final PrintStream e = System.err;
}


class Word {
    int mask;
    byte count[]= new byte[26];
    int total;
    String aword;
```

This is an important data structure for representing one word. We keep it as a string, we note the total number of letters in the word, the count of each letter and a bitmask of the alphabet. A zero at bit N means the letter that comes Nth in the alphabet is in the word. A one means that letter is not in the word. This allows for some fast comparisons later on for "how much overlap is there between these two strings?"

```
Word(String s)   // construct an entry from a string
{
    int ch;
    aword = s;
    mask = ~0;
    total = 0;
    s = s.toLowerCase();
    for (int i = 'a'; i <= 'z'; i++) count[i-'a'] = 0;

    for (int i = s.length()-1; i >= 0; i--) {
        ch = s.charAt(i) - 'a';
        if (ch >= 0 && ch < 26) {
            total++;
            count[ch]++;
            mask &= ~(1 << ch);
        }
    }
}
}
```

The program has the following steps:

1. Read in a list of real words, and convert each word into a form that makes it easy to compare on the quantity and value of letters.

2. Get the word or phrase we are anagramming, and convert it into the same form.

3. Go through the list of words, using our helpful comparison to make a second list of those which can be part of a possible anagram. Words that can be part of a possible anagram are those which only have the same letters as appear in the anagram, and do not have more of any one letter than appears in the anagram.

4. Go through our extracted list of candidate words. Choose the most difficult letter (the one that appears least often) to start with. Take words with it in, and call the anagram finder recursively to fill out the rest of the letters from the candidate dictionary.

The class "Word" above is the class that deals with one word from the wordlist and puts it in the special "easy to compare" form.

The class "WordList" below is the one that reads in a word list, and builds up an entire dictionary of all words in the special format:

```
class WordList implements UsefulConstants {
    static Word[] Dictionary= new Word[MAXWORDS];
    static int totWords=0;

    static void ReadDict(String f)
    {
```

The half dozen lines that follow are a very common idiom for opening a file. This can throw an exception, so we either deal with it here or declare it in the method. It is usually easiest to deal with exceptions closest to the point where they are raised, if you are going to catch them at all.

Here we catch the exception, print out a diagnostic, then re-throw a RuntimeException to cause the program to stop with a backtrace. We could exit the program at this point, but rethrowing the exception ensures that it will be recognized that an error has occurred. We throw RuntimeException rather than our original exception because RuntimeException *does not have to be handled or declared. Now that we have printed a diagnostic at the point of error, it is acceptable to take this shortcut:*

```
        FileInputStream fis;
        try fis = new FileInputStream(f);
        catch (FileNotFoundException fnfe) {
            e.println ("Cannot open the file of words '" + f + "'");
            throw new RuntimeException();
        }
        e.println("reading dictionary...");
```

It is better not to have any arbitrary fixed size arrays in your code. This one is done for convenience. Removing the limitation is one of the programming challenges at the end of this example. The buffer holds the characters of a word as we read them in from the word list and assemble them.

```
char buffer[] = new char[MAXWORDLEN];
String s;
int r =0;
while (r!=EOF) {
    int i=0;
    try {
        // read a word in from the word file
        while ( (r=fis.read()) != EOF ) {
            if ( r == '\n' ) break;
            buffer[i++] = (char) r;
        }
    } catch (IOException ioe) {
        e.println ("Cannot read the file of words ");
        throw new RuntimeException();
    }
```

This simple looking constructor to create a new Word object actually does the complicated conversion of a string into the form convenient for further processing (the dozen or so lines of code in class Word).

```
        s=new String(buffer,0,i);
        Dictionary[totWords] = new Word(s);
        totWords++;
    }


    e.println("main dictionary has " + totWords + " entries.");
    }



}
```

An example of a class that is both a subclass and an implementation follows. It extends and implements:

```
class anagram extends WordList implements UsefulConstants {

    static Word[] Candidate = new Word[MAXWORDS];
    static int totCandidates=0,
            MinimumLength = 3;
```

This is the main routine where execution starts:

```
public static void main(String[] argv)
{
    if ( argv.length < 1 || argv.length > 3) {
        e.println("Usage: anagram  string-to-anagram "
                    + "[min-len [word file]]");
        return;
    }
    if (argv.length >= 2)
        MinimumLength = Integer.parseInt(argv[1]);
```

If the name of a words list isn't explicitly provided as an argument, the program expects to find a file called "words.txt" in the current directory. This will simply be an ASCII file with a few hundred or thousand words, one word per line, no definitions or other information.

```
    // word filename is optional 3rd argument
    ReadDict( argv.length==3? argv[2] : "words.txt" );
    DoAnagrams(argv[0]);
}
```

```
static void DoAnagrams(String anag)
{
    Word myAnagram = new Word(anag);

    myAnagram.mask = ~myAnagram.mask;
```

The next couple of lines go through the list of words that we read in, and extract the ones that could be part of the phrase to anagram. These words are extracted into a second word list or dictionary, called "Candidates". The dictionary of Candidate words is sorted.

```
    getCandidates(myAnagram);

    int RootIndexEnd = sortCandidates(myAnagram);
```

This call says "Find an anagram of the string "myAnagram", using this working storage, you're at level 0 (first attempt), and considering candidate words zero through RootIndexEnd".

```
        FindAnagram(myAnagram, new String[50],  0, 0, RootIndexEnd);

        o.println("----" + anag + "----");
    }
```

This is how a word becomes a candidate:

1. The candidate must only have letters that appear in the anagram (this is the fast overlap test that a bit mask representation provides).

2. It must also be no shorter than the minimum length we specified.

3. It must not be too long.

4. And it must not have more of any one letter than the anagram has.

If the word meets all these conditions, add it to the Candidates dictionary.

```
static void getCandidates(Word d)
{
    for (int i = totCandidates = 0; i < totWords; i++)
        if (  (  (Dictionary[i].mask | d.mask) == (int)~0)
            && (   Dictionary[i].total >= MinimumLength   )
            && (   Dictionary[i].total + MinimumLength <= d.total
                || Dictionary[i].total == d.total)
            && ( fewerOfEachLetter(d.count,
                 Dictionary[i].count)  )  )

            Candidate[totCandidates++]=Dictionary[i];

    e.println("Dictionary of words-that-are-substring-anagrams has "
             + totCandidates + " entries.");
//      PrintCandidate();
}
```

```
static boolean fewerOfEachLetter(byte anagCount[], byte entryCount[])
{
    for (int i = 25; i >= 0; i--)
        if (entryCount[i] > anagCount[i]) return false;
    return true;
}


static void PrintCandidate()
{
    for (int i = 0; i < totCandidates; i++)
        o.print( Candidate[i].aword + ", "
                + ((i%4 == 3)?"\n":" " ) );
    o.println("");
}
```

Here's where we start trying to assemble anagrams out of the words in the candidates dictionary.

```
static void FindAnagram(Word d,
                        String WordArray[],
                        int Level, int StartAt, int EndAt)
{
    int i, j;
    boolean enoughCommonLetters;
    Word WordToPass = new Word("");

    for (i = StartAt; i < EndAt; i++) {
      if ( (d.mask | Candidate[i].mask) != 0) {
          enoughCommonLetters = true;
          for (j = 25; j >=0 && enoughCommonLetters; j--)
              if (d.count[j] < Candidate[i].count[j])
                  enoughCommonLetters = false;

          if (enoughCommonLetters) {
            WordArray[Level] = Candidate[i].aword;
            WordToPass.mask = 0;
            WordToPass.total = 0;
            for (j = 25; j >= 0; j--) {
```

The cast to (byte) is needed whenever a byte receives the value of an arithmetic expression. It assures the compiler that the programer realizes the expression was evaluated in at least 32 bits and the result will be truncated before storing in the byte.

```
        WordToPass.count[j] = (byte)
          (    d.count[j] -
               Candidate[i].count[j] );
        if ( WordToPass.count[j] != 0 ) {
            WordToPass.total +=
                (int)WordToPass.count[j];
            WordToPass.mask |= 1 << j;
        }
    }
    if (WordToPass.total == 0) {
        /* Found a series of words! */
        for (j = 0; j <= Level; j++)
            o.print(WordArray[j] + " ");
        o.println();
    } else if (WordToPass.total < MinimumLength) {
            ; /* Don't call again */
    } else {
```

The recursive call to find anagrams for the remaining letters in the phrase.

```
        FindAnagram(WordToPass, WordArray, Level+1,
            i, totCandidates);
        }
      }
    }
  }
}


static int SortMask;

static int sortCandidates(Word d)
{
    int [] MasterCount=new int[26];
    int LeastCommonIndex=0, LeastCommonCount;
    int i, j;

    for (j = 25; j >= 0; j--) MasterCount[j] = 0;
```

```
for (i = totCandidates-1; i >= 0; i--)
    for (j = 25; j >= 0; j--)
        MasterCount[j] += Candidate[i].count[j];


LeastCommonCount = MAXWORDS * 5;
for (j = 25; j >= 0; j--)
    if (    MasterCount[j] != 0
        && MasterCount[j] < LeastCommonCount
        && (d.mask & (1 << j) ) != 0   ) {
        LeastCommonCount = MasterCount[j];
        LeastCommonIndex = j;
    }


SortMask = (1 << LeastCommonIndex);


quickSort(0, totCandidates-1 );


for (i = 0; i < totCandidates; i++)
    if ((SortMask & ~Candidate[i].mask) == 0)
        break;
```

The root breadth is the first word in the sorted candidate dictionary that doesn't contain the least common letter. Since the least common letter will be hard to match, we plan to start out by using all the words with it in as the roots of our search. The breadth part is that it represents the number of alternatives to start with.

```
    e.println("least common letter is '"
            + (char)(LeastCommonIndex+'a') + "'" );
    e.println("words with least common letter: " + i + " words");
    return i;
}
```

Sort the dictionary of Candidate words, using the standard quicksort algorithm from any Algorithm book. This one was adapted from page 87 of K&R edition 2. Again, it shows that recursion is fine in Java.[2]

---

2. This anagram program was based on a C program that my colleague Brian Scearce wrote in his copious free time.

```
static void quickSort(int left, int right)
{
    // standard quicksort from any algorithm book
    int i, last;
    if (left >= right) return;
    swap(left, (left+right)/2);
    last = left;
    for (i=left+1; i<=right; i++)  /* partition */
        if (MultiFieldCompare( Candidate[i],
                              Candidate[left] ) == -1 )
            swap( ++last, i);

    swap(last, left);
    quickSort(left, last-1);
    quickSort(last+1,right);
}

static int MultiFieldCompare(Word s, Word t)
{
    if ( (s.mask & SortMask) != (t.mask & SortMask) )
        return ( (s.mask & SortMask)>(t.mask & SortMask)? 1:-1);

    if ( t.total != s.total )
        return (t.total - s.total);

    return (s.aword).compareTo(t.aword);
}

static void swap(int d1, int d2) {
    Word tmp = Candidate[d1];
    Candidate[d1] = Candidate[d2];
    Candidate[d2] = tmp;
}

}
.
```

1. After it's completed one anagram, make the program go back and prompt for more. Don't make it reload the wordlist! (Easy)

2. Modify the program so it doesn't use arrays of fixed size, but uses the Vector class from package "java.util" to grow arrays as needed at runtime. (Easy) Add this line to the start of the program:

```
import java.util.Vector;
```

3. Create a version of the program that has the word list compiled in to it. You'll probably want to first write a java program that reads a word list and prints out the array initialization literals for you to edit into your source program. What difference does this make to program start-up time? Run time? Size? (Medium)

4. Create a version of the program that uses several threads to sort the candidate words. Use a heuristic like "if the partition is larger than 4 elements, spawn a thread to sort it using quicksort, otherwise sort it directly by decision tree comparison." Decision tree comparison means

```
if ( a>b )
   if ( a>c )
      if (a>d)  // a is largest
      else      // d is largest, then a
         if (b>c) // order is d,a,b,c
         else     // order is d,a,c,b
// and so on
```

This challenge is of medium complexity.

5. What needs to be changed in the anagram program to make it capable of dealing with alphabets other than English? (Easy) Make it so (Medium to Hard, depending on whether you select a specific non-English alphabet or "all of them").

6. Have several threads calculating anagrams at once. This challenge is hard to get working correctly so the threads know how to stop when they reach the point of overlap.

When I wrote the above Java code, my first version had a bug in it. In the following code, I had omitted to subtract 1 from the String length, (also I did not check that the character was alphabetic before putting it in the data structure). Instead of looking like this:

GOOD CODE

```
for (int i = s.length()-1; i >= 0; i--) {
        ...s.charAt(i)...
```

I had it like this:

BAD CODE

```
for (int i = s.length(); i >= 0; i--) {
        ...s.charAt(i)...
```

In a C program, this would cause no anagrams to be found, but the program would run to completion. There would not be any indication that an error had occurred, or where. A naive tester would report that the program worked fine. Works fine? Ship it!

In my java program, this was the output from my first test run:

```
java.lang.StringIndexOutOfBoundsException: String index out of
range: 4
        at java.lang.String.charAt(String.java)
        at Word.<init>(anagram.java:35)
        at WordList.ReadDict(anagram.java:77)
        at anagram.main(anagram.java:104)
```

It told me an error had occurred, what the error was, why it was an error, where in the program it happened, and how execution reached that point. At that moment, as they say, I became enlightened.[3]

---

3. Some other languages have this kind of comprehensive runtime checking (Ada comes to mind), but Java is the only one that is also both object-oriented and has a C flavor.

Notes on Applications vs. Applets

As we mentioned in Chapter 3 when we touched on this topic, an applet is a Java program that is invoked not from the command line, but rather through a web browser reaching that page, or equivalently through the appletviewer that comes with the Java Development kit. We will stick with the appletviewer in this chapter because we are trying to teach the language not the use of a browser.

Reminder on Applets

There are two different ways to run a Java executable:

- as a stand-alone program that can be invoked from the command line. This is termed an "application".

- as a program embedded in a web page, to be run when the page is browsed. This is termed an "applet".

Applications and applets differ in the execution privileges they have, and also the way they indicate where to start execution.

The first thing to understand about applets is how they get run from a web browser, because the numerous methods that applets can override follow from that.

Web browsers deal with HTML (the HyperText Markup Language we mentioned in chapter 1). There are HTML tags that say "set this text in bold", "break to a new paragraph" and "include this GIF image here." There is now an HTML tag that says "run the Java applet that you will find in this .class file". Just as a GIF image file will be displayed at the point where its tag is in the HTML source, so the applet will be executed when its tag is encountered and the results displayed at that point in the web page.

An example of the HTML code that invokes an applet is shown below:

```
<title>
The simplest applet
</title>
<applet code=pentium.class width=300 height=50>
</applet>
```

The width and height fields are mandatory, and they are measured in units of pixels (dots of resolution on the computer monitor). Applets run in a window object called a panel, and you have to give the browser a clue as to how big a panel the applet should start with. Another useful tag is the "<codebase=codebaseURL>".

This optional attribute specifies the directory that contains the applet's code (this is termed the base URL of the applet, and if omitted is the URL of the directory of the document that contains the applet).

Since this is HTML, put the example above in a file called example.html . Figure 6-1 below shows how it will be run. The class needs to found somewhere along the CLASSPATH environment variable, or from the CODEBASE defined in the HTML tag. CODEBASE specifies a different directory that contains the applet's code. This is to help applets located on remote servers be accessed just as easily as those stored locally.

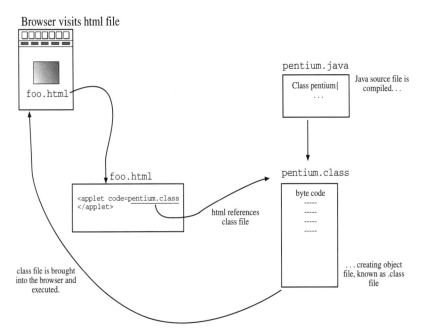

Figure 6-1

Are You Trying To Start Something? Executing an Applet

We've just seen that applets are started up in a different manner from applications. The difference is more than just command-line vs. HTML file. Applications start execution in a public function called "main()" similar to the convention used in C. Applets have a different convention, involving overriding certain pre-named functions.

The first thing to note is that an applet is a *window object* that *runs in a thread object,*[4] so every applet will be able to do window-y kind of things and thread-y kind of things. An applet's execution starts using the thread-y kind of methods that we have already seen in Chapter 5. You can override the start()/stop methods, but you do not call them yourself. This funny stuff exists because of the funny context that applets live in. They are loaded once, then subject to the kind of repeated execution that a hypertext web browser makes. The diagram in Figure 6-2 shows how.

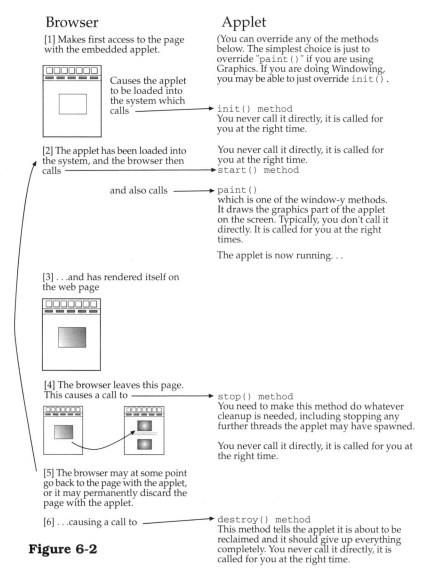

Browser

[1] Makes first access to the page with the embedded applet.

Causes the applet to be loaded into the system which calls ———

[2] The applet has been loaded into the system, and the browser then calls ————

and also calls ————

[3] . . .and has rendered itself on the web page

[4] The browser leaves this page. This causes a call to ————

[5] The browser may at some point go back to the page with the applet, or it may permanently discard the page with the applet.

[6] . . .causing a call to ————

Figure 6-2

Applet

(You can override any of the methods below. The simplest choice is just to override "paint()" if you are using Graphics. If you are doing Windowing, you may be able to just override init().

init() method
You never call it directly, it is called for you at the right time.

You never call it directly, it is called for you at the right time.
start() method

paint()
which is one of the window-y methods. It draws the graphics part of the applet on the screen. Typically, you don't call it directly. It is called for you at the right times.

The applet is now running. . .

stop() method
You need to make this method do whatever cleanup is needed, including stopping any further threads the applet may have spawned.

You never call it directly, it is called for you at the right time.

destroy() method
This method tells the applet it is about to be reclaimed and it should give up everything completely. You never call it directly, it is called for you at the right time.

4. We mean window in the general sense rather than Java-specific sense. In the Java specific sense, an Applet is a Panel.

You can almost always leave "destroy()" alone. The method "init()" is a good place to create GUI objects and threads. Similarly you will only override the methods "start()" and "stop()" if you have something that actually needs to be started and stopped, namely threads. If your applet doesn't start up any threads of its own, there's no need to supply your own version of start and stop. On the other hand, if your applet does create some threads, start() is probably where you will want to start them. And it is most important that you override stop() and explicitly stop all threads—otherwise they will continue to run even after you leave the page. If you want a thread to suspend when the browser leaves the page and resume where it left off if the browser returns, then use suspend() in method stop() and resume() in method start().

There is more housekeeping associated with threads in applets than in applications, because of the way pages (including their embedded running applets) are left behind and possibly revisited. An applet gets the ability to override all these thread method names for free—it does not need to import anything explicitly.

However, the window-y stuff needs to be imported ("import java.awt.*;") so that you can display window objects like menus and buttons. Here is an example of the minimal applet:

```java
import java.awt.Graphics;
public class HelloWorld extends java.applet.Applet {
    public void paint(Graphics g) {
        g.drawString("Beat it!", 15, 25);
    }
}
```

These magic methods init(), start(), stop(), and destroy() are defined in src/java/applet/Applet.java. These are exactly the methods that a thread has (see them in src/java/lang/Thread.java). What methods does an application have that correspond to these? None! An application isn't run under a browser, so it isn't liable to be stopped and started unpredictably as the browser moves to new pages.

The paint() method is a window-y thing, available to all window components. See Chapter 9.

Because an applet is a windowing thing (we will get back to more formal terminology eventually), it does not use the standard I/O that we have been using up till now for interactive I/O. Instead it uses the facilities that are available to windows, like drawing a string at particular coordinates. The coordinates system of every window has the origin in the top left as shown in Figure 6-3.

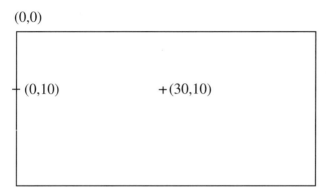

Figure 6-3

What are the other facilities that are available to windows? We will discuss these in greater depth in the last chapter which deals with the Abstract Window Toolkit. For now you can code review the classes that make up the AWT in directory java/src/awt. The file Container.java contains the superclass from which Applet is (eventually) derived. Container has the method "paint()" which is called by the Window toolkit whenever the applet panel needs to be refreshed.

You can look at the source for method drawString() in file java/src/awt/Graphics.java. This class has many methods concerned with rendering a shape, line, or text onto the screen. It will also let you select colors, and fonts.

The convention throughout Java is that class names begin with a capital letter, and method names start with a lower case letter, but subsequent words in the name are capitalized. This leads to odd looking names like "drawString" that make it seem as though someone had a previous job writing ransom notes wItH rAndOmlY caPitALiZeD LeTteRs. ("wE HaVe yOuR MiSsinG piXeL. seNd $10K iN sMaLL BilLS. dO nOt TeLl tHe PolICe. ThEy're sTuPId.")

When the compiler complains that it can't find one of the library methods, your first thought should be "did I get the capitals right?" It is not always consistent in that we have "MenuBar" and yet "Scrollbar" in the window toolkit. In cases like this, it's better to always be consistent or always be inconsistent, but not keeping changing between the two.

Set up the "pentium flaw" program as an applet. Modify the program so that it extends Applet and make sure that the class is public. Use g.drawString() instead of println(), in this method:

```
void paint(Graphics g) {
    g.drawString("text to display");
}
```

Write some html that points to the class. Invoke it through the appletviewer, and then try a Java capable web browser. (Medium).

Back in Chapter 5 we mentioned that some programs need to explicitly start threads, rather than have them created and started in one operation. An applet running in a web browser is one of those programs. It allows a closer fit to the "go back to a page you already visited, and which is likely to still be loaded" model. That is why init() (one time initialization) is separated from start() (called every time the page is accessed).

Summary

The browser will automatically instantiate an object of your Applet subclass, and make certain calls to get it running.

You can overload some of the called methods. The methods "init() and "paint()" are the ones you will mostly overload, unless you have threads in the applet, when you will want to overload "start()" and "stop()" too.

Typically you never call any of these methods. They are called for you by the window system/browser at appropriate times. As the browser visits pages and moves away from them these predefined Applet methods are invoked.

Hermaphrodite Applet-ications

You may have noticed that the way of starting an applet was not exclusive to the way of starting an application. Choosing one form did not preclude the other. It is permissible and feasible to have a class that is a subclass of Applet and also contains a public static void main. It can be used as an applet or an application.

It's mostly a novelty, but you might do this if you had a program that was useful both inside and outside a browser (perhaps it checks net connectivity which you might want to do in both situations) and you wanted to retain flexibility of invocation. You would be able to invoke it under the interpreter directly, and also via an html file read in a browser.

Also note that you can have a "main()" method in more than one class in your program. This means that you can have more than one entry point, allowing the program to do slightly different things depending on which class you tell the interpreter to start in. You can vary this from run to run.

Some Methods Useful in Applets, and when they are called, in the table below:

Method	Description
void init()	Called when the applet is first loaded into memory. Typically you override it with one-time initialization code.
void start()	Called each time the browser visits the page containing this applet. Typically you override it to start or resume any threads the applet contains.
void paint(Graphics g)	Will be called by the window system when the component needs to be redisplayed. You will not call this. You will override this if you dynamically change the appearance of the screen, and want to see it appear.
void stop()	Called when the browser leaves the page containing this applet. Typically you override it to stop or suspend any threads the applet contains.
void run()	Nothing to do with applets—this is the main routine in which thread execution starts.

Make the anagram application into an applet.

(Medium)

Passing Parameters to Applets

Just as we have command line arguments for applications, there is a similar feature for passing arguments from the HTML file to the applet it invokes. Parameters are indicated by an HTML tag of the form

```
<param    name=namestring    value=valuestring>
```

The param tags come after the <applet> tag, and before the </applet> tag. An example of some actual parameters in the applet version of the anagram program might be:

```
<applet  class=anagram.class  width=500, height=500>
     <param    name="target"    value="surfing the net">
     <param    name=wordlist    value="words.txt">
     <param    name=minsize     value="2">
</applet>
```

It does not matter if strings are quoted or not, unless the string contains embedded white space. Inside the program you call getParameter with the name as an argument, and it returns the string representing the value. If there isn't a parameter of that name, it returns null. Here is an example:

```
String s = getParameter("minsize");
// parse to an int.
int minsize = Integer.parseInt(s);
```

Notice that this follows the same conventions as "main(String argv[])" —all arguments are passed as strings, and programmers need to do a little processing to get the values of arguments that are numbers.

While we wait for all browsers to become Java-capable (and pretty soon you won't be able to give away a browser unless it understands Java), here's a useful tip.

All browsers ignore HTML tags that they don't understand. And they also ignore HTML tags that they do understand when they appear in unexpected places. These two facts together make it possible to write an HTML file that will invoke an applet in a Java-capable browser, and provide an alternative text or image for an incapable browser. Between the <applet> and </applet> tags, only a few tags, including <param> tags are recognized by applet-aware browsers. Browsers that cannot run Java will ignore these applet-specific tags.

So the HTML below will run the java applet if the browser can, and will display the alternative image instead if the browser is not Java capable.

```
<applet  class=anagram.class  width=500, height=500>
    <param   name="target"    value="surfing the net">
    <param   name=wordlist    value="words.txt">
    <param   name=minsize     value="2">

    <img src="NoJava4U.JPG">

</applet>
```

Security and Applets: Why We Need Security

The whole applet model, indeed the whole browser model is based on the idea that you can download things from anywhere on the Internet. When the things you download are just inert text and data there is no security issue. When Java gives you the ability to download executable code and run it in your environment security is very much an issue.

Unless measures are taken to prevent it, a malicious or buggy applet could delete your files, post your confidential data, or reformat your disk. The measures that have been taken to prevent this mostly consist of providing applets from the net with a very restricted environment in which to run—a padded cell if you like. There are no restrictions on applications or local applets because they do not appear on your system unless you put them there. Net applets on the other hand appear on your system and start executing just by virtue of visiting a web page that has a URL pointing to the applet.

The restrictions mean that an applet loaded from over the net:

- Cannot read and write your files (by default)

- Cannot make network connections to hosts other than the one it came from

- Cannot start a program on your system by using the equivalent of the system() call in C. An application or local applet can do this with the method
  "java.lang.Runtime.exec()".

- Cannot load a library

Some browsers may impose other restrictions on top of these. The eventual aim is to provide support for recognizing and executing trusted applets with more capabilities even over the net, without jeopardizing system security.

Note that there is a difference in default capabilities between a applet loaded from over the net, and an applet loaded from the local file system. Where an applet comes from determines what it is allowed to do. An applet brought from over the net is loaded by the applet class loader, and it is subject to the restrictions enforced by the applet security manager.

An applet stored on the client's local disk and accessible from the CLASSPATH is loaded by the file system loader. These applets are permitted to read and write files, load Java libraries and exec processes. Local applets are not passed through the byte code verifier, which is another line of defence against code from the net.

The verifier checks that the byte code conforms to the Java language specification and looks for violations of the type rules and name space restrictions. The verifier ensures that:

- There are no stack overflows or underflows.

- All register accesses and stores are valid.

- The parameters to all bytecode instructions are correct.

- No illegal type conversion are attempted.

Notes on Linking in Native Methods

Java provides support for linking in native methods. These are routines written in languages other than Java, to which Java can call out. Java I/O is accomplished by calls to the native I/O libraries on each platform. On Windows systems, arithmetic operations are done by calling out to the native runtime library.

Native methods are supported for reasons of performance and code reuse. Any Java application that uses them however has gone outside the Java language. The use of native methods destroys code portability, so you should be cautious in employing them.

Using native methods is inherently compiler, platform, and OS dependent. Here are the steps in the process for the ANSI C compiler on SPARC microprocessors under Solaris 2.x

1. Write a method with no body, and give it the access modifier "native".	`class peach {`
	`    static native void plum(int i);`
	`    ...`

2. The class that the method is in needs to have a static code segment that will load the native library. Use this statement: static { System.loadLibrary("plum"); } where the library is libplum.so So the rest of class peach will look like this:	`    ...`
	`    public static void main (String arg[] ) {`
	`        System.out.println("in main, calling plum");`
	`        plum(33);`
	`    }`
	
	`static { System.loadLibrary("plum"); }`
	`}`

3. Compile the java code,	`javac peach.java`

4. Create the C header file (.h) by running:

`javah peach`

this reads peach.class
and creates peach.h
The .h file can be included in any other C routines that want to call the native routine

create the C stub file (.c) by running:

`javah -stubs peach`

this reads peach.class
and creates peach.c (below)

The stub file peach.c will contain a function that is called from the Java interpreter, and this in turn will call the native C routine after converting any parameters from Java stack references to C data types. It's a little ugly, but it looks like this:

Note that the name of your native function is specified here, and it encodes the class name that it came from. You do not have the luxury of choosing the name of your native method. Also note the prototype. You must supply C code that matches this. Since we declared the native method as "static" the first argument is null, rather than a pointer to the "this" object. The implementation could equally have chosen to omit this first argument. Note also that i was declared as int in Java, but has shown up as long here. Longs are the same size as ints in this compiler (32 bits)

```
/* DO NOT EDIT THIS FILE - it is machine generated */
#include <StubPreamble.h>

/* Stubs for class peach */
/* SYMBOL: "peach/plum(I)V", Java_peach_plum_stub */
stack_item *Java_peach_plum_stub(stack_item
*_P_,struct execenv *_EE_) {
         extern void peach_plum(void *,long);
         (void) peach_plum(NULL,((_P_[0].i)));
         return _P_;
}
```

| 5. Write the native C function and compile it into a dynamic library by using the -G option. | ```c
#include <stdio.h>
void peach_plum(void* this, long i) {
    printf("in peach_plum, i=%d \n",i);
}
``` |
| Then compile this and the stub ("wrapper" would be a better name) file from step 4. You need to specify the path to these 2 include directories, because more header files are needed for a clean compilation. | ```
cc -G  \
    -I$JAVA_HOME/include \
    -I$JAVA_HOME/include/solaris \
    peach.c  plum.c \
    -o libplum.so
``` |
| 6. Make sure that the linker can see the directory that has libplum.so in it, by setting LD_LIBRARY_PATH to include it, then execute your Java program. | ```
% setenv LD_LIBRARY_PATH $OPENWINHOME/lib:.

% java peach
in main, calling plum
in peach_plum, i=33
``` |

ANSI C defines a sorting function with this prototype:

```c
void qsort(   void  * base,
          size_t  nmemb,
          size_t  size,
          int (* compar)(const void *, const void *)
        );
```

That last parameter is a pointer to a comparison function. It is not possible to call this native method directly from Java, as Java doesn't give us a way to express the concept of a reference to a method. The virtual machine allows this concept, so it would be easy to add in the future.

Only use native methods when you really have to.
```

Properties

Java has a platform independent way to communicate extra information at run time to a program. Known as "properties" these do a job like environment variables. Environment variables aren't used because they are too platform-specific. A programmer can read the value of a property by calling getProperty() and passing an argument string for the property in which you are interested.

```
String dir = System.getProperty("user.dir");
```

A long list of properties appears in the file java/lang/System.java. Some properties are not available in applets for security reasons. You can add a property on the command line when you invoke the program like this:

```
java -Drate=10.0 myprogram
```

That value "10.0" will be returned as a string when querying the property "rate". It can then be converted to a floating point number and used as a value in the program. In this case, it's an alternative to a command line argument.

Some Light Relief

There's an old story to the effect that "the people at Cray design their supercomputers with Apple systems, and the Apple designers use Crays!" Apart from this being a terrific example of recurring rotational serendipity (what goes around, comes around) is there any truth to it?

Like many urban legends, this one contains a nugget of truth. In the 1991 Annual Report of Cray Research Inc. there is a short article describing how Apple use a Cray for designing Macintosh cases. The Cray is used to simulate the injection molding of the plastic enclosure cases. The Mac II case was the first Apple system to benefit from the modelling, and the trial was successful. The simulation identified warping problems which were solved by prototyping thus saving money in tooling and production. Apple also uses their Cray for simulating air flow inside the enclosure to check for hot spots. The Cray house magazine reported that the Apple PowerBook continues to use supercomputer simulations. (CRAY CHANNELS, Spring 1992 pp.10-12 "Apple Computer PowerBook computer molding simulation").

The inverse story holds that Seymour Cray himself used a Mac to design Crays. The story seems to have originated with an off-the-cuff remark from Seymour Cray himself, who had a Mac at home, and used it to store some of his work for the Cray 3. Common sense suggests that the simulation of discrete circuitry (Verilog runs, logic analysis, etc.) which is part of all modern integrated circuit design, is done far more cost-effectively on a supercomputer than on a microprocessor.

Cray probably has a lot of supercomputer hardware laying around ready for testing as it comes off the production line.

It's conceivable that a Macintosh could be used to draft the layout of blinking lights for the front of a Cray, or choose some nice color combinations, or some other non-CPU intensive work. A Macintosh is a very good system for writing design notes, sending e-mail, and drawing diagrams, all of which are an equally essential part of designing a computer system.

The good folks at Cray Research have confirmed in a Cray Users Group newsletter that they have a few Macs on the premises. So while it's extremely unlikely that they run logic simulations on their Macs, we can indeed chalk it up as only-slightly-varnished truth that "the people at Cray design their supercomputers with Apple's systems, and the Apple designers use Cray's", for some value of the word "design"!

Further Reading

Instant Java

by John A. Pew

Publisher by Sunsoft Press

ISBN: 0-13-565821-7

This text contains dozens and dozens of useful applets written by a skilled graphics programmer, along with their source. Recommended if you want to see how certain effects are achieved, and learn more about Java at the same time.

CHAPTER
7

Overviewing the Java Libraries

> *A novice of the temple once approached the Chief Priest with a question. "Master, does Emacs have the Buddha nature?" the novice asked.*
>
> *The Chief Priest had been in the temple for many years and could be relied upon to know these things. He thought for several minutes before replying. "I don't see why not. It's got bloody well everything else."*
>
> *–Anonymous*

This chapter covers one of the last remaining topics of the Java language: the libraries that accompany it and how to use them. The libraries are dealt with last for two reasons: you really need to understand the Java language before you can understand how the libraries are used, and you can get a very long way with just the println and read-a-byte that we have used to date.

The chapter has two major sections: I/O, and the network facilities. The chapter provides a summary rather than an exhaustive list. There are three main reasons for this: it makes it easier to read the book; it provides a solid foundation for those requiring more in-depth knowledge; and, it gets the information that you need to start programming, to you more quickly. The biggest obstacle to learning about Java support for network programming is understanding network terms and capabilities. Accordingly, a summary of TCP/IP networking is presented, along with references for further study.

I/O

Java offers some simple I/O classes, organized in a hierarchy. Remember though that for protection of your data, I/O may not be available in an Applet. Simple I/O is simple to do, and the ability to do more structured I/O is also provided. Before you even get into the concept of I/O a number of methods are available in the class File to provide information about a file. Here are the methods:

```
public class File

    constructors:
        public File(String path)
        public File(String path, String name)
        public File(File dir, String name)

    deleting a file:
        public boolean delete()

    to do with file name:
        public String getName()
        public String getPath()
        public String getAbsolutePath()
        public String getParent()
        public boolean renameTo(File dest)

    getting the attributes of a file:
        public boolean exists()
        public boolean canWrite()
        public boolean canRead()
        public boolean isFile()
        public boolean isDirectory()
        public native boolean isAbsolute()
        public long lastModified()
        public long length()
        public boolean equals(Object obj)

    to do with the directory:
        public boolean mkdir()
        public boolean mkdirs()
        public String[] list()
        public String[] list(FilenameFilter filter)

    miscellaneous:
        public static final char pathSeparatorChar
        public int hashCode()
        public String toString()
```

The Programming Challenges come early in this chapter because the I/O material is so straightforward. Write a Java program that creates a subdirectory "Fruit" of the current directory if it does not already exist.

It should then create a file called "yam" in that directory, overwriting it if it already existed. Make the program print out what it is doing. Finally it should print the attributes of both the file and the directory it is in.

Interactive I/O

Java has the concept of a standard in, standard out, and standard error that Unix introduced. The class `System` contains these objects and they are known respectively as

```
System.in        System.out        System.err
```

We have already seen the println method used on standard out. It also has methods to print each of the built-in types. Standard error is very similar. Standard error is separate from standard out in order to provide a separate stream for error messages that might otherwise disappear down a pipe during I/O redirection. Standard in is just an interactive BufferedInputStream, and has the same "read" methods that are described below.

One routine that programmers always want to know about immediately is support for non-blocking I/O. Programmers want to know the method for getting a character from the keyboard without needing to press a carriage return, and returning at once if no character has yet been entered. This facility is much used when writing games software. (It has a much wider applicability for editors and all kinds of interactive software, but games programming is why a lot of programmers first start looking for it).

Java doesn't offer such a feature as part of an input stream (you could program it as a native method). But it is available in the window toolkit, and since most games will use the toolkit games programmers everywhere can breathe a sigh of relief.

Because the `in`, `out`, and `err` streams are used in just about every program, they have been placed in the `System` class in the `lang` package, which is imported automatically into each compilation unit. All other I/O is in the package `io`, which must be imported explicitly.

File I/O

Java I/O revolves around the concept of a "stream" which is a flow of data. A file in the filesystem can be thought of as a reservoir or pool of data. By itself it just lies there inertly. To make it flow into or out of your program, you use a stream object. Another way to understand this is to consider a stream as letting you do much the same things as an open file descriptor, but the focus is on the operations (flow of data) rather than the implementation (file descriptor). A Stream has a file descriptor as part of its private data.

You also have the ability to "push" streams on top of each other[1] to "stack up" several different kinds of processing and accessing data.

Input Classes and Methods

To get specific, the abstract class which is extended for all file input is `Input-Stream`. The Java source for these classes can (and should) be examined at `java/src/java/io/*`. You just instantiate a stream object and then can do I/O on it immediately. There is no separate "open()" step. If the instantiation didn't throw an exception, you are ready to go. And there's no concept of "I am opening this file for ASCII writes/binary data writes" as occurs on the PC with other forms of I/O. You write what you write, without making a needless distinction between character and other data.

Here are some examples of how to instantiate a FileInputStream. All of the constructors require that you provide the name of the file either directly, as a literal string or variable, or indirectly by giving a File object that has already been associated with a filename.

```
Example 1
    FileInputStream fis;
    try  {
        fis = new FileInputStream("animals.txt");
        ...
    }
    catch (FileNotFoundException fnfe) {
        ...
```

1. Just as with the STREAMS facility in the Unix kernel that connects device drivers to user processes. Java streams are not directly related to Unix kernel STREAMS, but are a similar kind of idea.

Example 2
```
File f;
FileInputStream fis;
try {
    f = new File("plum");
    fis = new FileInputStream( f );
} catch ...
```

Basic input operates on bytes, and there are 3 choices:

- to input a single byte, returning (int) -1 at EOF

- to input filling an array of bytes,

- to input filling a range within an array of bytes.

All reads are blocking reads: if the data is not there, it does not return from the read until it is. These 3 methods are the "read" methods shown in the class FileInputStream below. The hierarchy and the additional classes look like this:

InputStream The abstract class from which all input classes are derived.

FileInputStream   the basic input operations to read a byte or an array of bytes, skip over some bytes, and close the stream.

Commonly Used Methods:

```
// constructors
public FileInputStream(String name) throws FileNotFoundException
public FileInputStream(File file) throws FileNotFoundException

public native int read() throws IOException
public int read(byte b[]) throws IOException
public int read(byte b[], int off, int len) throws IOException

public native long skip(long n) throws IOException
public native int available() throws IOException
public native void close() throws IOException
```

ByteArrayInputStream implements a buffer (array of bytes) that can be used as an input stream. Although the byte array is in memory, this stream allows you to access it via read() calls.

Commonly Used Methods:

```
// constructors:
public ByteArrayInputStream(byte buf[])
public ByteArrayInputStream(byte buf[], int offset, int length)

public synchronized int read()
public synchronized int read(byte b[], int off, int len)

public synchronized long skip(long n)
public synchronized int available()
public synchronized void reset()
```

StringBufferInputStream implements a string buffer (modifiable string) that can be used as an input stream. Similar to the ByteArrayInputStream, in that it allows you to get data serially from a StringBuffer through read() calls.

Commonly Used Methods:

```
// constructor:
public StringBufferInputStream(String s)

public synchronized int read()
public synchronized int read(byte b[], int off, int len)

public synchronized long skip(long n)
public synchronized int available()
public synchronized void reset()
```

SequenceInputStream Takes a series of inputs streams, and effectively concatenates them, allowing the programmer to access them as though they were just one long stream.

Commonly Used Methods:

```
// constructors:
public SequenceInputStream(Enumeration e)
public SequenceInputStream(InputStream s1, InputStream s2)

final void nextStream() throws IOException
public int read() throws IOException
public int read(byte buf[], int pos, int len)
                         throws IOException
public void close() throws IOException
```

PipedInputStream This class is used in pairs with PipedOutputStream. It allows two threads to communicate using I/O calls.

What one thread writes into the PipedOutputStream, will be read by another thread that has instantiated PipedInputStream. These two classes mean that programmers have a ready-made producer/consumer buffer, and do not have to code this from first principles.

Commonly Used Methods:

```
// constructors:
public PipedInputStream (PipedOutputStream src) throws IOException
public PipedInputStream ()

public void connect(PipedOutputStream src) throws IOException
synchronized void receive(int b) throws IOException
synchronized void receive(byte b[], int off, int len)
                                   throws IOException
synchronized void receivedLast()

public synchronized int read()  throws IOException
public synchronized int read(byte b[], int off, int len)
                                   throws IOException
public void close()  throws IOException
```

FilterInputStream This is an abstract class derived from InputStream. It provides the ability to 'stack' or layer several input streams on top of each other. Each of these layers will modify the data as it passes it on.

The next four input classes extend the **FilterInputStream**:

BufferedInputStream An input class that does an initial read into an in-memory buffer (2Kbyte by default). Subsequent reads will supply data from this buffer (which is fast), rather than going to disk (which is slow). A few large accesses to disk are always quicker than many small accesses, so use this class when performance is a goal. The source is in java/src/java/io/BufferedInput-Stream.java

LineNumberInputStream An input class that keeps track of the number of lines that have been read. It also provides the ability to set and retrieve the line count. The source is in java/src/java/io/LineNumberInputStream.java

PushbackInputStream This class provides a method to "push back" a byte that has been read, back into the input stream. Pushback of a single character is an operation that is commonly required in the lexing phase of a compiler. It allows you to "lookahead" one and decide what to do with the current token based on the context of what comes before and after it. The source is in java/src/java/io/PushbackInputStream.java

DataInputStream So far all the above classes only allow you to read a byte or series of bytes. The DataInputStream class provides methods for all the built in types: booleans, floats, etc. These are written out (in DataOutput-Stream) as binary data and read in the same way here. So an integer with the value zero will be written out as 32 zero bits, rather than say, 4 bytes of 0x30, which would be the code for the printable ASCII string "0000".

Commonly Used Methods:

```
// constructor
public DataInputStream(InputStream in)

public final int read(byte b[]) throws IOException
public final int read(byte b[], int off, int len)
        throws IOException
public final void readFully(byte b[]) throws IOException
public final void readFully(byte b[], int off, int len)
                        throws IOException

public final int skipBytes(int n) throws IOException

public final boolean readBoolean() throws IOException
public final byte readByte() throws IOException
public final int readUnsignedByte() throws IOException
public final short readShort() throws IOException
public final int readUnsignedShort() throws IOException
public final char readChar() throws IOException
public final int readInt() throws IOException
public final long readLong() throws IOException
public final float readFloat() throws IOException
public final double readDouble() throws IOException

public final String readLine() throws IOException

public final String readUTF() throws IOException
public final static String readUTF(DataInput in)
                        throws IOException
```

The trick with DataInputStream is that you have to know what type of data to expect next so you can call the appropriate method to read it. This is a characteristic of input for all languages, but it bears repeating. Another possibility is to write the data in a format that precedes each data item with a pair of bytes that give type and length.

We have already seen in the case study in the previous chapter how to read from a file using a FileInputStream. The following are some examples of typical use of the other classes.

Here is an example using the StringBufferInputStream class to obtain characters from a string with "read()" calls. Bear in mind that this is a small example to show the concept.

```java
import java.io.*;
public class test7a {
    static String s = new String( "aardvark butterfly\n" +
            "cat dalmatian\n" +
             "eagle fish\ngopher hippo\ninyala jackal\nkyloe " +
             "lamb\nmoose nanny-goat\nopossum pandora\n" );

    static StringBufferInputStream sbis =
            new StringBufferInputStream( s );

    public static void main (String a[]) {
        int c;
            while ((c=sbis.read())!= -1) {

                System.out.print((char)c);

            }

        }

}
```

The result of running this program is that each call to sbis.read() comes back with one character, which is printed by the call to System.out.print(). The output looks like this:

```
aardvark butterfly
cat dalmatian
eagle fish
gopher hippo
inyala jackal
kyloe lamb
moose nanny-goat
opossum pandora
```

Pushing Streams to Combine Filtered Processing

Here is an example of how to push one stream onto another, to gain the filtered processing of both. The program reads from a string, but also keeps track of the lines in the input using the LineNumberInputStream.

```java
// shows the use of various input streams
import java.io.*;
public class test7b {
    static String s = new String(
            "aardvark butterfly\ncat dalmatian\n" +
            "eagle fish\ngopher hippo\ninyala jackal\nkyloe " +
            "lamb\nmoose nanny-goat\n" );

    static StringBufferInputStream sbis =
            new StringBufferInputStream( s );

    static LineNumberInputStream lnis =
            new LineNumberInputStream( sbis );

    public static void main (String a[]) {
        int c;
        try {
            while ((c=lnis.read())!= -1) {

                System.out.print((char)c);
                if (c=='\n') {
                    System.out.print("that finishes input line "
                        + lnis.getLineNumber() + "\n\n");
                }

            }
        } catch (IOException ioe) {
                System.out.println("Exception reading stream");
                ioe.printStackTrace();
                System.exit(0);
        }
    }
}
```

Note that (unlike when using StringBufferInputStream) the use of LineNumber-InputStream may involve an I/O exception, and you must make provision for this. The results of running this program are:

```
aardvark butterfly
that finishes input line 1

cat dalmatian
that finishes input line 2

eagle fish
that finishes input line 3

gopher hippo
that finishes input line 4

inyala jackal
that finishes input line 5

kyloe lamb
that finishes input line 6

moose nanny-goat
that finishes input line 7
```

Using the framework of the above example, push another input stream onto the existing two. Use SequenceInputStream to supply a FileInputStream as well as the StringBufferInputStream that we are using above. Create a file called animals.txt that contains a few more creatures. Instantiate the SequenceInputStream and push a LineNumberInputStream onto it, to demonstrate the seamless flow of data from two different sources. (Easy)

On MS-DOS based systems like Windows 95, a newline in an ASCII file is represented by two characters: ASCII linefeed followed by ASCII carriage return. On Unix systems, a newline is represented by just one character: an ASCII linefeed (0x0a). Having two characters to represent newline is a carryover from the days of mechanical teletypes[2], when it was useful to have one action to advance the roll of

2. Teletype is a trademark of an antique corporation. The sound of a teletype machine ("KERchunk-a-chunk-a-chunk") is often used as a radio special effect to indicate the arrival of timely news. No competent news organization has used teletypes in decades.

paper and another to move the print head back to the left margin. This hasn't been useful for twenty years or more now.

The different line delimiters can bedevil programs that are written to expect one convention but are run on a system with the other. For example, without taking this into account, the anagram program will run under Unix, but fail on Windows. The reason is this part of the source:

```
while ( (c=fis.read()) != EOF ) {
// how to read past EOLN on a PC?
    if ( c == '\n' ) break;
    buffer[i++] = (char) c;
```

The key statement says "if this is a newline character, break out of the loop and deal with the string we just completed reading." On a Windows system, this will leave a '\r' character jammed on the end of each token in the input stream.

There's a kludgey way to fix this and a proper way. The kludgey way is to explicitly check for the carriage return character following newlines, and throw it away if it's there. In the anagram program, it would be an extra read, like this:

```
while ( (c=fis.read()) != EOF ) {
// kludge up EOLN on a PC
    if ( c == '\r' ) c=fis.read();
    if ( c == '\n' ) break;
    buffer[i++] = (char) c;
```

A better way to accomplish this is to use the standard DataInputStream or LineNumberInputStream. Both of these Classes are capable of coping with an end of line conveyed by \n or \r\n or \r or EOF.

Modify the anagram program in the previous chapter so that it uses a DataInputStream instead of a FileInputStream, and can be run happily on both Unix systems and Windows systems.

There is also a `StreamTokenizer` class that can be pushed onto an input stream. It will attempt basic lexing of the stream, namely assembling sequences of characters into string tokens.

Output Classes and Methods

The abstract class which is extended for all file output is OutputStream. The Java source for these classes can (and should) be examined at java/src/java/io/*
The hierarchy and the additional classes are really just the counterparts of the Input classes that we have already seen. Instead of providing a couple of "read()" methods they provide some variations on "write()".

Basic output operates on bytes, and there are 3 choices:

- to output a single byte,

- to output an array of bytes,

- to output a range from within an array of bytes.

All writes are blocking writes: control does not return from the write until the I/O transfer is handed over to the operating system. These three methods are the "write" methods shown in the class FileOutputStream below.

The hierarchy and the additional classes look like this:

OutputStream   The abstract class from which all output classes are derived

FileOutputStream the basic input operations to write a byte or an array of bytes.

Commonly used Methods:

```
// constructors
public FileOutputStream(String name) throws IOException
public FileOutputStream(File file) throws IOException
public FileOutputStream(FileDescriptor fdObj)

public native void write(byte b) throws IOException
public void write(byte b[]) throws IOException
public void write(byte b[], int off, int len)
                            throws IOException

public native void close() throws IOException
public final FileDescriptor getFD()  throws IOException
protected void finalize() throws IOException
```

ByteArrayOutputStream Implements an in-memory byte array that can be written to as an Output Stream. The array grows as needed. There are two methods to read (retrieve) the data: toByteArray() and toString().

Commonly Used Methods:

```
// constructors
public ByteArrayOutputStream()
public ByteArrayOutputStream(int size)

public synchronized void write(int b)
public synchronized void write(byte b[], int off, int len)
public synchronized void writeTo(OutputStream out)
                          throws IOException

public int size()
public synchronized void reset()

public synchronized byte toByteArray()[]
public String toString()
public String toString(int hibyte)
```

PipedOutputStream Used in conjunction with a PipedInputStream to let threads pass data to each other by means of writes and reads on a common pipe.

Commonly Used Methods:

```
// constructors
public PipedOutputStream(PipedInputStream snk)
                    throws IOException
public PipedOutputStream()

public void connect(PipedInputStream snk) throws IOException

public void write(int b)  throws IOException
public void write(byte b[], int off, int len)
                    throws IOException

public void close()  throws IOException
```

FilterOutputStream This is an abstract class derived from Output-Stream. It supports an output stream of bytes that is filtered (processed) in some way, before being passed on for output.

Just as with input streams, several output stream filters can be pushed together, each modifying the data as it passes it on.

The next three output classes extend the **FilterOutputStream**:

BufferedOutputStream This stream acts as a buffer for data. The initial buffer size is 512 bytes, and the buffer is gradually filled by write() calls, and will only be written to the file when it is full, or a flush call is made.

Commonly Used Methods:

```
// constructors
public BufferedOutputStream(OutputStream out)
public BufferedOutputStream(OutputStream out, int size)

public synchronized void write(int b) throws IOException
public synchronized void write(byte b[], int off, int len)
                              throws IOException

public synchronized void flush() throws IOException
```

PrintStream   This class implements an output stream that has some additional methods convenient for printing the primitive (built-in) types. You can specify that the stream should be flushed whenever a newline is written.

System.out is just an instance of a PrintStream that has been connected to the terminal screen.

Commonly Used Methods:

```
// constructors
public PrintStream(OutputStream out)
public PrintStream(OutputStream out, boolean autoflush)

public void write(int b)
public void write(byte b[], int off, int len)

public void flush()
public void checkError()

public void print(Object o)
synchronized public void print(String s)
synchronized public void print(char s[])

public void print(char c)
                // & same for other primitive types
                // int, long, boolean, float, etc.

synchronized public void println(char c)
                // & same for other primitive types
                // int, long, boolean, float, etc.
```

DataOutput   The interface that defines output for the built-in types.

DataOutputStream This class provides portable output for the built-in data types. A value that is written by a method in this class is guaranteed to be readable by DataInput-Stream.

Commonly Used Methods:

```
// constructor
public DataOutputStream(OutputStream out)

public synchronized void write(int b) throws IOException
public synchronized void write(byte b[], int off, int len)
                          throws IOException
public final void writeBoolean(boolean v) throws IOException
public final void writeByte(int v) throws IOException
public final void writeShort(int v) throws IOException
public final void writeChar(int v) throws IOException
public final void writeInt(int v) throws IOException
public final void writeLong(long v) throws IOException
public final void writeFloat(float v) throws IOException
public final void writeDouble(double v) throws IOException
public final void writeBytes(String s) throws IOException
public final void writeChars(String s) throws IOException
public final void writeUTF(String str) throws IOException

public final int size()
public void flush() throws IOException
```

Here is an example of pushing a print stream onto a FileOutputStream. This provides the ability to use the print methods on a FileOutputStream.

```java
import java.io.*;
class test7f {

    static public void main (String a[]) {

        File f = new File("plum");
        FileOutputStream fos;
        PrintStream ps;

        try {
            f = new File("plum");
            fos = new FileOutputStream( f );
            ps = new PrintStream( fos );

            ps.println("The world needs more lerts");
        }
        catch (  ...
    }
}
```

That deals with the most commonly used Input and Output streams. There are a couple of other facilities to be aware of, too, such as random access I/O.

Random Access

The class RandomAccessFile allows the file pointer to be moved to arbitrary positions in the file prior to reading or writing. This allows you to "jump around" in the file reading and writing data with random (nonsequential) access. You provide a mode string when you open the file, specifying whether you are opening it for read access only "r", or read and update access "rw".

Here is an example of how you would append to a file, using the RandomAccess-File class. We will write a few more animals on the end of the "animals.txt" file created in the previous programming challenge.

```java
import java.io.RandomAccessFile;
class test7e {

    static public void main(String a[]) {
        RandomAccessFile rf;
        try  {
            rf = new RandomAccessFile("animals.txt", "rw");

            rf.seek( rf.length() );

            rf.writeBytes("ant bee\ncat dog\n");

            rf.close();

        } catch (Exception e) {
            System.out.println("file snafu");
            System.exit(0);
        }
    }
}
```

This example will extend the "animals.txt" file by appending the string on the end.

Write an elementary version of the Unix "cat" (concatenate) command. This should take a list of files on the command line, and type out their contents one after the other to the standard output device. (Easy to Medium difficulty)

Networking with Java

"If a packet hits a pocket on a socket on a port,

and the bus is interrupted and the interrupt's not caught,

then the socket packet pocket has an error to report.

—Programmer's traditional nursery rhyme

The biggest difficulty most people face in understanding the Java networking features lies in understanding the network part rather than the Java part. If you learn French, it doesn't mean that you can translate an article from a French medical journal. Similarly if you learn Java, you need to have an understanding of the network services and terminology before you can blithely write Internet code. This section provides a a solid review, followed by a description of the Java support.

Everything You Need To Know about TCP/IP But Failed to Learn in Kindergarten

Networking at heart is all about shifting bits from point A to point B. Usually we bundle the data bits into a packet with some more bits that say where they are to go. That, in a nutshell, is the Internet Protocol or IP. If we want to send more bits than will fit into a single packet, we can divide the bits into groups and send them in several successive packets. These are called "User Datagrams."

User Datagrams can be sent across the Internet using the User Datagram Protocol (UDP), which relies on the Internet Protocol for addressing and routing. UDP is like going to the post office, sticking on a stamp, and dropping off the packet. IP is what the mailman does to route and deliver the packet. Two common applications that use the UDP are: SNMP, the Simple Network Management Protocol, and TFTP, the Trivial File Transfer Protocol.

Just as when we send several pieces of postal mail to the same address, the packages might arrive in any order. Some of them might even be delayed, or even on occasion lost altogether. This is true for UDP too; you wave good-bye to the bits as they leave your workstation, and you have no idea when they will arrive where you sent them, or even if they did.

Uncertain delivery is equally undesirable for postal mail and for network bit streams. We deal with the problem in the postal mail world (when the importance warrants the cost) by paying an extra fee to register the mail and have the mailman collect and bring back a signature acknowledging delivery. A similar protocol is used in the network work to guarantee reliable delivery in the order in which the packets were sent. This protocol is known as Transmission Control Protocol or "TCP". Two applications that run on top of, or use, TCP are: FTP, the File Transfer Protocol, and Telnet.

TCP uses IP as its underlying protocol (just as UDP does) for routing and delivering the bits to the correct address. However, TCP is more like a phone call than a registered mail delivery, in that a real end-to-end connection is held open for the duration of the transmission session. It takes a while to set up this stream connection, and it costs more to assure reliable sequenced delivery, but often the cost is justified.

The access device at each end-point of a phone conversation is a telephone. The access object at each end-point of a TCP/IP session is a socket. Sockets started life as a way for two processes on the same Unix system to talk to each other, but some smart programmers realized that they could be generalized into connection end-points between processes on different machines connected by a TCP/IP network.

Sockets can deliver fast and dirty using the UDP (this is a datagram socket), or slower, fussier, and reliably using the TCP (this is termed a stream socket). Socket connections have a client end and a server end. Generally the server end just keeps listening for incoming requests ("operators are standing by" kind of thing). The client end initiates a connection, and then passes or requests information from the server.

There! Now you know everything you need to use the Java networking features.

Don't be mislead by the client/server terminology used in the X Window system.

In X terminology, the server is the software that owns the keyboard, display, and pointing device. The client is the software that talks to the server and makes window requests of it, i.e. the program you are running. This terminology is the opposite of what client/server means in all other contexts, and it is only one of several remarkable decisions the X-windows people have made.

What's in the Networking Library?

If you browse the network library source in java/src/java/net, you'll find these classes:

InetAddress	The class that represents IP addresses and the operations on them.
DatagramPacket	A class that represents a datagram packet containing packet data, packet length, internet addresses and port. Packets can be sent and received.
DatagramSocket	This class implements allows datagrams to be sent and received using the UDP.
PlainSocketImpl	This is the default socket implementation. It doesn't implement any security checks nor support firewalls.

SocketImpl	This is the Socket implementation class. It is an abstract class that must be subclassed to provide an actual implementation.
ServerSocket	The server Socket class. It uses a SocketImpl to implement the actual socket operations. It is done this way so that you are can change socket implementations depending on the kind of firewall that is used. The Unix Socket API does not distinguish between client and server sockets, but the Java API does.
Socket	The client Socket class. It uses a SocketImpl to implement the actual socket operations. Again, this permits you to change socket implementations depending on the kind of firewall that is used.
URL	This class is analogous to the InetAddress class, but at a higher level. The class represents a Uniform Reference Locator—a reference to an object on the Web.
URLConnection	A class to represent an active connection to an object represented by a URL. It is an abstract class that must be subclassed to provide an implementation of a connection.
URLEncoder	The class turns Strings of text into x-www-form-urlencoded format.
URLStreamHandler	An abstract class that opens a stream to the object referenced by the URL.
ContentHandler	A class to read data from a URLConnection and construct an Object. Specific subclasses of ContentHandler handle specific mime types.

There are a few other classes too, but these are the key ones.

TCP/IP Client Server Model

Before we look at actual Java code, a diagram is in order showing how a client and server typically communicate over a TCP/IP network connection. The way the processes contact each other is by knowing the IP address (which identifies a unique computer on the Internet) and a port number (which is a simple software convention the OS maintains, allowing an incoming network connection to be routed to a specific process). The client and server must use the same port number. The port numbers under 1024 are reserved for system software use. For simplicity, network socket connections are made to look like streams. You simply read and write data using the usual stream methods, and it automagically appears at the other end.

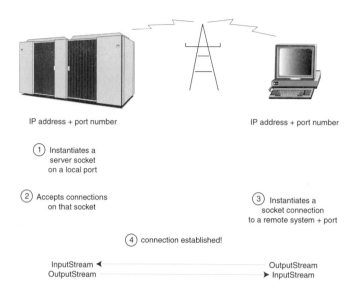

IP address + port number   IP address + port number

(1) Instantiates a
server socket
on a local port

(2) Accepts connections
on that socket

(3) Instantiates a
socket connection
to a remote system + port

(4) connection established!

InputStream ◄——————————————— OutputStream
OutputStream ———————————————► InputStream

On the Internet, no one knows you're a dog . . .

Let's make a brief digression at this point, and recall the phenomenon in which the Internet entered the public consciousness in a big way. One of the early indicators of this was a 1993 cartoon in the New Yorker Magazine, with the punchline "On the Internet nobody knows you're a dog!" This cartoon was cut out and displayed on every network programmer's office from Albuquerque to Zimbabwe. Mainstream recognition! On the Internet, nobody knows you're a dog.

Our code example is a Canine Turing Test—a Java program to distinguish whether the communicating party is a dog or not. People greet each other by shaking hands, while dogs sniff each other. Dogs are loyal companions, and part of their loyalty is absolute truthfulness. To tell if a dog is at the other end of a socket, just ask the question "If you met me, would you shake my hand, or sniff it?" Depending on the answer that the client sends back over the socket to the server, the server will know if the client is a dog or a human.

Obviously this program is only going to work if you at using a computer that has an IP address and a connection to a TCP/IP network. Or if you run it all on one system, and you have socket support working. On a Unix workstation TCP/IP support is a standard basic part of the operation system. On a PC you'll need to have the TCP/IP "protocol stack" installed. Calling this software a "protocol stack" is a bit of a misnomer, as it has nothing to do with LIFO stacks. "TCP/IP software" would be a more accurate name.

The code comes in two parts: a server that listens for clients and asks them the question, and clients that connect to the server. The server is going to detect whether clients are dogs or not. First the server code, which looks like this:

```
/**
 *   a network server that detects presence of dogs on the Internet
 *
 *   @version    1.1 Jan 21 1996
 *   @author     Peter van der Linden
 *   @author     From the book "Just Java"
 */
import java.io.*;
import java.net.*;

class server {
    public static void main(String a[]) throws IOException {
        int timeoutsecs = 600;
        int port = 4444;
        Socket sock;
        String query = "If you met me would you shake my hand, "
                        + "or sniff it?";

        ServerSocket servsock =
            new ServerSocket(port, timeoutsecs);

    while (true) {
        // wait for the next client connection
            sock=servsock.accept();

        // Get I/O streams from the socket
            PrintStream out =
             new PrintStream( sock.getOutputStream() );
            DataInputStream in  =
            new DataInputStream( sock.getInputStream() );

        // Send our query
        out.println(query);
        out.flush();

        // get the reply
        String reply = in.readLine();
        if (reply.indexOf("sniff") > -1)
            System.out.println(
            "On the Internet I know this is a DOG!");
        else System.out.println(
            "Probably a person or an AI experiment");

            // Close this connection, (not overall server socket)
            sock.close();
    }
  }
}
```

Drawing by P. Steiner; ©1993 The New Yorker Magazine, Inc.

"On the Internet, nobody knows you're a dog."

Now the client end of the socket, which looks like this:

```java
// On the Internet no one knows you're a dog...
// unless you tell them.

import java.io.*;
import java.net.*;

class dog {

    public static void main(String a[]) throws IOException {
        Socket sock;
        DataInputStream dis;
        PrintStream dat;

        // Open our connection to positive, at port 4444
        sock = new Socket("positive",4444);

        // Get I/O streams from the socket
        dis = new DataInputStream( sock.getInputStream() );
        dat = new PrintStream( sock.getOutputStream() );

        String fromServer = dis.readLine();

        System.out.println("Got this from server:" + fromServer);

        dat.println("I would sniff you");
        dat.flush();

        sock.close();
    }
}
```

When you try running this program, make sure that you change the client socket connect to refer not to "positive" (my workstation) but to a system where you intend to run the server code. You can identify this system by using either the name (as long as the name will uniquely locate it on your net), or the IP address. (If in doubt, just use the IP address).

Here's how to run the example:

1. Put the server program on the system that you want to be the server. Compile the server program, and start it:

```
javac server.java
java server
```

2. Put the client program on the system that you want to be the client. Change the client program so it references your server machine, not machine "positive". Then compile it.

```
javac dog.java
```

3. When you execute the client program, on the client system you will see the output:

```
java dog
```

```
Got this from server: If you met me would you shake my hand,
or sniff it?
```

4. On the server machine, you will see the output

```
On the Internet I know this is a DOG!
```

Make sure the server is running before you execute the client, otherwise it will have no-one to talk to.

Write a second client program that would reply with the "shake hands" typical of a person. Run this from the same or another client system. (Easy).

How to Find the IP Address Given a Machine Name

This code will be able to find the IP address of all computers that it knows about. That may mean all systems that have an entry in the local hosts table, or (if it is served by a name server) the domain of the name server, which could be as extensive as the entire Internet.

```java
import java.io.*;
import java.net.*;

class who {

    public static void main(String a[]) throws IOException {

        InetAddress InetAddr =
            InetAddress.getByName ("claycourt");
        System.out.println(
            "inet address is " + InetAddr.toString() );

    }
}
```

Some Notes on Protocol and Content Handlers

Some of the Java documentation makes a big production about the extensibility of the HotJava browser. If it is asked to browse some data whose type it doesn't recognize, it can simply download the code for the appropriate handler and use that to grok the data. Or so the theory runs. It hasn't yet been proved in practice.

A prime opportunity to showcase dynamic handlers arose when the Java Development Kit was switching over from the Alpha to Beta versions in late 1995. There were significant applet incompatibilities between the two. It provided a fine opportunity to use dynamic content handling. The browser source (which worked exclusively with Alpha applets) was widely available for the asking. No beta-capable version of the alpha Browser has appeared to date. The general wonderfulness of dynamic handlers in the browser has still to be proven in practice.

The theory of the handlers is this. There are two kinds of handler that you can write: protocol handlers and content handlers.

A **protocol handler** talks to other programs. Both ends follow the same protocol in order to communicate ("After you.", "No, I insist, after you.") If you wrote an Oracle database protocol handler, it would deal with SQL queries to pull data out of an Oracle database.

A **content handler** knows how to decode the contents of a file. It handles data (think of it as the contents of something pointed to by a URL). It gets the bytes and assembles them into an object. If you wrote an MPEG content handler, then it would be able to play MPEG movies in your browser, once you had brought the data over there. Bringing MPEG data to your browser could be done using the FTP protocol, or you might wish to write your own high performance protocol handler.

Content handlers and protocol handlers may be particularly convenient for web browsers, and they may also be useful in stand-alone applications. There is not a lot of practical experience with these handlers yet, so it is hard to offer definitive advice about their use. Some people predict they are going to be very important for decoding file formats of arbitrary wackiness, while other people are ready to be convinced by an existence proof.

Some Light Relief

The Nerd Detection System

Most people are familiar with the little security decals that electronic and other high-value stores use to deter shoplifters. The sticker contains a metallic strip. Unless deactivated by a store cashier, the sticker sets off an alarm when carried past a detector at the store doors.

These security stickers are actually a form of antenna. The sticker detector sends out a weak RF signal between two posts through which shoppers will pass. It looks for a return signal at a specific frequency, which indicates that one of the stickers has entered the field between the posts.

All this theory was obvious to a couple of California Institute of Technology students Dwight Berg and Tom Capellari, who decided to test the system in practice. Naturally, they selected a freshman to (unknowingly) participate in the trials. At preregistration, after the unlucky frosh's picture was taken, but before it was laminated into his I.D. card, Dwight and Tom fixed a couple of active security decals from local stores onto the back of the photo.

The gimmicked card was then laminated together hiding the McGuffin, and the two conspirators awaited further developments. A couple of months later they caught up with their victim as he was entering one of the stores. He was carrying his wallet above his head. In response to a comment that this was an unusual posture, the frosh replied that something in his wallet, probably his bank card, seemed to set off store alarms. He had been conditioned to carry his wallet above his head after several weeks of setting off the alarms while entering and leaving many of the local stores.

The frosh seemed unimpressed with Dwight and Tom's suggestion that perhaps the local merchants had installed some new type of nerd detection system. Apparently the comment got the frosh thinking though, because the next occasion he met Dwight, he put Dwight in a headlock until he confessed to his misdeed. **Moral**: never annoy a nerd larger than yourself.

Further Reading

"More Legends of Caltech"

William A. Dodge, Jr.
published by the California Institute of Technology, Pasadena, Calif., 1989.
(This book has no ISBN).

TCP/IP Network Administration

Craig Hunt
O'Reilly & Associates, Sebastopol CA, 1994
ISBN 0-937175-82-X
The modest title hides the fact that this book will be useful to a wider audience than just network administrators. It is a very good practical guide to TCP/IP, written as a tutorial introduction.

Teach Yourself TCP/IP in 14 Days

Timothy Parker
Sams Publishing, Indianapolis, 1994
ISBN 0-672-30549-6
When a book starts off with an apology for the dullness of the subject material, you just know that the author has some unusual ways about him.

Answer To Programming Challenge

Here is a Java program that creates a subdirectory, and a file in it.

```java
// create a subdirectory Fruit
// then create a file called yam in that directory
import java.io.*;
class files {
    public static final PrintStream o = System.out;

    public static void main(String a[]) throws IOException {
        File d = new File("Fruit");
        checkDirectory(d);
        checkFile("Fruit/yam");
    }

    static void checkFile(String s) {
        File f = new File(s);
        if (!f.exists() ) {
            o.println("File " + f.getName() + " doesn't exist");
            FileOutputStream fos;
            try { fos = new FileOutputStream(f);
                fos.write(' ');
            } catch (IOException ioe) {
                o.println("IO Exception!");
            }
        } else {
            o.println("File " + f.getName() + " already exists");
        }
    }

    static void checkDirectory(File d) throws IOException {
        boolean success;
        if (!d.exists() ) {
            o.println("Directory "
                        + d.getName() + " doesn't exist");
            if (success=d.mkdir())
               o.println("Have created directory " + d.getName());
            else
               o.println("Failed to create directory "
                            + d.getName());
        } else {
            o.println( d.getName() + " exists already");
            if (d.isDirectory()) {
                o.println( "and is a directory.");
            } else {
                o.println( "and is a file.");
                throw new IOException();
            }
        }
    }
}
```

Answer To Programming Challenge

This program uses a SequenceInputStream to jam two different sources of data seamlessly together. It pushes a LineNumberInputStream on top of that, to keep track of line numbers.

```java
// shows the use of various input streams
import java.io.*;
public class test7c {
    static String s=new String("aardvark butterfly\n" +
                "carp dalmatian\n" +
                "eagle fish\ngopher hippo\ninyala jackal\nkyloe " +
                "lamb\nmoose nanny-goat\nopossum pandora\n" );

    static StringBufferInputStream sbis=
            new StringBufferInputStream(s);

    public static void main (String a[])
            throws FileNotFoundException {
        int c;
        FileInputStream fis = new FileInputStream("animals.txt");

        SequenceInputStream sis =
            new SequenceInputStream( sbis, fis );

        LineNumberInputStream lsis =
            new LineNumberInputStream( sis );

        try {
            while ((c=lsis.read())!= -1) {

                System.out.print((char)c);
                if (c=='\n') {
                    System.out.print("that finishes input line "
                            + lsis.getLineNumber() + "\n\n");
                }

            }
        } catch (IOException ioe) {
                System.out.println("Exception reading stream");
                ioe.printStackTrace();
                System.exit(0);
        }
    }
}
```

The file "animals.txt" contains
```
queenbee raven
swan terrier
urchin  vixen
wallaby xoachi
yellowjacket  zebra
```

Running the program results in
```
aardvark butterfly
that finishes input line 1
```
```
carp dalmatian
that finishes input line 2
```
```
eagle fish
that finishes input line 3
```
```
gopher hippo
that finishes input line 4
```
```
inyala jackal
that finishes input line 5
```
```
kyloe lamb
that finishes input line 6
```
```
moose nanny-goat
that finishes input line 7
```
```
opossum pandora
that finishes input line 8
```
```
queenbee raven
that finishes input line 9
```
```
swan terrier
that finishes input line 10
```
```
urchin  vixen
that finishes input line 11
```
```
wallaby xoachi[3]
that finishes input line 12
```
```
yellowjacket  zebra
that finishes input line 13
```

3.   An "xoachi" is a little-known animal whose name I made up.

CHAPTER 8

The Abstract Window Toolkit

T he Java Abstract Window Toolkit (AWT) continues the portability goals of the language. It provides a single windowing user interface on systems with wildly different native window systems. It does this in a clever way: it supports only the functions that are common to all the window systems. The Java window system then uses the underlying native window system to actually render the screen images, and manipulate GUI objects.

One word of caution: as with any significant piece of software, there are some remaining bugs in the January 23, 1996, 1.0 release of the AWT. If something doesn't work quite the way this text suggests it should, then collect some further information and see if you can categorize the conditions under which it fails.

You may have found a bug in the AWT (in which case report it by sending e-mail to java@java.sun.com), you may have found a bug in this text (in which case claim your bounty as described at the front), or you may just fill a gap in your understanding of what is supposed to happen.

For example, FileDialogs work under Windows 95, but do not always work under Solaris 2. Objects of class Window can be displayed using Windows 95, but not currently under Solaris 2.

The Role Of Objects

Object-oriented programming fits well with window systems. The concept of making new widgets by subclassing existing ones, and overriding part of their behavior is a time-saver. Another philosophical similarity is the way that widgets have to handle events just as objects handle messages.

Method inheritance is a key part of the window interface in Java. Programmers are expected to overload routines and extend classes to gain the exact behavior that they want. The basic components of a GUI (buttons, textfields, scroll bars, lists, and so on) are all created by subclassing the superclass called "Component".

How the Java Abstract Window Toolkit Works

The AWT requires the native window system to be running on the platform, as it uses the native window system to implement windows within Java. Figure 8-1 (opposite page) shows this. Be warned that this means the behavior of the AWT widgets is that provided by the native window toolkit. This can be subtlely different on different platforms. For example, the TextField widget behaves differently between Motif and Windows.

Mnemonic: Peer objects let your Java runtime "peer" at the underlying window implementation. They are only of interest to people porting the Java Development Kit. To a Java applications programmer all window system code is written in Java.

The policy of supporting the "highest common factor"[1] of all the supported native window toolkits works well. The windowing operations that are common to all toolkits tend to be the most useful ones. Highest common factor GUI toolkits are not a new idea. It is a new idea to support a highest common factor toolkit as a class library that is highly integrated with its own general purpose programming language.

It would be possible to approach the GUI with a different philosophy and have the Java AWT support on every platform every operation that is supported by one native toolkit. This would require a huge amount of extra implementation and maintenance effort for a small increase in functionality.

---

1.   Some people call it the "lowest common denominator" instead.

Where there are big differences in Window toolkit, Java adopts conventions that smooth over the differences. For example, Mac's have one button on the mouse, PC's have 2 buttons on the mouse, Unix has 3 buttons on the mouse (left, right, and center)

Java deals with this hardware difference by adopting the convention that mice have three buttons. If the GUI invites a user to "click on the right button", mice with fewer than three buttons can simulate it by holding down the meta and alt keys while mousing clicking. This shows up in the "modifiers" field of the event. However this isn't a perfect solution, as it doesn't detect when multiple mouse buttons are pressed simultaneously. Some more cooking is needed here.

How the Java abstract window toolkit works

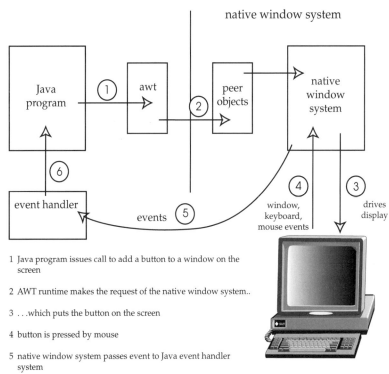

1 Java program issues call to add a button to a window on the screen

2 AWT runtime makes the request of the native window system..

3 . . .which puts the button on the screen

4 button is pressed by mouse

5 native window system passes event to Java event handler system

6 and from there into Java app's code

Figure 8-1

Window systems have become too complicated and overblown in recent years. When there are 1,000 page manuals explaining the Microsoft Windows API, and when it takes hundreds of lines of code to put a window on the screen (using X-windows) you know that it's time for something simpler and better. Supporting only the window operations that are common to all toolkits means that programmers have an easier job learning the window toolkit. Software gets written faster and it is less buggy. Sure, it may not feature "balloon help", but you can have it now and it works.

You can write Java windowing programs with one specific platform in mind, but you get code that runs on all the other platforms for free.

Application software companies no longer have to produce different versions of their software for each supported platform. As soon as these companies transition their products to Java, we will no longer need to see "123 for Windows 3.x, 123 for Windows 95, 123 for Solaris." There will just be "123 for Java". It's a huge and compelling reason to program in Java.

General Remarks on Window Systems

A few words of explanation about the programming model for window systems are in order. Unlike procedural programs in which things happen sequentially from beginning to end, windowing programs are asynchronous. You cannot predict at any given instance which of the on-screen buttons, menus, frames etc., the user will touch. Accordingly a model known as "event-driven programming" is used.

In event-driven programming, the logic of your code is inverted. Instead of one flow of control from beginning to end, the program mostly waits for user input. When the user touches something on screen with the mouse pointer, the window system catches that event and passes it on to a handler that you earlier supplied. This is known as a callback, and your handler is a "callback routine" because the window system calls back to it when the event happens. Your handler will deal with the graphics event, and the action that is associated with it. If a button says "press here to read the file", then your button handler must handle the button event, and also read the file in. Handling a button event just means noticing that it occurred, but other events like dragging something with the mouse take a bit more work.

Almost the whole of window programming is learning about the different objects that you can put on the screen (windows, scrollbars, buttons, etc.). Your event handling code for each widget (as these windowing objects are termed) will be invoked as needed. Let's take a look at the very simplest example just to get started.

We have already seen the code to pop-up a window for an applet (since all applets run in a window, having an applet at all means that we have already implicitly created a window). The most frequently-used kind of window is a subclass of Window, known as a Frame. Here is the code to put up a Frame from an application.

```
import java.awt.*;
public class cherry {
    static Frame f = new Frame("cherry");

    public static void main(String[] a) {
        f.resize(300,100);
        f.show();
    }
}
```

Compiling and executing this program will cause a Frame like this to appear on the screen:

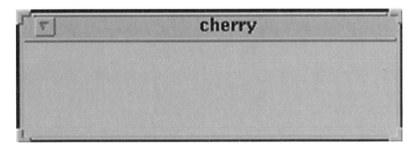

Figure 8-2 A Frame

As is usual in a programming language, there is more than one way to accomplish this. As an alternative, we could have made class cherry extend class Frame, and instantiate itself inside cherry. A "Frame" is a window with a title bar on which title strings and pull-down menus can be placed. Here, we just gave it the title on the title bar of "cherry".

Almost everything that you can see on the screen from Java is ultimately taking place in a Frame or a Panel. These are the "corkboards" or backdrops to which we attach scrollbars, textfields, menu items, etc.

Details of the AWT

The AWT provides five services to the programmer:

- A set of the usual GUI widgets[2]: buttons, pull-down menus, choices, checkboxes, text input fields, and so on.

- An event handling system that notices when the user adjusts one of these widgets, and conveys that information to the program.

- The concept of "containers"—objects that you attach a widget to. A container can hold a number of related widgets, and deal with them as a group. Typically you do not display an individual widget, you add it to a container. It is the container that is displayed.

- Some "layout managers" that provide help in automatically positioning where a widget goes when you add it to a container. This frees up the programmer from the responsibility of prescribing where every last widget in the GUI should go. (Although you can do it that way too, if you want). Each container will have a layout manager associated with it.

- Simple support for graphics operations: draw an arc, fill a polygon, etc.

AWT Containers

We have already seen how to get a basic backdrop on the screen both with an applet, and with an application. Here is a little more information about these backdrops, or containers. Containers are a subclass of something called a Component. Almost everything in the AWT is a subclass of Component. Having an ultimate common parent makes it easy to build up GUIs recursively: all these components fit in this container, which fits in this component. . . It is easy to render everything onto the screen, by simply painting the backdrop, and then having all the nested Components paint themselves too.

Components do two principal things:

1. Display themselves and all contents on the screen.

2. "widget" is a term popularized by the X-Window system. It conveys the idea of "window gadget"—a gadget or thingummy that has some handy interaction with the user in a window. For example, scrollbars, cursor icons, and buttons are all widgets.

> **2.** Catch and handle events relating to the widgets, keyboard and mouse when the focus is on the Component.

Containers are the backdrops to which you will add your GUI widgets. The two important things you do with a Container:

> **1.** Add/remove widgets from it, according to some layout policy.

> **2.** Override a method in a Component, for event handling.

The class hierarchy looks like this:

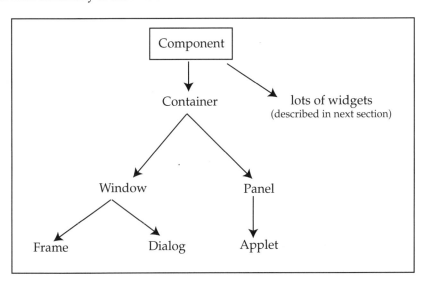

Figure 8-3

As Figure 8-3 above shows, "Containers" are of two kinds:

- Subclasses of Window, which are separate pop-up windows in their own right, and

- Subclasses of Panel, which are containers that generally represent a smaller part/area of a larger Window (that is to say, they will have been added to a Window). Applets appear on the screen as a Panel.

A description of Component and its container subclasses follows.

Component   Everything on the screen is built out of Components. A Component has a a size and position, and can be rendered onto the screen. This is a very general class that has methods to check whether the instance is on screen, is visible, what its size and location is, and whether to show it or not. It also has methods to capture events and deal with them (described below).

Component also has a method

```
public boolean handleEvent(Event evt)
```

to process user input events when the user presses a button, drags the mouse, and so on.

```
handleEvent()
```

is the most basic handler. It does some analysis of the input event, and will call one of about a dozen other methods like these:

```
public boolean action(Event evt,Object what)
public boolean keyDown(Event evt, int key)
public boolean mouseMove(Event evt, int x,int y)
```

The programmer overloads these to provide the callback routines that window systems use for event handling.There are also methods in Component to set colors, fonts, and new sizes and places on the screen.

Finally, Component gets painted on the screen when the runtime system calls its method:

```
public void paint(Graphics g)
```

We have seen this method several times before, and now we know the class to which it belongs.

Container   A data structure class that is used to hold several widgets, and treat them as a related group. Typically, all the widgets in one window, or one part of a window will be in the same container, and the container will be displayed. It has the method:

```
public Component add(Component comp)
```

to add a widget to the container. Most of its other methods are to do with layout managers, or choosing a size for the container.

A container in itself is not displayable. It is only when you get down to the subclasses of Container that you have something that can be shown on the screen. Container has 2 subclasses: Window and Panel.

Window   This is a totally blank window. It doesn't even have a border or a menu bar. It could be used to implement a pop-up window. Typically you don't use Window directly, but use its more useful subclasses (**Frame** and **Dialog**). There appears to be a bug in the January 23 initial 1.0 version of Java preventing a Window from being displayed on Solaris.

Window has a few methods to do with showing and hiding the window, bringing it to the front and back, and packing together the components in the window.

Frame   This is a specialization of Window, on which Menu bars (which can be multilevel) are created and processed. Menubars are very similar to Choices, as described in the next section.

It has a border and possibly a menu bar attached to it. When you create a **Frame**, it is not physically displayed inside the applet or other Container, but is a separate free floating window on the display monitor.

An example of the code to create a Frame, and how it looks on the screen appears in Figure 8-2 earlier.

Dialog   The Dialog class can be used to pop-up a window that has an area where the user can type a line of text. There is also a subclass called **FileDialog** that brings up the native "file chooser" window, allowing a filename to be selected. Because of the file access restrictions on applets FileDialog is most useful in applications.

The code to put up a FileDialog is:

```
import java.awt.*;
public class fd {
    static Frame f = new Frame("cherry");

    public static void main(String[] a) {
        FileDialog fd = new FileDialog(f, "grapes");
        fd.show();
        f.add(fd);
        f.show();
    }
}
```

It will display a window like the one in Figure 8-4 (opposite page):

The code to retrieve the filename string that the user chose looks like this.

```
String s = fd.getFile();
```

FileDialogs don't seem to be fully functional in the Java 1.0 release of January 23, 1996, for Solaris 2.

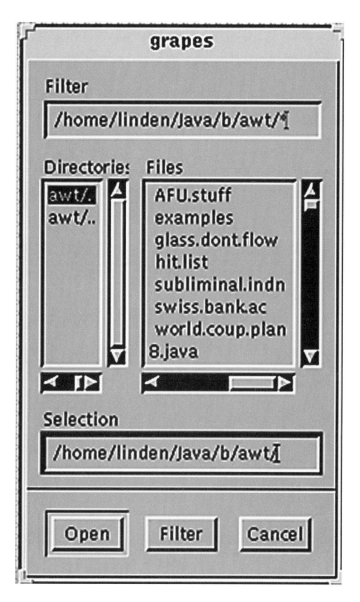

Figure 8-4

Panel   A container with a built-in way to layout on the screen everything it contains. A Panel is a smaller region that is usually contained within a Frame.

Here is a picture of a panel that has been nested within an applet. The panel has been colored so you can see it. By default it has the same color as the applet, so is invisible. Many smaller panels can be added to one applet container. Each panel can then be treated as a container in its own right: have things added to it, catch events, and have a layout policy.

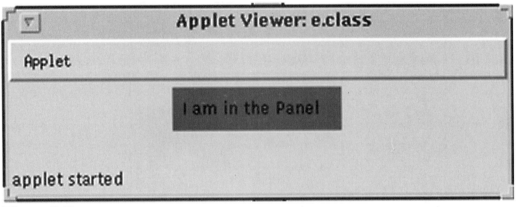

Figure 8-5

Panel has almost no methods of its own, and none of general interest. The major purpose of the Panel class is to provide a default "FlowLayout" manager for its Applet subclass. The code to display this panel is:

```
import java.awt.*;
import java.applet.*;
class MyPanel extends Panel {
    public void paint(Graphics q) {
        resize(200,25);
        setBackground(Color.green);
        g.drawString("I am in the Panel",10,10);
    }
}
public class cucumber extends Applet {
    MyPanel p = new MyPanel();
    public void init() {
        add(p);
    }

}
```

Applet   Applet is a subclass of **Panel**. The major thing this
says is that Applets come readymade with some GUI stuff in place.
We've seen applets many times now, but here is another example
screendump of one.

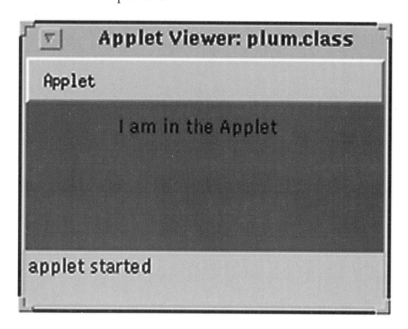

Figure 8-6

Here is the code that created that applet:

```
import java.awt.*;
import java.applet.*;

public class plum extends Applet {

    public void init() {
        setBackground(Color.green);
        resize(250,100);
    }

    public void paint(Graphics g) {
        g.drawString("I am in the Applet", 35,15);
    }

}
```

One advantage of an applet over an application for a GUI program is that you can start adding components and displaying them without needing to create an underlying backdrop, as one already exists.

Here are some popular methods of Applet:

```
public URL getDocumentBase()
public URL getCodeBase()

public String getParameter(String name)
public void resize(int width, int height)

public void showStatus(String msg)
public Image getImage(URL url)
public Image getImage(URL url, String name)

public AudioClip getAudioClip(URL url)
public void play(URL url)
```

These four methods are for the stages in the applet lifecycle (shown also in Figure 6-2):

```
public void init()
public void start()
public void stop()
public void destroy()
```

As you can see, Applet has several methods that deal with sounds and pictures. For both of these, it uses a URL (the "Universal Resource Locator" that we met in Chapter 1) to pinpoint the file containing the goodies. You do not have to do anything special to make an Applet retrieve an image from its server over the Internet—it is a built-in method for you. A URL can locate something that is local to your system, or anywhere remote on Internet. Some people like to imagine that is why it is a "Universal" resource locator. It will look anywhere in the Universe.

The DocumentBase referred to in the first method, is simply the directory containing the HTML page that you are currently visiting. Similarly, the CodeBase is the directory that contains the applet you are currently executing. Often these two directories will be the same.

Applet has other methods too. The source can be seen in

```
java/src/java/applet/Applet.java
```

AWT Widgets

This section describes how to add widgets to Frame or Panel, and how to process the input that you get back from widgets. The widgets that we will cover here are buttons, textfields, scroll bars, mouse events, and so on. The class hierarchy is quite flat. The widgets are subclasses of the general class Component that we have already seen above.

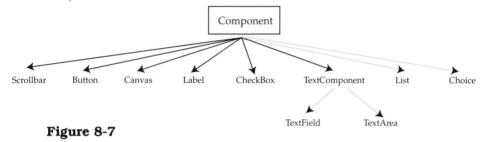

Figure 8-7

These classes are the widgets or building blocks from which you will create your GUI. What you do with all these components is:

1. Add them to a Frame or Applet, then display it.

2. Get back input when the user presses buttons, makes selections, etc., and process it.

Fortunately both of these activities are quite straightforward, and we'll cover them here in source code, words, and pictures. The add method can be applied to a Frame in an application, like this:

```
Frame f = new Frame();
    ...
f.add( something );
```

Or it can be applied to the Applet's panel in an applet, like so:

```
public static void init () {
    this.add( something );
```

or, more simply:

```
public static void init () {

    add( something );
```

Recall the Applet lifecycle described in Chapter 6. That made clear that there is an "init()" method which each Applet can overload. It will be called when the Applet is loaded, and it is a good place to place the code that creates these GUI objects. We will use "init()" for that.

A Few Words on Getting a GUI Event

Just as adding widgets to a panel or frame is easy, so getting back user input is also straightforward. Everything hinges on the method with this signature:

```
public boolean action( Event e, Object o)
```

The method is part of every Component, so all of the buttons, choices lists, etc., inherit it and can overload it.

Whenever a user operates a Component (presses a button, clicks on a choice), the action event is called. The "Event e" argument is a class that can be seen in the awt directory. It contains much information about the coordinates of the event, the time it occurred, and the kind of event that it was. If the event was a keypress, it has the value of the key. The other argument is a generalized object that contains extra information in some cases.

For each container that a widget is added to, the programmer has the opportunity to provide an overriding version of:

```
public boolean action(Event e, Object o)
```

and to use that to determine exactly what the event was, and from that take action to deal with it.

Having explained the theory of widgets and widget input, lets take a look at how they appear on the screen, and typical code to handle them.

Scrollbar

what it is

In fancy words, a Scrollbar is a draggable analog component. The user slides a bar along, and the program gets back a numeric value from that. A Scrollbar can be freestanding, or attached to a canvas or other component.

what it looks like on screen

You will typically overload the init() method to add these objects to the Applet's panel. In an application, you can set them up where you like. (Note: in future examples in this section, we won't bother repeating the context that this is part of the init() method in an applet).

the code to create it

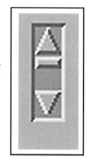

Figure 8-8

```
public void init() {
    Scrollbar s  =
        new Scrollbar(Scrollbar.VERTICAL,20,10,5,35);
    add(s);
```

The arguments are

- Whether the bar should go up, or along (Scrollbar.HORIZONTAL)
- The initial setting for the slider (bar)
- The size of the visible portion of the scrollable area
- The value at the low end of the scale
- The value at the high end of the scale

The code to retrieve user input from a Scrollbar:

Scrollbars are the only widget that does not have an action() method. Scrollbar events use the underlying method "handleEvent()". All widget events start out in handleEvent(), but the Event class does some preprocessing, and splits out most of them into a call to action() or one of the mouse action methods. This isn't done for Scrollbars. The method handleEvent() is used to get the position of the slider when it is moved.

```
public boolean handleEvent(Event e) {
    if (e.target instanceof Scrollbar) {
        value = ((Scrollbar)e.target).getValue();
        return true;
    }
}
```

Scrollbars are often teamed up with another widget, for example, a text entry field. This allows a limited screen area to be assigned to it, while allowing the whole thing to be viewed in pieces. Scrollbars cause a whole series of events the whole time you are moving the slider. The runtime system doesn't wait until you have stopped and call handleEvent once; it may call it dozens of times as you scroll.

Button

what it is

This is a GUI button. You can program the action that takes place when the button is pressed.

what it looks like on screen

Figure 8-9

the code to create it

```
Button b = new Button("peach");
add(b);
```

the code to retrieve user input from it

```
public boolean action(Event e, Object o) {
    if (e.target instanceof Button)
        if( "peach".equals( (String) o ) ) {
          System.out.println("peach button pressed");
          return true;
      }
  }
```

Note: there is an alternative, perhaps uglier way to obtain the label of the button that was pressed, using the Event e:

```
if( "peach".equals( ((Button)e.target).getLabel()) )
```

You can only cast the target to a button if it actually is a button or button subclass.

Program an "Alice in Wonderland" applet: a panel with two buttons, one of which makes the panel grow larger, the other smaller. resize(int width, int height) will resize a Container. (Easy—about 20 lines of code).

Canvas

what it is

A Canvas is a screen area that you can use for drawing graphics or receiving user input. A Canvas contains almost no methods. All its functionality is inherited from Component (setting font, color, size, and receiving events) or from you giving it functionality when you extend the class. When you extend the class, you can override the "paint()" method for this Canvas, and *that* gives you a Graphics context in which to use the Graphics methods. There's more about Graphics in a later section.

what it looks like on screen

Figure 8-10

The screen dump is not very exciting, merely showing a rectangular area that has been highlighted with a different color to make it visible (see code below). Canvases are pretty inert until you extend them and use them to display images, or do other graphics programming.

the code to create it

This code gives the Canvas a red color, so you can distinguish it from the Panel (as long as your Applet panel isn't red to begin with of course). It then gives the Canvas a size of 80 pixels wide by 40 high, and adds it to the Applet.

```
Canvas n = new Canvas();
n.setBackground(Color.red);
n.resize(80,40);
add(n);
```

Here is how you would extend Canvas to provide a surface that you can draw on, like any Graphics context.

```
import java.awt.*;
import java.applet.*;
public class can extends Applet {
    myCanvas c = new myCanvas();

    public void init() {
        c.resize(190,65);
        resize(200,75);
        add(c);
    }
```

```
    }

class myCanvas extends Canvas{
    public void paint(Graphics g) {
        g.drawString("don't go in the basement", 10,25);
        g.drawLine(10,35, 165,35);
    }
}
```

The HTML that initiates this applet is simply:

```
<head><title>Components</title><head>
<p>
<applet code=can.class  width = 150 height =100>
</applet>
```

And you would get it compiled and executing by typing:

```
javac can.java
appletviewer can.html
```

It will put a window like this on the screen:

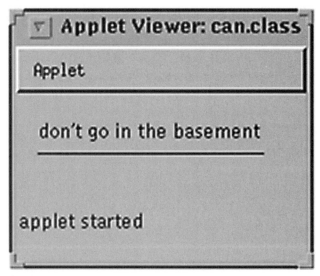

Figure 8-11

A canvas is similar to a Panel, in that you can draw on it, render images, and accept events. A Canvas is not a container however, so cannot hold other components.

Label

what it is

This is a very simple component. It is just a string of text that appears on screen.

What it looks like on screen

Figure 8-12

the code to create it

```
Label la = new Label("Grapes");
add(la);
```

Labels are write only, so there is no code to retrieve user input from it. Labels are typically used as a cheap fast way to get some text on the screen, and to label other widgets with descriptions or instructions.

CheckBox

what it is

A screen object that represents a boolean choice "pressed" or "not pressed" or "on" or "off". Usually has some text (often a label) explaining the choice, e.g. "Press for fries" would have a Checkbox "button" allowing yes or no.

what it looks like on screen

Figure 8-13

the code to create it

```
Checkbox cb  = new Checkbox("Fries?");
add(cb);
```

the code to retrieve user input from a CheckBox:

```
public boolean action(Event e, Object o) {
    if (e.target instanceof Checkbox) {
        System.out.println("Fries status flipped");
        return true;
    }
}
```

Note that you the programmer have to keep track of the state of Checkboxes, as the event only tells you that it changed state, not what the new state is. Also note that there is a way to group a series of Checkboxes together to create a Checkbox-Group of "radio buttons". The term "radio buttons" arises from the old manual station selection buttons in car radios. When you pressed in one of the buttons, all the others would pop out and be deselected. CheckboxGroups work the same way. The file CheckboxGroup.java in the awt directory has the details.

TextField

what it is

A single line of text that the user can type in. The number of characters shown is configurable.

what it looks like on screen

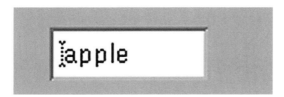

Figure 8-14

the code to create it

This creates a TextField with eight characters showing, and initialized to with the characters "apple". You type different characters in there and more than eight, but only eight will show at a time.

```
TextField tf = new TextField("apple",8);
add(tf);
```

the code to retrieve user input from it

A TextField causes an event when a return is entered in the field. At that point you can retrieve the text.

```
public boolean action(Event e, Object o) {
    if (e.target instanceof TextField) {
        String readthis = (String) o;
        return true;
    }
}
```

Note that this widget doesn't offer an event for each character entered, only when the carriage return is pressed at the end of the String.

List

what it is

A scrolling list of text strings, from which the user can select one or several (single or multiple selection is configurable).

what it looks like on screen

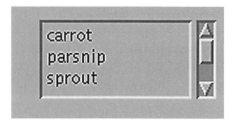

Figure 8-15

the code to create it

This creates a scrolling list with three items visible initially, and does not allow multiple selections at the same time (multiple selections is false).

```
List li = new List(3,false);
li.addItem("carrot");
li.addItem("parsnip");
li.addItem("sprout");
li.addItem("cabbage");
li.addItem("turnip");
add(li);
```

the code to retrieve user input from it

```
public boolean action(Event e, Object o) {
if (e.target instanceof List) {
    String readthis = (String) o;
```

The action handler is called when the selection is made by clicking on the list entry.

If you have allowed multiple selections to be active in the list at one time (the list represents say pizza toppings, where you might want pepperoni and black olives and mushrooms), then you should use a different widget to signal that the input is ready. A button or a checkbox can be used for this. The list has a method called "getSelectedItems()" that will return each of several one by one.

Choice

what it is

A selection from several text strings. This is a pop-up list, akin to a pull-down menu. When you hold the mouse button down on the choice, a list of all the other choices appears, and you can move the mouse over the one you want.

what it looks like on screen

Figure 8-16

when you select the list, it pops up the full range of choices, looking like this

Figure 8-17

the code to create it

```
Choice c = new Choice();
c.addItem("lemon");
c.addItem("orange");
c.addItem("lime");
add(c);
```

the code to retrieve user input from it

```
public boolean action(Event e, Object o) {
if (e.target instanceof Choice) {
    String result = (String) o;
```

TextArea

what it is

A TextField that is several lines long.

what it looks like on screen

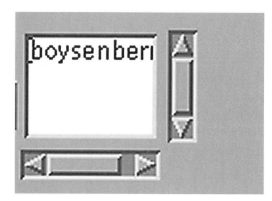

Figure 8-18

the code to create it

```
TextArea t = new TextArea("boysenberry", 4, 9);
add(t);
```

This creates a text area of four lines, each showing nine characters. The first line shows the first nine characters of the string "boysenberry". You can place text on the next line in the initializer by embedding a '\n' character in the string. TextAreas come with scrollbars, so you can type an unbounded amount of text.

the code to retrieve user input from it

Unlike a TextField, a TextArea might have embedded newlines, so a newline can't be used to cause the event that says "I am ready to present my value".

The same solution is used as with a multiple-selection list. Use another widget, say a button, or checkbox, to signal that the text is ready to be picked up.

```
public boolean action(Event e, Object o) {
if (e.target instanceof Button)
   if( "text ready".equals( (String) o ) ) {
    String my_text = t.getText();
    return true;
   }
```

Finally, here is the applet that consists of all the widgets described above, placed in the Applet panel.

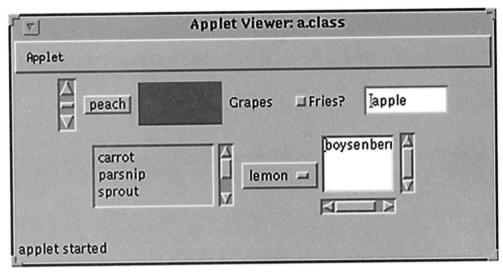

Figure 8-19

The code for this is on the CD in the directory containing all the other AWT programming material.

Rewrite the above program so that it is an application not an applet. Create a Frame, add all the components to it, and then "show()" the Frame. (Easy)

Note that there is a significant GUI difference between applications and applets. Applets display their components as soon as they are added to the panel, but in an Application you must call "show()" to display the Frame and widgets you created. E.g. one way to do it would be:

```
Frame f = new Frame("Even more Fruit");
   ... lots of widget adding ...

f.show()
```

Obtaining Mouse and Keyboard Input

The previous section described how various widgets interact with the user. This section describes how mouse and keyboard events are passed to your program. It is done in a very similar way to what we have already seen for widgets,

Events go to the Component that is the immediate Container of the place where the event happened. The class Component has a method `handleEvent()` with this signature:

```
public boolean handleEvent(Event evt)
```

If you look at handleEvent in file java/awt/Component.java, you'll see that it contains a switch statement based on what the event was, and it really factors out all the keyboard and mouse events calling individual methods to handle all the possibilities for those.

A list of some of the specific Event handlers that `handleEvent()` factors out is:

```
public boolean mouseDown(Event evt, int x, int y)
public boolean mouseDrag(Event evt, int x, int y)
public boolean mouseUp(Event evt, int x, int y)
public boolean mouseMove(Event evt, int x, int y)
public boolean mouseEnter(Event evt, int x, int y)
public boolean mouseExit(Event evt, int x, int y)

public boolean keyDown(Event evt, int key)
public boolean keyUp(Event evt, int key)

public boolean action(Event evt, Object what)
```

The programmer can override these to provide the callback routines that window systems use for event handling.

To see what's really going on with events, insert this line at the start of your version of handleEvent.

```
System.err.println("Event: " + e.toString() );
```

You'll be amazed at the number of events that are generated by the simplest mouse motions. This method converts each to a string and prints it.

Use inheritance to create your own version of the Button and Choice classes in an example Applet. Override "action()" within each of these two classes. Now it is much easier to decode which event has come in. If the "myButton.action()" has been invoked, it must have been an instance of myButton that was operated. (Easy).

Write an action() method that will handle all of the widgets in the previous section, and for each print out what the event is. (Medium).

Here is an example of how a game program might capture individual key presses as they are made. Note that only certain events are available from certain widgets. In particular, non-blocking key presses are available in Panels, but not in TextFields. This can be even more annoying than those smirking kids in the Mentos commercials.

```java
import java.awt.*;
import java.applet.*;
public class game  extends Applet {

    public void init() {
        resize(450,200);
    }

    public boolean keyDown(Event evt, int key) {
        System.out.println("Got: " + (char)key );
        return true;
    }

}
```

What could be simpler?

You will usually want to put the three or four lines of code that deal with a window being quit or destroyed (when the user has finished with it—this is usually a standard choice on the frame menu bar). The code looks like:

```java
public boolean handleEvent(Event e) {
    if (e.id == Event.WINDOW_DESTROY) {
        System.exit(0);
    }
    return false;
}
```

You don't have to exit the program. That would be appropriate when the user quits from the top level window. For a lower-level window, the right thing to do may be to hide the window, and release the resource for garbage collection by removing any pointers to it.

All the Event handling methods have a boolean return type. This is used to answer the question "Did this method fully handle the event?" If it did, return true. If it did not, (Whoa! Trick answer coming!) return the result of calling the superclass's event handler to propagate the event up the containment hierarchy. To understand why, let's look at a partial solution to the previous Programming Challenge.

Programming Solution!

```java
import java.awt.*;
import java.applet.Applet;

public class mb extends Applet {
    myButton mb;

    public void init() {
        add(new myButton("press me") );
    }
}

class myButton extends Button {

    public myButton(String s) {
        super(s);
    }

    public boolean action(Event e, Object arg) {
        System.out.println("myButton pressed!");
        return true;
    }
}
```

Here we see a very common form of inheritance: subclassing an AWT widget to provide some slight refinement of behavior. Normally, our "action()" method is a common method that might handle a dozen kinds of event. In this case, when the button is pressed, control is transferred to the myButton.action() method and no decoding of "what Event was this?" is needed. We know it must have been a myButton that was pressed.

Now, we may have created several levels of subclass of Button, myOtherButton extends... extends myButton extends Button. Each adds some slight twist, and each has its own overriding action() routine. Our intent will be to first try handling the special button event in the lowest subclass. If that doesn't want it, then we almost certainly want to pass the event up the inheritance hierarchy. (If that isn't what we want then why did we bother creating the inheritance hierarchy?) However, what will actually happen is that the runtime system will propagate the unconsumed event up the containment hierarchy.

For Advanced Students Only:

The fact that you return "true" from the Event handler leads the normal programmer to assume that one should return "false" if more processing is required by the containing class.

Bzzzt! The idiom is that you "return super.handleEvent(e)" to pass the event up the inheritance chain if your method doesn't consume the event.

This is because there are two possible chains to follow to look for the event handler:

1. Up the chain of containers: (Event is in a Panel which is in a Frame which is in a Window...)

2. Up the chain of subclasses: (Event is from myOtherButton which is a subclass of myButton, which is...)

What you usually want to happen is for the runtime to try both hierarchies. The runtime system should make the event go up the chain of superclasses for a given widget, and then go to the enclosing container, exhaust all its superclasses, and so on.

This will occur if your Event handler, instead of returning false, does:

```
return super.handleEvent(e);
```

None of this is necessary if you do not have a chain of subclassed widgets. On the other hand, it doesn't hurt to write the statement this way regardless. If you don't have a big inheritance hierarchy myButton.action() will call Button.action() which simply returns false anyway.

Layout in a Container

You may be wondering how the Applet knows where to put the individual elements that we have been adding to it. The answer is Layouts. Layout Managers are classes that specify how components should be placed in a container. Here is a Frame full of widgets laid out with "FlowLayout".

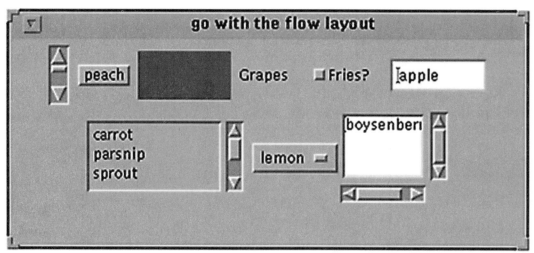

Figure 8-20

Here is the same frame, with a one line change in the program to use a GridLayout of 2 rows and 5 columns.

Figure 8-21

Panels (which includes Applets) have a "Flow" layout by default—this means that components are added left to right, keeping them centered in the container. If the container isn't wide enough, new rows are used as needed. Users can stretch the window to reveal anything that doesn't fit on the screen image. There are several other layout strategies, including providing the absolute coordinates of components. The LayoutManager can be set by the Container with the call like:

```
setLayout( new GridLayout(2,5) );
```

Predefined LayoutManagers are:

`FlowLayout`	We have already described the default behavior of FlowLayout: components are placed centered from left to right in a row. When there is no longer room for the next component to be added, a new row is started. The layout doesn't have to be centered; it can be aligned on the left or right. All Panels (including Applets) use flow layout, unless you provide something different.
`BorderLayout`	You add components around the edge, and the last component gets all the remaining space in the middle. BorderLayout is the default layout manager for Windows and their subclasses (Frames and Dialogs).
`GridLayout`	You specify an N by M grid, and the components are placed one to each grid position, left-to-right, top to bottom.
	Components like buttons and scrollbars change their size to match the grid they are in. This behavior always surprises and frustrates programmers when they first try it. One solution is to nest a Panel of fixed size in the grid, and attach your component to the Panel.
`GridBagLayout`	This is a variation of GridLayout, but it does not force fit components one per grid position. GridBagLayout allows the programmer to let a component take up the space of several adjacent grid positions if it wishes.

CardLayout — This layout is named with a deck of playing cards in mind. You can only see one card at a time, but you can shuffle through the deck and pull another card to the top to display at any time. Each "card" in the Card-Layout will typically be a Panel with its own layout, with the two tied together by a "Choice" selection.

Layouts are funky. You probably won't find any one layout that does exactly what you want. The solution is to divide your Panels and Frames into sub-panels, and use a different layout manager (as appropriate) for each panel. Then display the different panels together in a single frame.

The source for each of the layout managers can be read in directory java/src/java/awt, on the CD.

Graphics Programming

We have now seen all the involved parts of the AWT. The final piece of AWT functionality we are going to cover is quite simple. It is the Graphics class, which provides support for some elementary graphics operations.

If you look at the source for the Graphics class in java/src/java/awt/Graphics.java, you will note that it is an abstract class:

```
public abstract class Graphics { ...
```

Therefore, it cannot be instantiated directly, so you will never see code like:

```
Graphics gr = new Graphics();   // NO! NO! NO!
```

Instead, it will be subclassed and extended, with the abstract methods filled in.

Here is a list of the more common methods from Graphics that you might use.

So when will I use the `paint()`, `repaint()`, or `update()` methods?

If you just use the static display typical of a GUI, you might never need to overload any of the three above methods. You can often just hide() and show() them as needed. Let's explain when you use paint().

Normally the window system keeps track of what you have put on the screen. If you obscure it with other windows and then bring it to the front, the window system is responsible for restoring the state.

If, however, you wish to *change* what you have put on the screen (say you have displayed a GIF that you now want to replace with something else), this would be accomplished by over-riding paint(). Code in init() can get something on the screen to begin with. Code in paint() can change the screen and get something different up there. You call repaint() to signal to the window system that it needs to update the screen. The window system will then call your paint() method to put the new image on the screen. It's done this way because paint takes an argument (a Graphics context) that you don't normally have (or need to have) access to. Repaint() doesn't need any arguments.

Repaint() calls update() which calls clear() and then paint(). You might override update() if you are doing some advanced graphics work, and you know that you only need a small por-tion of the screen to be changed (e.g. in an animation). Update give you the opportunity to achieve this, by providing a point where you can insert your own code between repaint() and paint(). In addition,

    repaint(x,y,w,h);

will repaint just the stated size rectangle at the given coordinates. Paint may be called by the runtime independent of update.

Summary: You never call paint() yourself. You may override it, but the understanding is always that it will be called for you at the times the window system thinks it need to update the screen. If you want to force the window system to think that, then call "repaint()".

Repaint() simply lodges a request to update the screen, and returns immediately. Its effect is asynchronous, and if there are several paint requests outstanding it is possible that only the last `paint()` will be done.

Method	Description
void repaint()	You or the window system may call this to request that the window be refreshed. Typically, you would call it if you have changed the appearance of something, and you want to see it on the screen. It calls update()
void update(Graphics g)	This is a step in repainting the window. It defaults to calling clear() then paint() but you can conceivably override it to do something additional. However, most of your programs will not override this, and will not call this.
void paint(Graphics g)	Will be called by the window system when the component needs to be redisplayed. You will not call this. You will override this if you dynamically change the appearance of the screen, and want to see it appear.

These are quite basic as far as graphics toolkits go.

```
Color getColor();
void setColor(Color c);

Font getFont();
void setFont(Font font);

void drawLine(int x1, int y1, int x2, int y2);

void drawString(String str, int x, int y);

void drawRect(int x, int y, int width, int height) {
void fillRect(int x, int y, int width, int height);

void drawOval(int x, int y, int width, int height);
void fillOval(int x, int y, int width, int height);

void clipRect(int x, int y, int width, int height);
void copyArea(int x, int y, int width, int height, int dx, int
dy);

void drawArc(int x, int y, int width, int height, int startAngle,
int arcAngle);
void fillArc(int x, int y, int width, int height, int startAngle,
int arcAngle);

void drawImage(Image img, int x, int y, ImageObserver observer);
```

There is also support for drawing and filling polygons. There is no support for drawing lines thicker than one pixel. Thicker lines can be accomplished by drawing a filled polygon.

The `clipRect()` method cuts down the size of the area that is painted, to just the stated area. This is to help performance — never paint more than you need to. Successive calls to clipRect cut the size down further to just the <u>intersection</u> of what it was and the new area. This is counter-intuitive, and many people think this it a misfeature that should be fixed. The workaround is to create a new Graphics object for each of the smaller areas you want to clip to.

Here is an example program that draws a rectangle, a line, an oval, some strings and an arc onto a canvas, and changes fonts midway. First the screendump of the applet:

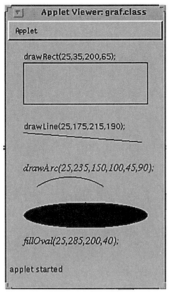

Figure 8-22

And here is the program that generated it:

```
// let's get some graphics up on the panel!
// PvdL, January 1996.
import java.awt.*;
import java.applet.*;
public class graf  extends Applet {

    Font banana = new Font("TimesRoman", Font.ITALIC, 16);

    public void init() {
        resize(250,350);

    }

    public void paint(Graphics g) {
        g.drawString("drawRect(25,35,200,65);", 25,30);
        g.drawRect(25,35,200,65);

        g.drawString("drawLine(25,175,215,190);",25,140);
        g.drawLine(25,145,215,190);

        g.setFont(banana);
        g.drawString("drawArc(25,235,150,100,45,90);",25,205);
        g.drawArc(25,215,150,100, 45, 90);

        g.fillOval(25,255,200,40);
        g.drawString("fillOval(25,285,200,40);",25,320);
    }


}
```

About the only point worth commenting on is that we always want our graphics rendering routines to be as fast as possible, so don't do anything in "paint()" that takes a long time, or isn't directly related to putting an image on the screen. In particular, although we only use the new Font "banana" in paint(), it's better to declare it and have it all set up ready before you even enter paint(). There is just one more graphics related topic to cover, and that is the Image Observer and the Media Tracker (which do related things). The MediaTracker is a class in the AWT that is intended to provide support for putting several media objects (sound files, or images, say) in a group, and indicating when they are loaded into memory.

Here's how an applet could use MediaTracker to wait for an image to be loaded.

```
public void init() {

    MediaTracker t = new MediaTracker (this);

    Image i = getImage (getDocumentBase(),

    t.addImage (i,1);

    try    t.waitForID(1);

    catch  (InterruptedException ie) return;

    //Image is now in memory, ready to draw

}
```

The ImageObserver class does a similar job, but can report incremental progress in loading a single .GIF or .JPEG file. When you call the method getImage(), it finds the image, and starts to retrieve it but returns before bringing it all back into memory. This is partly an optimization aimed at avoiding needless loads (perhaps the image is on a part of the page that is scrolled off out of sight), and partly a human interface feature (rather than force the user to sit there while you load a GIF scanline-by-scanline, you can entertain the user with various other diversions until the image has been read in).

The ImageObserver interface lets you monitor the incoming image, and can provide updates on the size it will take on the screen. The good news is that an Applet contains a default implementation of ImageObserver. So if you're running in an applet, wherever you need to provide an ImageObserver argument, just use "this".

When you want to learn about the progress of loading the image, you can provide a method `imageUpdate()` that will override the regular version in the implementation of class ImageObserver. Your imageUpdate will be called repeatedly until you return a value of false to indicate that you've got enough information. Perhaps a code example will help to clarify how this works:

```
import java.applet.*;
import java.awt.*;

public class iu extends Applet {
    Image    i;
        int times=0, flags=0,x=0,y=0,w=0,h=0;

    public void init() {
        i = getImage(getDocumentBase(), "spots.jpeg" );
        w = i.getWidth(this);   System.err.println("INIT:w="+w);
        h = i.getHeight(this);  System.err.println("INIT:h="+h);
    }

    public boolean imageUpdate(Image i, int flags,
                        int x, int y, int w, int h) {
            if (times++<5)
                System.err.println("my IMAGEUPDATE: flags="
                                +flags+ " w="+w+ " h="+h);
            return true;
    }

    public void paint (Graphics g) {
        g.drawImage(i,50,50, this);

    }

}
```

This clearly shows how imageUpdate is a callback routine. Experiment with this example (invoke with the usual html file), including removing the limitation of 5 prints in the middle of imageUpdate (done so that the information doesn't scroll off the screen the first time you try it).

Many people find the principle of ImageObserver hard to grasp. Perhaps it would have been better if the AWT designer had chosen a simpler, more familiar model to indicate progress in loading. For example, each Image could have been associated with a couple of off-screen scrollbars to indicate the incoming image height and width. Programmers would override the action routine for scrollbars to read the progress of loading in realtime.

How to Display an Image File in an Application

If you're in an application, use Toolkit.getImage(). You can use the getToolkit() method from any Component or the Toolkit.getDefaultToolkit() like this:

```
import java.awt.*;
import java.net.*;
public class load {
    static public void main(String a[]) {
        myFrame m = new myFrame();
        m.resize(200,200);
        m.show();
    }
}

class myFrame extends Frame {
    static Image i;
    static String where = "file:\\\\c:\\java\\pvdl\\jack.gif";
    static URL url;
    static {
        try { url = new URL(where); }
        catch (MalformedURLException mue) {
            System.out.println("Bad URL: " + where); }
        i =Toolkit.getDefaultToolkit().getImage(url);
    }

    public void paint (Graphics g) {
        g.drawString("Greetings",20,20);
        g.drawImage(i,50,50, this);
    }
}
```

Note all those backslashes! They really are necessary to indicate a pathname using the MSDOS conventions. Java really shows its Unix origins here by specifying that backslash is an escape character. Backslash is also the MSDOS (and Windows 95) default file separator character, that separates names in a file path. When backslash appears in a Java String, e.g. a pathname, it has to appear twice: once as the escape character and once as the character being escaped. C suffers from the same defect, but C was created long before MS-DOS was thought of. It would have been better for Java to choose a different character for escape, "#" say.

Other Aspects of the AWT

The purpose of the previous section is to introduce you to the highlights of GUI programming in Java. The AWT is a large library. We have covered all the high-points here, but it does feature some additional functionality. There are also a number of specialized techniques used for programming GUI's. Be alert to the fact that there are other features of the Window toolkit, which you will find if you explore the library source on your own a little.

Graphics programming (just as much as GUI programming) is an extensive topic that really needs much more space to do it justice than can be given here. We have not covered animation (which is just the display of successive images rapidly), nor the popular technique of double-buffering—better described as "off screen imaging" in which you draw an image into a graphics context that is in memory rather than on the screen. When it is drawn, it can be loaded onto the screen almost instantly, rather than with the delay typical of network connections.

All these topics really deserve a book of their own, and this isn't it. However, we have covered all the important material and in sufficient depth for you to write proper java GUI programs.

Here, by way of a final example, is the answer to one very frequently asked question. How do I load and display images in Applets? There is a method called getImage(URL) in the Applet class for retrieving an image from the server. You can also getImage() with a (Base URL, file-name) pair of arguments to retrieve something local. The Graphics class has a method called drawImage(). Putting it all together, the code looks like this:

```java
import java.awt.*;
import java.applet.*;

public class gif extends Applet {

    Image i;

    public void init() {
        add( new Label("Here's a GIF") );
        i=getImage(getDocumentBase(), "dickens.gif");
        resize(450,200);
    }

    public void paint(Graphics g) {
        boolean b = g.drawImage(i, 25, 25, this);
    }

}
```

If you copy the file "dickens.gif" from the images directory on the CD, into the same directory as you type this applet source, it will compile and run fine. Don't forget to invoke it via the usual HTML file.

A GIF is a file format for storing pictures. GIF stands for Graphic Interchange Format, and it was originally developed by CompuServe to be a system-independent way to store images. GIFs only store 8 bits of color information per pixel. Just adequate for run-of-the-mill PC's that only allow 256 different colors on screen at once, it is rapidly heading for technical obsolescence. Only use GIFs for cartoons and line drawings. GIF includes compression based on the Lempel-Ziv-Welch (LZW) algorithm, so the files are smaller than they would otherwise be. LZW compression is protected by a software patent filed by Unisys a few years ago. A copy of the public record for this patent is on the CD in justjava/ch1. If you've never seen a software patent before, take a look at this example.

A JPEG is a newer and superior file format for compressing images. It's an acronym for Joint Photographic Experts Group (the committee that wrote the standard). An image in JPEG format can take much less storage space than the same picture in GIF format. However, the JPEG format also allows you to tradeoff image quality against storage needs—more requires more. When you save an image in JPEG format, you can specify a percentage for the image quality. JPEG stores full color information: 24 bits per pixel.

Java doesn't currently have any library routines to capture an image and write it out to disk. It doesn't really need them—if you are viewing an image, you probably have it in GIF or JPEG format already. If not, use a converter program.

Some Light Relief

Satan: oscillate my metallic sonatas.

Some people claim that "backwards masking" conceals satanic messages in popular music. They believe that if you play the music backwards (like reading the phrase above backwards) a hidden message will be revealed.

You can easily play a piece of music backwards by recording it onto a cassette tape. Then take the cassette apart by unscrewing the little screws, and swap the reels left to right (don't flip them upside down). You will have to thread the tape a little differently onto one spool.

You've done it correctly if the feed and take-up spools revolve in opposite directions to each other when you hit "play." Rewind once to remove this anomaly, and away you go with your backwards masking. This experiment is so much fun, you should drop whatever you're doing (you're probably reading a book) and go and try this *right now.*

For advanced students: overdub a tape to produce a gimmicked version on which you have added some suitable wording ("Sacrifice homework. Cthulu is our thesis advisor. Wear leather and stay out late on Fridays. Stack dirty dishes in the sink, and cut in line at supermarkets"). Leave the tape out for a suitable colleague to "discover" your backwards masked work.

Where this fits into Java is not hard to see. Applets have some simple methods to play sound files. The 1.0 release can deal with sounds in the .au format, but support for more formats is surely on the way. There are a number of sound files on the CD that comes with this book, in the top level "noises" directory.

You can use these as datafiles to experiment with.

You can search at http://www.yahoo.com on ".au" to find dozens and dozens more sites and soundfiles.

You can also browse the site   http://cuiwww.unige.ch/OSG/AudioFormats

which describes the implementation of all the popular sound file formats including:

.WAV	**Windows**
.au	**Sun and NeXT.**
.AIF	**Mac and SGI**

On a Sun workstation, you can find much information under

`/usr/demo/SOUND`, including source code and a few more example sound effects.

Here is a minimal applet to play a sound effect:

```java
import java.applet.*;
public class noise extends Applet {
    public void init() {
        play( getCodeBase(), "danger.au");
    }
}
```

The file "danger.au" is on the CD. It makes a noise like a drumstick rattling on the side of a tin cup. The program would be invoked from the usual html file:

```
<head><title>noisy</title><head>

<p>

<applet code=noise.class  width = 150 height =100>

</applet>
```

The applet directory src/java/applet contains several other useful methods:

```
public AudioClip getAudioClip(URL url)
```

Once you have retrieved an AudioClip from a URL, you can play it once, play it in a loop continuously, or cease playing it with these methods:

```
play()
loop()
stop()
```

If you play it continuously, make sure that you stop playing it in the stop() method, called when the applet's Panel is no longer on the screen. Otherwise the noise will continue longer than you probably want.

Write an applet that plays a sound file, and evaluates it for hidden Satanic messages. There is an easy way to do this and a hard way. The easy way is to play the sound file, and then conclude:

```
println("That contained 0 Satanic messages \n");
```

The hard way would actually involve some analysis of the sound waveforms, but it would probably produce exactly the same result.

A second programming challenge is to figure out the format of a .au file using the references above, and code a program to play one backwards. This is a hard programming challenge, and if you complete it, mail the code to pvdl@best.com (or indeed any interesting Java code) and maybe I'll put it on the book website, along with your name in a Java programming Hall of Fame.

Answer to Programming Challenge

Here is a Java applet that displays a window with two buttons, one labelled "eat me" and the other labelled "drink me"— rather like the two flasks that Alice in Wonderland was confronted with. When you press the "eat me" button, the window grows slightly larger; when you press the "drink me" button (again like Alice in Wonderland) the window gets smaller.

```java
import java.awt.*;
import java.applet.Applet;
public class alice extends Applet {

    static Button g = new Button ("eat me");
    static Button s = new Button ("drink me");

    public void init() {
        add (g);
        add (s);
        resize (150,55);
    }

    public boolean action(Event e, Object o) {
    Dimension d = size();
        if (e.target.equals(g) ) resize (d.width+10,d.height+10);
    else if (e.target.equals(s) ) resize (d.width-10,d.height-10);
    return true;
    }
}
```

The program can be invoked by an html file like this:

```html
<head><title>Alice's dilemma</title></head>
<p>
<applet code=alice.class  width = 150 height = 100>
</applet>
```

Try running it. This is a windowing programming with objects you can interact with and cause something to happen on the screen. It's only about 20 lines long, so it's pretty exciting.

CHAPTER

9

Future Developments

"Lord Hippo suffered fearful loss.
By putting money on a horse
Which he believed, if it were pressed,
Would run far faster than the rest."

—*Hilaire Belloc, Selected Cautionary Verses.*

Java is still at an early stage in its lifecycle. The version 1.0 software only became available to the public on January 23, 1996[1]. However many related products have already been announced, or are being frantically worked on in great secrecy.

Java Developments

The development of Java-related products can be classified under six primary headings: performance, development tools, library enhancements, networking, security, and hardware. Here are the high points of each.

---

1. This is the version on the CD accompanying this book, with the final API's so readers do not have to worry about all the incompatible and changing Alpha and Beta versions.

Performance

This is the number one request from users, and probably the single highest priority item. Java, being an interpreted system, is currently an order of magnitude slower than C. But C was designed to be close to the hardware and only has built-in data types that are directly supported in hardware.

You have to pay something for the abstractions that Java provides and for the built-in structured types like String. On the positive side, modern workstations have MIPS to burn compared with earlier hardware, and are only going to improve. But there are a number of improvements that can be made in the software too.

Performance-oriented implementations of the Java virtual machine are on the way. We can expect optimizing runtimes that detect the frequently traveled paths in a program, and compile down to native code as the program is being executed. More performance improvements can come from a "Just-In-Time" compiler that does early binding by loading classes in anticipation, rather than on demand at runtime in an applet. Early symbol binding can be done in a separate thread, with otherwise unused CPU cycles put to use.

Some people have suggested compressing the byte code of an applet (or anything that is downloaded), and uncompressing it at the client end. This is likely to yield useful results for distributed applications, as the network download time is often the bottleneck.

Development Tools

Just as C is ubiquitous on hardware now, there will be Java ports to many more platforms—everything from a Cray to your TV remote control. At that point the consumer electronics goal of the original project will have been met, proving that if you wait long enough the world will eventually pass by your front door. But for some of the world it's only because they're lost.

We've already mentioned the just-in-time compilers, and we can expect the full range of conventional development tools too. I, for one, would like "indent" to properly format programs, and "java lint" to warn about questionable code constructs. Tip: the Unix C version of indent works fine on Java source and does 95 percent of what you want.

Java is a perfect match for the kind of integrated development environment which is commonplace in the PC space, but which has yet to become established among Unix professionals. If such an environment is written in Java (and it's hard to believe that anyone would be dumb enough to use a different language), then of course it is instantly portable to Unix, Windows, Macs, etc.

Some of the first IDE's on the market are quick adaptions of C++ IDE's, with time-to-market as a major goal. Hence these are not written in Java, and not available for all platforms yet.

The Abstract Window Toolkit is in need of some help: a GUI-builder that lets a programmer draw images on the screen showing how the interface should look, and which then generates the Java to implement it. And how about some test tools to measure code path coverage? Reliable Software Technologies is releasing a Beta version of their code coverage tracker for Java. It is a coverage assessment tool that measures what parts of the code were exercised during test.

RST is making this tool freely available and it can be obtained from the web site http://www.rstcorp.com. Oh yes, and some better profiling and performance measurement tools. The opportunities are here in abundance, but you'd better act fast!

Symantec Corporation is working on an integrated Java development environment, as is Borland, and several other companies.

Library Enhancements

The 1.0 release of Java provides only the basics of audio and graphics: little more than an existence proof, really. There is a ready market right now for third party Java libraries that provide video in and video out, especially now that desktop workstations and even some high-end PCs are powerful enough to sustain real time full motion video (on small parts of the screen). Audio input is one opportunity. A Java binding to the Virtual Reality Modelling Language is another. Java might just be the killer application needed to help make Virtual Reality become reality instead of just virtual.

A key requirement is that the solutions that emerge become open standards, not closed proprietary APIs. Silicon Graphics and Macromedia have announced that they are cooperating with Sun to develop APIs for multimedia and 3D graphics. Persistent objects—objects that exist longer than the program that created them, then be read in again later and reanimated—will surely be coming.

The Javascript language will get some practical use. Javascript is a simple scripting language which can be embedded in an HTML file. It offers loops, and conditional tests. The idea is to put some of the power of a programming language in the hands of non-programmers who want to create web pages with applets, without needing to become Java-heads. Javascript was briefly named "Livescript" before Netscape saw which way the wind was blowing. The intersection of Java and Javascript is the empty set.

Networking and Distributed Processing

In its brief life, Java has already become the de facto WWW programming API, and may soon become the Internet programming API. There are more innovations possible, including client/server windowing. At present, the Java AWT and its native peer window component have to be on the same system. There is no technical reason why they cannot be separated, so that users can run a window system down a PPP connection[2]. In practical terms this would allow you (well, alright, me) to dial into the office and run Java applets on a powerful office workstation, displaying the results on a PC at home. One of the design achievements of NeWS (Sun's Network-extensible Window System) was the decoupling of displays. A NeWS program could send its results to any workstation on the same net. This can soon become true for Java.

Java will consolidate its distributed processing and windowing capabilities, and move to provide a common windowing front end to databases, in particular. Several companies announced that they are developing tools in this area.

1. Oracle is making its corporate "PowerBrowser" Java-capable. Oracle recently stunned the computer industry by demonstrating a prototype $500 "Internet terminal."

2. Sybase announced it is licensing the Java system for use with its database products.

3. WebLogic is planning a portfolio of DBMS tools and services based on Java connectivity and portability. These are further described at: http://weblogic.com/

Adobe has licensed Java and announced that it will integrate Java into both its PageMill authoring tools, and Adobe Acrobat. Adobe Acrobat is a software product aimed at interactive browsing. Just as Postscript is a language that describes how a document should look, allowing different output devices to do the best they can to render it, Acrobat is a language that describes in a device-independent manner how a screen should look. Acrobat is really just a sophisticated version of HTML. A publisher can put text on a CD in Acrobat format, and anyone with an Acrobat browser can view the text in a nice formatted and font-rich form, regardless of whether they are on a Unix system, a Mac or a PC.

---

2. Think of PPP ("Point to Point Protocol") as carrying TCP/IP services to a system without a dedicated IP address. PPP is often run down a telephone line, e.g. between your workstation and your home PC, so you can work from home.

Security

The restrictions imposed on applets for security reasons are a little onerous. Everyone wants Java to be free from the kinds of viruses that pervade the MS Windows environment. No one wants to see the return of the 1988 Internet worm[3]. Much work remains to be done to ease the restrictions without compromising system integrity. The Java security FAQ at the javasoft site gives some intriguing hints about the encryption, digital signatures and secure transactions that will come. Features like these will encourage more commerce on the net. Java doesn't actually have a security model right now. It has a series of disabled features intended to make it harder for crackers to tamper with remote systems. Of course, some people just regard this as a challenge. Marianne's Java security FAQ contains the fine details on what applets can and cannot do. It can be found at:

    http://www.javasoft.com/sfaq

Sun has stated that it plans to add loading and authentication of signed classes in future, which will make it safe for browsers to run applets with full privileges. A "signed class" is one that has a unique and unforgeable signature on it (just like the signature on your checks) so browsers can be confident in entrusting the class with file access permission, knowing that it comes from someone they trust, and has not been altered. It will be possible for a class to have multiple signatures. Sun has announced that digital signatures for classes is a feature that will be in the next release.

In most cases, the Netscape browser imposes stricter restrictions on the applet than does Sun's applet viewer. It is possible to set the Access Control List (ACL) of a file, to allow the appletviewer to access it for instance. File protection by ACL's is common in the mainframe data processing world, and was introduced into Solaris with release 2.5. Windows 95 doesn't have ACL's.

Hardware and Firmware

A recurring idea in computer science is designing an architecture that is particularly convenient or efficient at executing a specific language. Past attempts include:

Algol-60:	early Burroughs processors
Lisp:	the Symbolics Lisp Machine
COBOL:	many processors optimized for BCD arithmetic.
Ada:	Rational Computers

3. See "With Microscope and Tweezers: An Analysis of the Internet Virus of November 1988" by Mark W. Eichin and Jon A. Rochlis, Mass. Institute of Technology, February 1989. This paper starts off describing the Internet as "a collection of networks linking 60,000 host computers" which seems hilariously insignificant in contrast to today's Internet. We've come a long way.

None of the examples to date have been conspicuously successful. The Lisp Machine was driven out of business by general purpose Unix workstations. The end of the Cold War spelled the end of massive budgets for defense contractors to blow on "cost-plus" contracts, taking the Ada machine down with it. Burroughs was swallowed by Unisys which in turn isn't exactly breaking any new ground in computing these days. Will the Java machine fare any better?

A lot of companies think so, and are betting on it. It costs upwards of $1 billion to design and build a completely new computer architecture these days. If you can leverage existing facilities and technology, you can possibly do it on a shoestring of just $100 million, so anyone betting on a Java-specific chip is making a pretty significant investment.

Oracle has already demonstrated their Internet terminal, and you don't exactly have to be Nostradamus to predict that the lights are burning late in their handsome Redwood Shores, CA, offices as they try to figure out exactly how best to bundle Java with it. Silicon Valley is a pretty small community when you get right down to it, and one hears all kinds of talk about Java chips, Java workstations, Java PC's, Java terminals, Java supercomputers and Java microcomputers. Who knows, some of it may even be true.

What is The Future For This Hardware?

The Oracle Corporation's $500 Network Computer.

model name:	NC (Network Computer)
CPU:	Acorn ARM7500 RISC
OS name:	NC-OS (no prizes for creativity in naming) based on Acorn Computer Group Plc' s RISC OS
	NC-OS will be ported to x86 platforms, and is also intended to be portable to any WWW, Internet, or communications device.
enclosure design:	Frog Design Inc. (The same creative consultants who worked on the Mac packaging with great success).

Acorn is an enormously capable British computer engineering company. They have been held back by their small size and limited installed base, but have a long track record of innovative and well-thought-out designs.

These are about the only features of the NC system that are known at this point. Oracle's plan for marketing, supporting, or even manufacturing the NC has yet to be announced.

Sun Microsystems has announced a family of Java chips, Pico Java, Micro Java, and Ultra Java, covering a range of price performance points. Availability for the entry level Pico Java is targetted for mid-1996, at a price around $25.

LSI Logic at least has gone public with some of its plans for what they call the "Internet on a Chip". This chip is targeted at Java/Internet terminals and other embedded systems. The chip uses one of the MIPS RISC microprocessor designs. More information is at http://www.lsilogic.com/mediakit/unit3_1x.html.

Two big characteristics working in favor of Java-on-a-chip are: 1) the performance speed-up; and, 2) the well-defined virtual machine which makes the task easier than trying to "siliconify" other high-level languages. Java is built on a well-defined stack-based virtual machine with the byte code instruction set, supported by a run-time library. It's also possible that tighter integration into the operating system could provide some of the benefits of a Java chip at a fraction of the cost.

The virtual machine was defined with the Java language in mind, but people were quick to realize that other compilers could be targeted to it. This would provide them with instant ports to any platform that supported Java. Not all languages are good candidates for meeting the requirements of the Java VM. C++ is a little too lax in its use of pointer arithmetic to be a good fit. However, the language experts at compiler company Intermetrics have already targeted their Ada 95 compiler to the Java VM, and created quite a stir by demonstrating it working at a 1995 Ada convention. Their web site is at http://www.inmet.com

We can also expect to see a lot more demand for graphics designers, illustrators, and artists. Java can animate your web page, true, but you still need something to say, and an interesting way in which to say it. Consider the "Neon sign" applet that used to be at

http://java.sun.com/JDK-prebeta1/applets/contest/NeonSign/index.html.

This is an impressive looking applet that shows a flickering neon sign, spelling out the name of the applet author. The more you look at this, the less there is to it. The applet just consists of two images, one with the neon sign dark, and one with it lit up. The applet randomly switches back and forth between them, so it appears that the sign is flashing. But all the cleverness of this applet is in the glossy artwork—and *that* is precisely the part that most programmers cannot supply for you.

What Will Microsoft Do?

One of the big wildcard questions is "what does Microsoft intend to do?" Microsoft has signed a letter of intent saying it wants to license Java from Sun.

Opinions differ as to whether Microsoft sincerely plans to embrace the technology, or will somehow try to act as a spoiler. Some people wonder if it is just pre-announcing Java vaporware as a strike against Netscape. Certainly it is very hard to find examples of companies that have succeeded in a collaborative venture with Microsoft. The mighty IBM was humbled, burned even, by its abortive attempt at joint development on OS/2 with the Redmond giant. Stac Electronics tried to make a deal with Microsoft for Stac's data compression software. According to court documents, the deal fell apart on Microsoft's unwillingness to pay per copy royalties. But Microsoft just went ahead and put Stac's software technology into MS-DOS 6 anyway[a]. Stac won a court judgement for $120 million against Microsoft in February 1994, later settling for $90M to avoid a lengthy appeal. In the book "Start-Up", Jerry Kaplan claims that Microsoft pinched his idea for pen computing when he showed them the concept to ask for applications porting. Instead Microsoft started a project to produce their own pen computing OS.

The whole concept of platform independence strikes at Microsoft's lock on desktop software. Microsoft must be uneasy about this, to say the least. It was faced with choosing between embracing the technology (perhaps offering a poor implementation to frighten people away) or ignoring it. If Microsoft embraced Java, Microsoft risked appearing to endorse a competing technology. If Microsoft ignored Java, Microsoft risked being left behind.

In the end Microsoft chose not to ignore the Internet, and not to ignore Java. Microsoft recently made moves suggesting that its private user network would be migrated to the Internet, and announced that it planned to license Java. That announcement, in early December 1995, was the final seal of mainstream corporate approval for Java. But a lot of industry players are still very suspicious about Microsoft's real motives and plans.

---

[a] One journalist asked "Just what kind of game does Microsoft think it's playing here?" and immediately provided his own answer: "Monopoly." Monopoly is a trademark of Waddington Brothers.

Other Java Resources

Half the point of Java is accessing the resources of the WWW. Here is a collection of favorite sites. If you check in with the Java ones periodically, you will always be well-informed about new developments.

http://www.javasoft.com (also reachable as http://java.sun.com)   The Sun Java site. Download software, look at applets, read the most up-to-date documentation and user guides.

http://www.gamelan.com   The Gamelan site. Named after an Indonesian musical ensemble, the Gamelan (pronounced to rhyme (approximately) with "come along") site is a rich resource for Java code, Java applets, hints, libraries and all kinds of information.

Gamelan is sponsored by the EarthWeb organization, an Internet consulting and services company. The Gamelan site is a treasure house that should be your second port of call after the Sun site.

http://www-net.com/java/faq   The mother of all FAQ lists. This site contains pointers to the various and several Java FAQ lists that public-spirited programmers are maintaining to help spread the information.

You can also access some of these individual FAQ sites directly at:

http://sunsite.unc.edu/javafaq/javafaq.html
http://www-net.com/java/faq/faq-java.txt
http://www.city-net.com/~krom/java-faq.html
http://java.sun.com/faqIndex.html
http://www.digitalfocus.com/digitalfocus/faq/index.html

http://www.io.org/~mentor1/jnIndex.html   This is the URL for Digital Espresso—a weekly summary of traffic on the comp.lang.java newsgroup. The volume of traffic there is enormous (several thousand messages per week), so a weekly summary really helps those who want to keep up without getting mired in the detail.

http://www.kinetiks.com/apisearch.html   Use this site to search the Java API.

http://hornet.mmg.uci.edu/cgi-bin/nph-fwais.pl   Use this site to search recent postings in the Java newsgroup.   Perhaps someone had exactly the same question as you, and perhaps someone else was able to answer it.

http://www.yahoo.com   Yahoo started life as a part-time project by a couple of Stanford students. It has rapidly blossomed into one of the premier web searching and indexing sites. You are not a web aficionado until you have a "connection timed out" while trying to reach yahoo.

http://www.dimensionx.com   or http://www.dnx.com   Another early
adopter of Java. This site is rich with applets, ideas and general Java
know-how. Well worth a visit.

http://www.fbi.gov/topten.htm   The FBI "Top Ten most wanted" list. Check
this every month to see if any of your co-workers have made it onto the
list. If so, make history and be the first to turn them in by e-mail.

http://www.ccil.org/jargon/jargon.html   The Jargon File. Everything you
don't need to know about programmer slang, and less. Also available as
a book, lord help us. Version 3.0 came out in August 1993 as The New
Hacker's Dictionary second edition (ISBN 0-262-68079-3), published by
MIT Press. They finally re-edited that bizarre and confusing saga of Guy
Steele's about the Palo Alto ice cream store. It's still not a very funny
story, but at least now you can understand what the point would be, if it
had one. Guy Steele is currently responsible for writing the Java Language Specification.

http://www.ora.com/gnn/bus/ora/win/regwiz.html   Find out the truth
about the Microsoft Registration Wizard snooping your hard disk for
competitors' products! Learn how expert programmers use debugging
and file monitoring tools to see what is really happening in a system.
A detective story with a moral at the end.

Conclusion

Programmers get interested in Java for many different reasons. Perhaps you
started out by hearing that Java made possible executable content in web pages.
Perhaps your initial reaction, like mine, was "So what?" Maybe your boss asked
you to investigate Java after reading something in "The Economist" magazine, or
the Wall Street Journal, or Time, or Newsweek, or the New York Times. It's highly
unusual for a programming language to receive so much attention from the main-

© 1996 Matthew Burtch

stream media, especially before the product has even reached the First Customer Shipment milestone.

The amount of media coverage of Java naturally raises some questions in the minds of programmers. It begins to look like the kind of exaggeration more usually associated with the entertainment industry. But that is not what is happening here at all. Sun was completely taken by surprise by the Java phenomenon, just as much as everyone else. As the significance of the language grew and grew, a series of increasingly senior managers were brought in to lead the program. Investment in the language—inside Sun and outside—grew too.

Scott McNealy, the CEO of Sun, has occasionally remarked that Sun made a mistake by not whole-heartedly backing the NeWS window system when it was first developed in 1987. As a result, it has taken nearly a decade for the Unix world to resolve the conflicting windowing system alternatives. Scott has commented in the past that he will personally ensure that superior Sun software technology is never again stifled through wavering commitment, and he is certainly delivering on his promise. The chief architect of NeWS was James Gosling—the chief architect of Java.

Sometimes tremendous interest in a product is not the result of overselling or collective trend-following. Sometimes it really does happen because the world recognizes the right product, in the right place, at the right time. Java is a better mousetrap, and the world is beating a path to Sun's door. There has been a convergence of mighty trends that Java is well-placed to address.

Not much in Java is completely new. What is new is the combination of all the things, put together in a simple package, and made available on highly-generous terms from computer industry technology leader, Sun Microsystems. While executable content in web pages is novel, it isn't such a big deal in itself. Java is an enabling technology for what will follow.

Java is producing a "paradigm shift"—a fundamental rethinking of the established ways of software development. Paradigm shifts lead to tremendous upsets, but also tremendous opportunities. The development of the internal combustion engine was a paradigm shift, and there were undoubtedly people in 1876 who were asking "But Herr Otto, so what if you can spin that big flywheel with a petrol motor?" What implications does it have for software distribution channels if you can pull applets to your system with a web browser?

Convergence of Mighty Trends

As the computer industry closes out the last 5 years of the Millennium, the times are characterized by the following mighty trends:

- popularization of the Internet

- computer industry blending into telecom industry

- consumer electronics merging with PC technologies

- computer industry drive to multimedia everything

- rejection of the complexity of C++

- desire for independence from Intel and Microsoft desktop monopolies

- resurgence of threads and object-oriented programming.

and, as always,

- more and more computing power for less and less investment.

Partly by accident, partly by design, Java is located at the point where all these paths come together.

Past computer industry paradigm shifts have included the trend to minicomputers, which DEC rode to great prosperity throughout the 1970s. That was followed by the "migration to the desktop" spearheaded by the Apple II PC and reinforced (tardily) by the IBM PC. The "migration to the desktop" paradigm shift almost bankrupted DEC as they failed to anticipate it and then came up with a succession of failing strategies to cope with it. It did bankrupt other, even less well prepared companies like Wang.

This time around we are just at the beginning of the cycle, but already it is clear—there are fortunes to be made and lost out there. This is an exciting time to be in the computer business, and an especially exciting time to be a computer programmer. As the turbo-talk goes, "Java is a simple, object-oriented, distributed, interpreted, robust, secure, architecture-neutral, portable, high performance, multithreaded, and dynamic language." The importance is not really in any one of these but in the combination of all of them. How will the computer industry be changed by the client/server metaphor extending across the Internet? Who will be the first to offer a computer system with a web browser as its primary interface to everything? What happens next is up to you.

Important! Above all, remember: have fun!

Some Light Relief

The Origami Kamikaze water bomber.

Sometimes people criticize the work done by programmers as "paper pushing". That's not really accurate, what we do is more "electron pushing", but there is one way we can make the label "paper pusher" come true. Do you want learn how to create little paper airplanes loaded with annoying cargo, and launch them at your work colleagues? Yes, of course you do. Here's how.

Origami is a ancient and honorable technique of delicate paper folding. It takes finesse, skill, and subtlety. So we certainly won't be considering *that* any further. Instead, this section explains how to make a paper airplane that takes a payload. Not only can you impress your co-workers with paper airplanes, but you can also bombard them with an air delivery of confetti, glue, or shaving cream from the far side of the room. People will be talking about you for days to come, and your manager will certainly remember your achievements when the review period comes around.

One warning here, at the age of 14 I dropped a paper waterbomb on the head of schoolfriend "Piffer" Tully from an upstairs classroom. He didn't see who did it, and I felt it better not to burden him by claiming responsibility. Now 25 years later it is probably safe to own up (Ha, ha, ha, Piffer!), and also alert you to the fact that not everyone appreciates the drollness of saturation bombing by paper airplane.

So pick your targets carefully, or stick to launching blanks. As always, observe the three cardinal safety rules when working around electronic equipment: 1) make sure you know where the main circuit breaker is located; 2) keep a grounding strap around your wrist, and most important; 3) wait till your boss goes on a lunch break before starting this project. Here's how you make the Kamikaze water bomber.

First, take an ordinary sheet of 8.5" by 11" paper, and make it narrower by cutting off 1.5" or so, to make 7 by 11. Then follow these instructions:

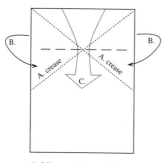

A. fold over and crease twice
B. Bring sides in, so the 2 B's touch
C. fold top down into triangle

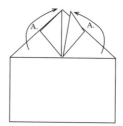

A. fold corners up to apex

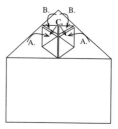

A. fold in the side corners
B. fold down the top corners
C. tuck corners of top triangle into pocket of lower triangles

NOW TURN THE PAPER OVER

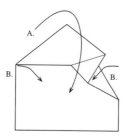

A. fold big triangle over and crease
B. tuck corners in under as you fold big triangle down again, (similar to the Valley fold done as Step 1B, the two B's come together underneath the pointed flap marked A).

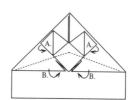

A. tuck flaps in and behind
B. Tuck second flaps up and behind to secure and hold the first tucks

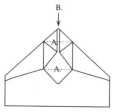

A. firmly crease
B. inflate by gently holding wings, pulling accordian folds & blowing into nose to expand cargo cabin
C. fill with payload through hole in nose.

Locate enemy forces and launch!

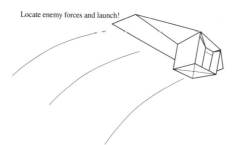

Fold up wings, and fill with payload through hole in nose. Umm, the hole in the *plane's* nose, that is. Launch and enjoy.

Origami is relaxing and fun. Just the thing for unwinding after a busy day chasing electrons. If you've really got a lot of spare time[4], check the origami models at http://www.cs.ubc.ca/spider/jwu/origami.html

There's a praying mantis there that takes 100 steps to complete!

P.S. My Origami Java chip will be released soon.

By The Way. . .

Some companies are so desperate for Java programmers, that they are stating their requirements in terms of "hours of experience"!

Seen recently on comp.lang.java

```
From: (name removed to protect the guilty)
Newsgroups: comp.lang.java
Subject: Freelance job for C++/Java Programmer
Date: 27 Jan 1996 23:26:28 -0800
Distribution: world

We are now looking for: an experienced C/C++, Java program-
mer.

Around 4 years experience on Windows & Mac preferred,
minimum of 100 hours with Java required.
```

Personally, I never hire programmers based on how long they have been in the workforce. It's much more relevant to find out what programs they have written and what they're interested in. But this posting is an interesting insight into market economics.

4.   Or if your boss takes really long lunch breaks.

APPENDIX

A

- Getting Internet Access

- Getting a Browser

- Getting Java Updates

- Summary

- Further Reading

Getting the Net Connection and Software

As everyone knows, the only real way to learn a programming language is to write some programs in it. For that you need the Java system, and a Java-capable web browser. This book comes with a CD that contains the version 1.0 Java compiler system for Windows NT, Windows 95 and Solaris 2.x. However, you may want to download a web browser, or later releases of Java. This chapter explains how to get these pieces of software. It assumes elementary familiarity with utilities like anonymous FTP for retrieving files from Internet hosts.[1]

In theory, you could forego the web browser and Internet access, and just learn Java application programming on your local system. In practice, however, this would be a mistake. You would be missing a key part—seamless client-server programming on the network—which is responsible for the vast interest in Java.

Getting Internet Access

As a preliminary to obtaining the software, you should get an Internet connection. Many readers of this book will already have Internet access through their employer or educational institution. If neither of these sources is available to you, perhaps your town has a library service that offers an online connection, or perhaps you can sign up for a computer class that comes with a student account at a local college. Or

---

1. If you do not have this knowledge, the Krol book referenced at the end of the chapter will provide it.

you may just prefer the convenience of Internet access in your own home, just as most people have a phone connection and some people have a cable TV connection. An Internet connection at home is readily obtained in most parts of the developed world with a commercial Internet Service Provider (ISP). You connect to the ISP via a phone call, and the ISP is directly connected to the Internet.

Choosing your ISP

In many cases, you will have a choice of Internet Service Provider (ISP), so these two checklists indicate the ways to evaluate them. The first checklist is mostly about the way you connect to the ISP. The second checklist covers the services the ISP offers.

You will need some kind of personal computer at home: a Macintosh, a "Wintel" (MS Windows/Intel) box, a workstation running Unix or one of its variants like Linux. Your system must support a graphical user interface. A VT100 compatible ASCII terminal is no longer good enough.

ISP connections are invariably provided by dialling in from your home, so a large part of the first check list has to do with the telephone service. You may well find that the other members of your household make you get a second phone line instead of tying up your family's main number.

Checklist—ISP connectivity

[   ] **Local calling area** (not a toll call)

So that you don't bankrupt yourself with long distance phone charges you need an ISP to have a Point of Presence (POP) local to your home. An acceptable alternative is a dial-back system where you call in, and they immediately call you back so that the call is billed to them (their size gives them bulk discount with the Telco). A toll-free call-in number is also acceptable.

[   ] **Free communications software**

You will likely need some communications software for your system. This software is needed to make the connection and keep it going. The ISP should know what is needed for the different Operating Systems, and supply it without charge.

[   ] **28.8kbps lines (V34) or better**

The phone line between your home and the ISP is going to be the slowest link in the system. The ISP needs to use the fastest commercially-available modems. At the time of writing (10:17pm, Saturday December 2 1995) these are 28.8Kbps modems. These will adapt to slower speeds automatically, so even if your modem is not rated that high, it can still communicate. You will get frustrated with a slow modem before very long, and when you finally upgrade no change is needed at the ISP end. If you need to buy a modem, don't fall for the false economy of a slow one.

[   ] An adequate modem pool

It's frustrating to get a busy signal when you dial in to your ISP. They need to keep adding modems as their business grows, and preferably have a policy such as "at least one SS20 class machine per 100 users" or "no new clients if the modem pool is maxed out more than 3 hours/day."

[   ] SLIP/PPP

To run a web browser on the Internet, your computer system will need an IP connection. This can be provided over a phone line by one of two alternatives:

- SLIP   Serial Line Internet Protocol
- PPP   Point-to-Point Protocol

Either is adequate, but PPP provides more features (none of which you will be using if you only ever connect to your ISP from home).

[   ] No or low hourly connect fee

The Internet can be an interesting place, and you might spend more than a few hours there. Ideally, there will not be a "per-hour" connection time fee. Some ISP's offer no fee access outside normal business hours. It's also OK if there is a large monthly allowance of free connect time, with a low hourly charge when that is used up.

[   ] Base monthly charge

You'd like the monthly charge to be as low as possible. Expect to pay about the same as basic cable tv service costs. In my area (Silicon Valley, California) that's about $25–30 per month.

[   ] System support

This is where most ISPs fall down. Support is expensive to provide, but usually generates no revenue. As a result, you may find almost no help is available if you have an unusual connection or set up problem. Ask questions to gauge how much system support is offered. What happens if you delete a file by accident? Will they recover it from backup for you?

Sometimes a lively user community can partly compensate for lack of support, by answering common questions.

[   ] Amount of disk space provided

You are going to be downloading files, and perhaps saving them temporarily in your ISP account. How much disk space is bundled in with your account, and how much do they charge for extra use? Some ISP's will provide bulk storage for short periods of time so that large file transfers will complete, but you must dispose of the file shortly thereafter.

There are certain items that the ISP may boast, which you don't actually care about. These include:

- **56K, T-3, or T-1 service**
  You don't care about the bandwidth of the ISP's pipe to the Internet. As long as it's big enough, that's all that matters.

- **Internic registration**
  Most people don't need their own domain name.

- **Static vs. dynamic IP addressing**
  Either is fine for you.

- **Co-location (where you have your machine at their site)**
  This is really for business and commercial users. For you, half the fun is frobbing the hardware personally.

That covers the connection between your home and the ISP. Now you need to consider the range of Internet services that you will get.

Checklist—ISP Services

[   ] Web access and a Java-capable Web browser

You absolutely need access to the World Wide Web, through a browser with a graphical user interface (not text-only). This is why you need a computer system at home, rather than just an ASCII terminal. The browser must be Java capable.

You will want to put up a web home page announcing your existence to Cybernauts. The ISP should provide you the disk space and connectivity to create your own home page.

[   ] FTP access

The File Transfer Protocol allows you to retrieve files from remotes sites. Eventually this will all be done with WWW access, but until the entire world has converted, you still need the lower-level functionality that FTP provides.

There are different levels of Internet connectivity, each providing different services and applications. Although the terminology is not yet in general use, Internet document RFC1775 describes the hierarchy of services.
You can retrieve the description via anonymous FTP from "ftp.internic.net" in file /pub/rfc1775.txt

The levels of service available through most ISPs are:

Client Access

The user runs applications that employ Internet application protocols directly on their own computer platform, but might not be running underlying Internet protocols (TCP/IP), might not have full-time access, such as through dial-up, or might have constrained access, such as through a firewall. When active, Client users might be visible to the general Internet, but such visibility cannot be predicted. "Visibility" means "able to chat on-line."

Mediated Access

The user runs no Internet applications on their own platform. An Internet service provider runs applications that use Internet protocols on the provider's platform, for the user. User has simplified access to the provider, such as dial-up terminal connectivity. For Mediated access, the user is on the Internet, but their computer platform is not. Instead, it is the computer of the mediating service (provider) which is on the Internet.

Messaging Access

The user has no Internet access, except through electronic mail and through netnews, such as Usenet or a bulletin board service. Since messaging services can be used as a high-latency (i.e., slow) transport service, the use of this level of access for mail-enabled services can be quite powerful, though not interactive.

Your ISP needs to offer "client access" in the above sense. Mediated access or messaging access are not good enough for the WWW.

[   ] **WAIS, gopher, and archie**

These are all ways to search the Internet, to locate sites and files of interest. The ISP must provide easy access to these utility programs.

[   ] **No censorship**

Some ISP's (notably AOL) impose censorship on their customers. This behavior is often a misguided response to pressure from political or watchdog groups flexing their muscle. Censorship occasionally makes ISP's look ridiculous, as in 1993 when Prodigy was using an automated screening program. One contributor to a musical discussion had a posting returned on the grounds that he was using language "inappropriate to the Prodigy service." He was discussing Bach's B Minor Mass—the movement titled "Cum Sancto Spiritu." America Online committed the same faux pas in November 1995, when they declared the word "breast" taboo—thereby making it impossible for breast cancer patients to contact one another for information and support. The major use of the keyword was allowing these patients to find each other. Check the censorship policies of your ISP, and give your business to companies that provide unrestricted access.

[   ] **Usenet news and other services**

If the ISP provides Web access (which is essential), they are almost certain to provide Usenet news access, telnet, and e-mail services too. These are not essential, but they are very nice to have and there is no reason to exclude them. Usenet news should include the alt or alternative newsgroups, not just the mainstream collection. Check whether these services are bundled in with your Internet access.

ISDN: Integrated Services Digital Network

For now, the most common dialup connection is via a modem. Even the fastest modems are several orders of magnitude slower than dedicated network connections. People use modems because there has been nothing better.

The better alternative will not be long in coming. In fact it has been waiting in the wings for at least a decade. ISDN or "Integrated Services Digital Network" is a digital service (in contrast to the existing analog phone wiring) providing an effective 128Kbit/sec channel across a phone line. Compare that to the best modems that are only one quarter the rate. Faster throughput speeds can be achieved by installing higher rated lines with multiple ISDN channels. The key fact about ISDN is that it brings the speed and reliability of digital transmission to the desktop, rather than relying on analog technology for the last leg.

Your ISP should have an ISDN plan. ISDN is currently only available in urban areas.

Engineers used to joke that ISDN meant "It Still Does Nothing" because the service is taking so long to catch on. In truth, it was a solution in search of a problem. That will change when ISDN finally solves the "vicious circle" that has bedeviled it:

> ISDN is not popular because it is costly.

> ISDN is costly because it is not popular.

The Web is the problem that ISDN has been waiting to solve.

It is no exaggeration to say that Java is being ported to more platforms, with more urgency than any other piece of software in the history of the computer industry. People want this software and they want it now.

The market share among high volume desktop platforms looks roughly like this:

IBM PC and PC compatibles	90%
Macintosh	9%
Unix (all versions)	1%

However a different picture emerges if you tabulate only desktop platforms that are connected to the Internet. The breakdown is roughly:

Unix (all versions)	90%
IBM PC and PC compatibles	9%
Macintosh	1%

For this reason, the first 3 ports were done in this order. Coming from Sun, Java was naturally developed on Sun workstations under the Solaris 2.x (Unix) Operating System. A port to Windows 95 and Windows NT rapidly followed, and was released at the same time as the Solaris version. Sun staff are also completing the Mac port and have announced availability beginning in March 1996.

Ports are also underway or nearing completion to most other platforms of significance. Details can be obtained from these sites:

Other Platforms

IBM: Windows 3.1, AIX and OS/2 ports are underway by IBM, they have announced products for the first quarter of 1996, under the code name of "Cyberparts". See the IBM web page at   http://ncc.hursley.ibm.com/javainfo/

DEC: a port to Alpha OSF/1 is being done by the Open Software Foundation. For information, see   http://www.gr.osf.org:8001/projects/web/java/

Sun: Solaris on x86 an unsupported version of JDK for Solaris x86 can be found at   ftp://xm.com:/pub/

SGI: At least one port outside SGI is taking place. See   http://liawww.epfl.ch/~simon/java/irix-jdk.html

Hewlett-Packard: The Open Software Foundation (OSF) is working on a port to HP/UX on the Precision Architecture. For information, see http://www.gr.osf.org:8001/projects/web/java/

linux: Several independent ports to Linux have been made. See http://www.science.wayne.edu/~joey/java/linux.html or http://www.blackdown.org

NeXT: A port to the NeXTstep environment is underway. See http://www.next.com

AT&T: The Open Software Foundation (OSF) is working on a port to AT&T Unix. For information, see http://www.gr.osf.org:8001/projects/web/java/

Amiga: http://www.yahoo.com/Computers/PCs/Amiga http://www.lls.se/~matjo/PJAmi/PJAmi.html

Hardware Needs

Java itself doesn't lay down any specific demands on the hardware. The web browser probably will. For example, Netscape Navigator 2.0 specifies that users need:

Unix

+ 16Mb memory

+ Solaris 2.3 or later

Windows

+ Windows 95 or Windows NT

+ i386 processor or later

+ 8Mb memory

+ sound blaster card

Macintosh

+ Macintosh System 7.5 or later

+ 8Mb memory

+ PowerPC

Java itself is not a resource hog. If the system is sufficiently configured to run a fully-featured Web browser, it meets the minimum needs for Java too.

The system is referred to as the JDK—Java Development Kit. It includes a java compiler (javac), a java bytecode interpreter (java), a debugger (jdb), and an applet viewer ("appletviewer") that lets you run an applet in the absence of a web browser.

Getting a Browser

The next piece of software you need is a Java-capable web browser. At the start of 1996, that means Netscape Navigator version 2.0 or later, or Sun's own HotJava browser. These are the first two Java-capable browsers available, but all other browser suppliers are racing fast to catch up. Simply put, if a web browser is not Java-capable from this point on, it will not be purchased by anyone knowledge-able. You need a Java-capable browser so you can:

- experiment with www browsing

- run applets (little Java applications) that are embedded in Web pages.

In these early days of the Web and Java, companies are eager to meet the pent-up demand for products. They are releasing early so-called Beta versions of their software. They are even making the Beta versions available without charge. The Beta versions are not supported products, and often are very buggy. It can be a frustrating experience trying to learn a language with Beta software.

Software is often available on a choice of media, commonly CD and diskettes. If your system has a CD ROM reader, look for the software on CD ROM, because it avoids swapping 11 diskettes in and out (e.g. to install Win-95).

The classic model for software product releases follows three phases:

Alpha release. The alpha software is the first version that has the major functionality in place. The software will still be very buggy, but enough of it works well enough to release to other departments in the company for test and use. As the inevitable defect reports come back, the problems will be tracked and fixed, so it can move to the next phase of the cycle.

Beta release. You enter the Beta cycle immediately after the alpha cycle is complete. As many as possible of the bugs have been found and fixed, and a new release is generated. This Beta software is made available to outside testers. It may be made widely available to anyone who asks for it (like Windows NT Beta) or it may be given only to a small group of highly qualified partner companies.

The point of Beta test is to locate bugs that can only be found with use and misuse in typical customer environments. The big problem with Beta testing is that you are now so far advanced in the development cycle that it may not be possible to fix any but the most heinous bugs that are uncovered, and perhaps not all of them.

FCS release. FCS stands for "First Customer Shipment." As the Beta period (typically some multiple of months) winds up, the bug-fixing criteria get stricter and stricter. This is because unrestricted bug fixing will destablize the product, at a time when you are aiming for maximum reliability. Typically no new functionality is allowed in the Beta period, and towards the end, only really serious bugs can be fixed: bugs that eat data (data corruption) or bugs that cause core dumps. Finally 6-8 weeks before the end of Beta the software is built for the final time, and put through in-house regression testing. Any last minute problems are noted and either reported in the release notes, or fixed on a case-by-case basis. The CDs are duplicated, sent out to the distribution channels and become available for purchase on the FCS date.

Getting the Netscape Software.

Here's how to get the latest Netscape release. Netscape has released several updates to the original Beta release, so there has been more than one Beta.

1. Use anonymous FTP to the Netscape site ftp.netscape.com. The netscape site is very heavily used. You might consider access outside prime hour. There are no mirror sites (except inside certain educational institutions).

2. The directories are named to reflect their contents. If you wanted the original Beta release (you don't) you could retrieve it from the pathname that matches your system:

Unix

> /2.0beta/unix/netscape-v20b2-export.alpha-dec-osf2.0.tar.Z
>
> netscape-v20b2-export.hppa1.1-hp-hpux.tar.Z
>
> netscape-v20b2-export.i486-unknown-linux.tar.Z
>
> netscape-v20b2-export.sparc-sun-solaris2.4.tar.Z

Windows

> /2.0beta/windows/n16e20b2.exe
>
> n32e20b2.exe

Mac

> /2.0beta/mac/netscape-2.0b2.hqx

The point is that you have to use some intelligence to choose which file to download. The Beta 3 release used pathnames of a different form.

Unix

> /2.0b3/unix/netscape-v20b3-export.i486-unknown-linux.tar.Z
>
> netscape-v20b3-export.sparc-sun-solaris2.4.tar.Z

Windows

> /2.0b3/windows/n16e20b3.exe
>
> n32e20b3.exe

Mac

> /2.0b3/mac/netscape-2.0b3.Hqx

Use the most recent release that is on the site. The name of the directory should be obvious when you get to the netscape site.

3. Do a binary transfer on the file whose name matches your platform.

If you are running windows on your system, there are two choices for the executable file:
n16e20b3.exe -- for Windows 3.x
n32e20b3.exe -- for Windows 95 and NT.

If running windows you must choose the 32 bit version for windows 95 and NT. Java will not run under Windows 3.x yet (and perhaps never in Netscape).

4. The Netscape binary is several Mb in size, and will take about 25 minutes to download using a 28.8Kbps line.

When you finally have the Netscape binary on your system, unpack it. On Windows it is a self extracting archive: just execute it, and it will create several programs in the directory. On Unix, it is a compressed tar file, so run uncompress, followed by tar -xvf.

At this point you will have several files in the directory, one of which is called setup. Run the setup program, choose where you want to install it, look at the readme file (it says you promise not to give Netscape to any Syrians, Libyans, North Koreans, Yugoslavs etc.)[2] choose the default security level, configure in the TCP/IP support according to the instructions in the Netscape support/client support/release notes or handbook at http://www.netscape.com and you are ready to go.

The Beta versions of Netscape have a limited shelf life. They expire after a predetermined date, to encourage you to either retrieve a newer beta, or buy the FCS product.

Microsoft Trojan Horse?

In a news report headlined "Microsoft Trojan Horse stymies net use" Interactive Week reported in September 1995, that the use of Microsoft Network removed a file that was essential for network software (like Netscape Navigator) from competitors.

The news story went on to explain if you upgrade from Windows 3.x to Windows 95, it automatically replaces the windows socket library Winsock.dll with a new version that only works with Microsoft's Internet access software. Not only is Microsoft Network given the most prominent place of display on the window interface, it also disables all its competitors.

Only the most knowledgeable of users will be able to track down the problem, and reconfigure the compatible version of the library. Suppliers of competing software only had two options: rewrite their software to use the new Microsoft library—except that Microsoft was very reluctant to release information on the Application Program Interface (API) of the new Winsock environment. The only other choice, which Netcom and many others took, was to immediately abandon use of the new winsock.dll, move the old compatible winsock code elsewhere and hide it from the Microsoft upgrade program that overwrites it.

In December 1995, the United States Department of Justice (the arm of the Federal Government that enforces anti-monopoly laws) announced it was investigating the incident.

---

2. This is because the encryption software in Netscape is deemed a "munition" by the U.S. Government.

Getting Java Updates

Finally, you want to acquire updates to the Java software. As with Netscape there have been several preliminary releases, leading up to an FCS on January 23, 1996. If the Java FCS version is available for your platform, use it in preference to Beta. The FCS version contains fewer bugs, is better documented, and is better supported. Beta software is for the adventurous.

The business model for selling Java is not yet completely worked out. For the immediate future, the priority is to build volume and market presence. This is much more important than an immediate return on Phil Samper's $5M long shot bet.

From reading the "Help Wanted" ads in the Silicon Valley newspapers, and looking at the programmers the Java team wants to recruit, we can predict that some form of licensing will eventually be built into the product. Perhaps users will even be able to download the software, then activate it by phoning in their credit card information and receiving a customized password.

One possible business model that company vice presidents dream about is to first get everyone using Java, which looks like it is happening of its own accord. Then figure out a way to shave a minute fraction (say 1/100th of one percent) of every transaction. Finally, retire to your own island in the South Pacific. The rewards are immense for whoever figures out a standard way to extract a toll from those using the information superhighway.

How to Download Java

Assuming you need to download Java, the process is very similar to downloading Netscape.

1. Use anonymous FTP to your closest mirror to the Java site. The mirrors are:

USA: Wayne State University

  ftp://ftp.science.wayne.edu/pub/java

USA: SunSITE at University of North Carolina

  ftp://sunsite.unc.edu/pub/languages/java

USA: The Blackdown Organization

  ftp://www.blackdown.org/pub/Java

USA: Dimension X

ftp://java.dnx.com or

ftp://www.dnx.com

UK: SunSITE Northern Europe, Imperial College, London

ftp://sunsite.doc.ic.ac.uk/packages/java

Sweden: Luleå University

ftp://ftp.luth.se/pub/infosystems/www/hotjava

Germany: SunSITE Central Europe, Aachen

ftp://sunsite.informatik.rwth-aachen.de/pub/mirror/java.sun.com

Japan: Center for Global Communication (GLOCOM), Tokyo

ftp://ftp.glocom.ac.jp/mirror/java.sun.com

Singapore: SunSITE Singapore, National University of Singapore

ftp://ftp.iss.nus.sg/pub/java

Korea: Korea Advanced Institute of Science and Technology CAIR, Taejon

ftp://ftp.kaist.ac.kr/pub/java

If none of these work for you, the Sun Java site is at ftp.javasoft.com. The Java site and its mirrors are very heavily used. You might consider access outside prime hours. Log on for anonymous ftp.

2. At the Java site, the files are in the pub directory, and are named to reflect their contents.

Alpha release

/pub/hotjava-alpha3-solaris2-sparc.tar.Z

/pub/hotjava-alpha3-win32-x86.exe

Pre-Beta releases

/pub/JDK-prebeta1-solaris2-sparc.tar.Z

/pub/JDK-prebeta1-patch-solaris2-sparc.tar.Z

/pub/JDK-prebeta1a-solaris2-sparc.tar.Z

Beta release

/pub/JDK-beta-solaris2-sparc.tar.Z

/pub/JDK-beta-win32-x86.exe

Beta 2 release

/pub/JDK-beta2-solaris2-sparc.tar.Z

/pub/JDK-beta2-win32-x86.exe

Although the Java system is architecture neutral to programmers and users, the software that implements the system is different for each platform [1 second puzzler for readers: explain why.]

3. Switch to binary mode, and get the file whose name matches your platform. You only need get the most recent version of the JDK, as indicated by its name.

What's in the JDK

When you unpack the Java Development Kit and install it, you'll find that you have these components:

filename	what it is
javac	compiler, java source to byte code
java	interpreter, runs byte code
jdb	debugger
appletviewer	Allows java programs in Web pages to be run without using a Web browser.

These are the tools you will use most frequently. There are also a few special purpose utilities.

javadoc	Creates html documentation files from clues embedded in Java source.
javah	Creates C header files that correspond to Java objects. This is useful when creating programs that mix languages.
javap	A tool to print out byte codes
javaprof	A profiling tool to tell you which statements in your program were executed the most often.

The 1.0 FCS version of the Java Development Kit does not contain the HotJava browser, though the team is frantically working on that. If you want to try Hot-Java, you will need to download the Alpha version of the software or wait for HotJava to come out in Beta form.

Potential Pitfall

Many aspects of the Java packages changed between Alpha and Beta. As a result, you cannot mix objects between the two. Specifically, you cannot run the Alpha HotJava on Beta applets. This will not work. Use the appletviewer instead.

This incompatibility is one of the reasons for declaring alpha, beta and FCS versions of software. Implementors are allowed to make incompatible changes in the early stages.

Summary

This chapter described the steps you need to do to assemble a computer system that allows you to run Java. The steps are:

1. Obtain Internet access.

2. Get a web browser, such as Netscape version 2.0 or later, install it on your system.

3. Get the Java Development Kit (either from the CD that came with this book, or by downloading it) install, and test it on your system. The installation and testing is described in the Introduction at the front of this book.

Further Reading

LAN Times Encyclopedia of Networking

by Tom Sheldon

publ by Osborne McGraw-Hill, 1994

ISBN 0-07-881965-2

The back cover describes this as "covering A (Appletalk) through X (X Windows)" and it is absolutely right: the sections on Y and Z were completely missing from my copy. Har har. Just funning you. This is an excellent and easily-understood encyclopedia of anything and everything to do with networks. If you can only afford one book on data communications, this is absolutely the one to buy.

The Whole Internet

by Ed Krol,

publ. O'Reilly & Associates, Sebastapol CA, 1992.

ISBN 1-56592-025-2

An excellent and exceptionally able description of all key aspects of the Internet for the intelligent lay-reader. Also contains detailed descriptions of the applications that you can run on Internet.

APPENDIX B

With n bits in integer two's complement format, you can count:

unsigned from 0 to (one less than 2^n)
signed from -2^{n-1} to (one less than 2^{n-1})

Powers-of-two from 2^1 to 2^{64}

2^1	2	2^{17}	131,072	2^{33}	8,589,934,592	2^{49}	562,949,953,421,312
2^2	4	2^{18}	262,144	2^{34}	17,179,869,184	2^{50}	1,125,899,906,842,624
2^3	8	2^{19} megabyte	524,288	2^{35}	34,359,738,368	2^{51}	2,251,799,813,685,248
2^4	16	2^{20}	1,048,576	2^{36}	68,719,476,736	2^{52}	4,503,599,627,370,496
2^5	32	2^{21}	2,097,152	2^{37}	137,438,953,472	2^{53}	9,007,199,254,740,992
2^6	64	2^{22}	4,194,304	2^{38}	274,877,906,944	2^{54}	18,014,398,509,481,984
2^7	128	2^{23}	8,388,608	2^{39} terabyte	549,755,813,888	2^{55}	36,028,797,018,963,968
2^8	256	2^{24}	16,777,216	2^{40}	1,099,511,627,776	2^{56}	72,057,594,037,927,936
2^9 kilobyte	512	2^{25}	33,554,432	2^{41}	2,199,023,255,552	2^{57}	144,115,188,075,855,872
2^{10}	1,024	2^{26}	67,108,864	2^{42}	4,398,046,511,104	2^{58}	288,230,376,151,711,744
2^{11}	2,048	2^{27}	134,217,728	2^{43}	8,796,093,022,208	2^{59}	576,460,752,303,423,488
2^{12}	4,096	2^{28}	268,435,456	2^{44}	17,592,186,044,416	2^{60}	1,152,921,504,606,846,976
2^{13}	8,192	2^{29} gigabyte	536,870,912	2^{45}	35,184,372,088,832	2^{61}	2,305,843,009,213,693,952
2^{14}	16,384	2^{30}	1,073,741,824	2^{46}	70,368,744,177,664	2^{62}	4,611,686,018,427,387,904
2^{15}	32,768	2^{31}	2,147,483,648	2^{47}	140,737,488,355,328	2^{63} bubbabyte	9,223,372,036,854,775,808
2^{16}	65,536	2^{32}	4,294,967,296	2^{48}	281,474,976,710,656	2^{64}	18,446,744,073,709,551,616

APPENDIX
C

Characters 0x0 to 0x1F are the C0 (control) characters, defined in ISO/IEC 6429:1992

Characters 0x20 to 0x7E are the G0 graphics characters of the 7-bit code set defined in ISO/IEC 646-1991(E) — essentially the 7-bit ASCII characters.

Characters 0x80 to 0x9F are the C1 (control) characters, defined in ISO/IEC 6429:1992

The unshaded characters comprise the Latin-1 code set defined in ISO/IEC 8859-1:1987 (though the symbols "Φ" and "Φ" (0xDE and 0xFE) are approximations to the capital and small Icelandic letter "thorn." The actual letters are too weird to be in character sets anywhere outside a 12 mile radius of Reykjavík.

Table C-1

ISO 8859 8-bit Latin-1 character set and control characters

Least significant 4 bits of the byte

	0	1	2	3	4	5	6	7	8	9	A	B	C	D	E	F
0	nul	soh	stx	etx	eot	enq	ack	bel	bs	ht	lf\n	vt	ff	cr\r	so	si
1	dle	dc1	dc2	dc3	dc4	nak	syn	etb	can	em	sub	esc	is_4	is_3	is_2	is_1
2	space	!	"	#	$	%	&	'	(	)	*	+	,	-	.	/
3	0	1	2	3	4	5	6	7	8	9	:	;	<	=	>	?
4	@	A	B	C	D	E	F	G	H	I	J	K	L	M	N	O
5	P	Q	R	S	T	U	V	W	X	Y	Z	[	\	]	^	_
6	'	a	b	c	d	e	f	g	h	i	j	k	l	m	n	o
7	p	q	r	s	t	u	v	w	x	y	z	{	|	}	~	del
8	*n/a*	*n/a*	bph	nbh	*n/a*	nel	ssa	esa	hts	htj	vts	pld	plu	ri	ss2	ss3
9	dcs	pu1	pu2	sts	cch	mw	spa	epa	sos	*n/a*	sci	csi	st	osc	pm	apc
A	nbsp	¡	¢	£	¤	¥	¦	§	¨	©	ª	«	¬	shy	®	¯
B	°	±	²	³	´	µ	¶	•	¸	¹	º	»	¼	½	¾	¿
C	À	Á	Â	Ã	Ä	Å	Æ	Ç	È	É	Ê	Ë	Ì	Í	Î	Ï
D	Ð	Ñ	Ò	Ó	Ô	Õ	Ö	×	Ø	Ù	Ú	Û	Ü	Ý	Φ	β
E	à	á	â	ã	ä	å	æ	ç	è	é	ê	ë	ì	í	î	ï
F	∂	ñ	ò	ó	ô	õ	ö	÷	ø	ù	ú	û	ü	ý	Φ	ÿ

Most Significant 4 bits of the byte

APPENDIX
D

- Using the CD-ROM on Windows 95 and Windows NT

- Using the CD-ROM on Solaris 2

- Using the CD-ROM on Macintosh (System 7.5 or later)

The SunSoft Press Java Series CD-ROM

Thre are currently four books in the SunSoft Press Java Series: Core Java, Instant Java, Java by Example, and Just Java. The same CD-ROM is included with each book and contains examples from all of the books. The CD also contains the Java Developer's Kit (Release 1.0) for Solaris 2.x, Windows 95, and Windows NT.

A Beta version of the Macintosh Java Developer's Kit was released as this book went to press and was added to the disc. It was not possible to test all of the Java programs on the disc with the Macintosh JDK. If you experience any problems with the Beta release, check the SunSoft Press Java Series Web page for updates (http://www.prenhall.com/~java_sun).

Using the CD-ROM on Windows 95 and Windows NT

In addition to the JDK and Java applets and applications from the four books, the Win95nt directory contains Symantec's Café Lite and shareware versions of WinEdit and WinZip. **This CD-ROM does not support Windows 3.1.**

The Win95nt directory structure is as follows:

Directory/File	Contents
Booksjdk	Contains the installation program for the Java Series books and the JDK (1.0)
Cafelite	Contains the installation program for Café Lite
Readme.txt	Installation notes for Windows users
Winedit	Contains the installation program for WinEdit
Winzip	Contains the installation program for WinZip

To install the JDK or Java programs from the books:

1. Click the Start button and choose Run. (Windows NT users, Select Run from the Program Manager File menu.)

2. Type D:\WIN95NT\BOOKSJDK\Setup.exe and click the OK button. (If your CD-ROM drive is not drive D, substitute the appropriate letter.)

3. The installation program will prompt you to select the components you wish to install. You may install the JDK by itself or the JDK and any combination of files from the four books.

4. The installation program will prompt you for the drive and directory to use for each of the components you select.

(Please note that the Café Lite installation program also installs a copy of the JDK on your system.)

NOTE: On Windows 95 systems, the installation program adds the Java bin directory to the PATH statement in your AUTOEXEC.BAT file and adds a CLASSPATH assignment or modifies your existing CLASSPATH to point to the Java runtime library. You must reboot for these changes to take effect. On Windows NT systems, you will have to change the environment variables manually.

Please note that UNIX and Windows text files have slightly different conventions for end-of-line. UNIX expects a newline character (linefeed) and Windows expects a carriage return and a linefeed. Many Windows editors (including WinEdit) are able to cope with UNIX conventions and vice versa. Be aware, however, that some Windows editors will not display line breaks properly if you try to read text files that were created on a UNIX system. The Java compiler handles source files created under either convention.

Using the SunSoft Press Java Series Sample Programs

Core Java

When you have finished installing the Core Java files on your system, there should be thirteen subdirectories in the CoreJavaBook directory. The source code for the programs described in this book can be found in the 12 directories named ch2, ch3…ch13. There should also be a directory named corejava that contains java files and class files needed to run various applications.

For example, if you open up the ch10 directory, you will see 5 subdirectories:

    MessageCrackerTest
    ExceptTest
    ExceptionalTest
    DebugWinTest
    BuggyButtonTest

These directories contain the class files and java files for the programs discussed in Chapter 10.

Instant Java

The Java programs described in Instant Java are all available on the CD-ROM and can easily be customized. After installing the programs onto your system, you should have 7 subdirectories in your InstantJavaBook directory. Five of the directories correspond to chapters in the book:

fund	Chapter 2 Fundamental Applets
text	Chapter 3 Text Applets
image	Chapter 4 Image Applets
animate	Chapter 5 Animation Applets
assorted	Chapter 6 Assorted Applets

The other two directories contain images and additional source code and classes:

images	Image files (GIF and JPEG formats)
classes	Additional source code and classes

Java by Example

After copying the files for Java by Example to your system, you should have 2 subdirectories in the JavaByExampleBook directory you created. This directory contains the applications and applets from the book that are marked with a CD-ROM icon. The applications directory contains Java applications illustrating everything from interfaces to memory management to encapsulation. You should see the following subdirectories:

Calculator1
Calculator2
IO
Intro
Lisp
Parser
TreeSort
LinkedList

The applets directory contains a selection of applets that illustrate use of the Java graphics library, multiple threads, multimedia, and more.

Just Java

After installing the files for Just Java, you should have 3 subdirectories in the JustJavaBook directory you created:

examples
images
noises

The programs referred to in Just Java are contained in the examples directory. There is one directory for each chapter, containing the small example programs from that chapter.

The images directory contains half a dozen image files for you to experiment with loading and manipulating using the Java features that allow you to display and change images on screen.

The noises directory contains selected sound effects files from the Java release that illustrate how Java can be used to play audio files.

To install Café Lite:

Café Lite is a trial version of Symantec Café, the Integrated Java Development Environment. A coupon for an upgrade to the full version of Symantec Café is included at the back of this book. Please note that the Café Lite installation program also installs a copy of the JDK on your system.

1. Click the Start button and choose Run. (Windows NT users, Select Run from the Program Manager File menu.)

2. Type D:\WIN95NT\CAFELITE\Cafelite.exe and click the OK button. (If your CD-ROM drive is not drive D, substitute the appropriate letter.)

To install WinEdit:

1. Click the Start button and choose Run. (Windows NT users, Select Run from the Program Manager File menu.)

2. Type D:\WIN95NT\WINEDIT\Setup.exe and click the OK button. (If your CD-ROM drive is not drive D, substitute the appropriate letter.)

NOTE: The installation program adds the directory you specified for installing WinEdit to the PATH statement in your AUTOEXEC.BAT file.

To customize WinEdit for Java Programming

If you would like to customize WinEdit to make Java programming easier, the book Core Java describes useful modifications to the standard WinEdit configuration (See Chapter 2). This CD-ROM contains a batch file named Wepatch.bat that you can run to make these modifications.

Wepatch.bat and the other files needed to modify WinEdit are on the CD-ROM in a subdirectory of Winedit named Winedita.

To run Wepatch.bat:

1. Install WinEdit as described above.

2. Change to the Winedita directory on the CD-ROM. D:\WIN95NT\WINEDIT\WINEDITA

3. Run Wepatch <WinEdit directory> <Windows directory>

For example, if you installed WinEdit in a directory on your hard drive named C:\Programs\WinEdit and your Windows directory is C:\Windows, at the system prompt you would type:

> Wepatch C:\Programs\WinEdit C:\Windows

To install WinZip:

1. Click the Start button and choose Run. (Windows NT users, Select Run from the Program Manager File menu.)

2. Type D:\WIN95NT\WINZIP\Winzip95.exe and click the OK button. (If your CD-ROM drive is not drive D, substitute the appropriate letter.)

3. The setup program will display a dialog box asking you where to install WinZip.

4. A dialog box containing information about the WinZip license agreement will also be displayed.

Using the CD-ROM on Solaris 2.x

Because this CD-ROM is a standard ISO-9660 disk that does not support long file names and other UNIX extensions, the Java programs and the Java Developer's Kit (JDK) for Solaris 2.x are stored as tar archives. Use the *more* command or *vi* to read the readme.txt file.

The solaris2 directory structure is as follows:

corejava.tar	Programs from Core Java
instjava.tar	Programs from Instant Java
javaexam.tar	Programs from Java by Example
jdk_1_0_.tar	Solaris 2.x JDK (Release 1.0)
justjava.tar	Programs from Just Java
readme.txt	Installation notes for Solaris users

To install the Java programs:

1. Make a directory on your UNIX filesystem and change to that directory. Then copy the appropriate tar file to that directory.

2. Use the command *tar -xvf* to unarchive the file. For example:

   tar -xvf corejava.tar

To install the Java Developer's Kit (Solaris 2.3 or later):

1. Make a directory on your UNIX filesystem and change to that directory. Then copy the file jdk_1_0_.tar to that directory.

2. Use the command *tar -xvf* to unarchive the file. For example:

   tar -xvf jdk_1_0_.tar

3. Add or modify the appropriate variables in your .cshrc (or whatever initialization file is appropriate for the shell you use) to put the Java bin directory in your path and to set a CLASSPATH environment variable to point to the Java runtime library, which is in the lib directory under the JDK. For example:

   setenv CLASSPATH "where-you-put-java"/lib/classes.zip.

4. Logout and login again so the new variables take effect.

Using the CD-ROM on Macintosh (System 7.5 or later)

The MAC_OS directory contains a Beta release of the Macintosh JDK. Java programs from the books have also been included. Please note, however, that these Java programs have NOT been tested using the Macintosh JDK.

You should also note that Macintosh, Windows, and UNIX text files have slightly different conventions for end-of-line. Macintosh expects a carriage return, Windows expects a carriage return and a linefeed, and UNIX expects a newline character (linefeed)

Most Macintosh editors are able to cope with UNIX and Windows conventions. Be aware, however, that some Macintosh editors will not display line breaks properly if you try to read text files that were created on a Windows or UNIX system. Even though some text files may not appear to be properly formatted, however, the Java compiler handles source files created under either convention.

The MAC_OS directory structure is as follows:

COREJAVA.SEA	Programs from Core Java
INSTJAVA.SEA	Programs from Instant Java
JAVAEXAM.SEA	Programs from Java by Example
JUSTJAVA.SEA	Programs from Just Java
MJDK10B1.SEA	Macintosh JDK (Beta)

To install the JDK or program files from the books:

Because this is an ISO-9660 CD-ROM, the JDK and the program files from each of the books are stored on the disc as self-extracting archives. Copy the files that you want to use to your hard drive and double-click to open.

Index

349

DESIGNING VISUAL INTERFACES:

Communication Oriented Techniques

Kevin Mullet and Darrell K. Sano

Useful to anyone responsible for designing, specifying, implementing, documenting, or managing the visual appearance of computer-based information displays, this book applies the fundamentals of graphic design, industrial design, interior design, and architecture to solve the human computer interface problems experienced in commercial software development. It describes basic design principles (the what and why), common errors, and practical techniques (the how). Readers will gain a new perspective on product development as well as an appreciation for the contribution visual design can offer to their products and users. Six major areas: Elegance and Simplicity; Scale, Contrast, and Proportion; Organization and Visual Structure; Module and Programme; Image and Representation; and Style.

1995, 304 pp., Paper, 0-13-303389-9 (30338-8) (includes 4-color plates)

DEVELOPING VISUAL APPLICATIONS OPENXIL:

An Imaging Foundation Library

William K. Pratt

A practical introduction to imaging into new, innovative applications for desktop computing. For applications in the technical, commercial, and consumer environments, imaging should be considered as basic as putting text or user interface elements into an application. This book breaks down the barriers that developers may have in integrating imaging into their applications. It acquaints developers with the basics of image processing, compression, and algorithm implementation by providing clear, real-world examples of how they can be applied using OpenXIL, a cross-platform imaging foundation library. This book acquaints knowledgeable imaging developers with the architectural features and capabilities of OpenXIL. It can also serve as a primer for new OpenXIL programmers.

1996, 400 pp., Paper, 0-13-461948-X (46194-7)

HTML FOR FUN AND PROFIT Gold Signature Ed.

Mary E. S. Morris

This book is about writing HTML pages for the World Wide Web. Written in a step-by-step, hands on, tutorial style, it presents all the information needed by an aspiring web page author. Platforms are also discussed. Includes:

- Setting up your server
- Learning HTML formatting basics, including lists and special characters
- Integrating multimedia into web pages
- Formatting tables in HTML
- Creating interactive HTML documents with CGI scripting
- Customizing HTML pages with Server Includes
- Designing effective web page layouts
- Appendices on installing and using Xmosaic, WinMosaic, and MacMosaic browsers are included.
- A CD-ROM containing shareware and extensive examples of sample HTML pages and sample perl scripts is also provided.

This book also includes a chapter on Netscape with HTML examples on the CD-ROM. The CD-ROM includes a web server for Microsoft Windows 3.1, NT, Macintosh and UNIX.

EXPERT C PROGRAMMING:

Deep C Secrets

Peter van der Linden

Known as "the butt-ugly fish book" because of the coelacanth on the cover, this is a very different book on the C language! In an easy, conversational style, *it* reveals coding techniques used by the best C programmers. It relates C to other languages and includes an introduction to C++ that can be understood by any programmer without weeks of mind-bending study. Covering both the IBM PC and UNIX systems, this book is a *must read* for anyone who wants to learn more about the implementation, practical use, and folk lore of C!

1994, 384 pp., Paper, 0-13-177429-8 (17742-8)

1996, 330 pp., Paper, 0-13-242488-6 (24248-7) Book/CD-ROM

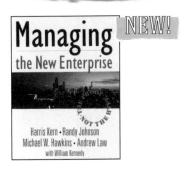

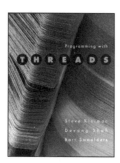

environments. Topics covered include:

- Why rightsize?
- What business results can rightsizing produce?
- Key technologies critical to rightsizing
- Good starting points for rightsizing
- What is the process to rightsize an information system?
- Cost considerations and return on investment (ROI) analysis
- How to manage the transition

Throughout the book, case studies and `lessons learned' reinforce the discussion and document best practices associated with rightsizing.

1995, 272 pp., Paper,
0-13-123126-X (12312-5)

SOLARIS IMPLEMENTATION:

A Guide for System Administrators
George Becker, Mary E. S. Morris and Kathy Slattery

Written by three expert Sun system administrators, this book discusses real world, day-to-day Solaris 2 system administration for both new installations and for those migrating an installed Solaris 1 base. It presents tested procedures to help system administrators to improve and customize their networks by eliminating trial-and-error methodologies. Also includes advice for managing heterogeneous Solaris environments and provides autoinstall sample scripts and disk partitioning schemes (with recommended sizes) used at Sun. *1995, 368 pp., Paper,*
0-13-353350-6 (35335- 9)

SOLARIS INTERNATIONAL DEVELOPER'S GUIDE, Second Edtion
Bill Tuthill and David Smallberg

Written for software developers and business managers interested in creating global applications for the Solaris environment (SPARC and x86), this 2nd edition expands on the 1st edition and has updated information on international markets, standards organizations, and writing international documents. New topics in the 2nd edition include CDE/Motif, NEO (formerly project DOE)/OpenStep, Universal codesets, global internet applications, code examples, and success stories.

1996, 250 pp., Paper,
0-13-494493-3 (49449-2)

SOLARIS PORTING GUIDE, Second Edition
SunSoft Developer Engineering

Ideal for application programmers and software developers, the Solaris Porting Guide, Second Edition, provides a comprehensive technical overview of the Solaris 2.x operating environment and its related migration strategy. The second edition is current through Solaris 2.4 (both the SPARC and x86 platforms) and provides all the information necessary to migrate from Solaris 1 (SunOS 4.x) to Solaris 2 (SunOS 5.x). Other additions include a discussion of emerging technologies such as the Common Desktop Environment (CDE), hints for application performance tuning, and extensive pointers to further information, including Internet sources.

1995, 752 pp., Paper,
0-13-443672-5 (44367-1)

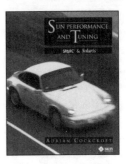

SUN PERFORMANCE AND TUNING:
SPARC and Solaris
Adrian Cockcroft

An indispensable reference for anyone working with Sun workstations running the Solaris environment, this book provides detailed performance and configuration information on all SPARC machines and peripherals, as well as on all operating system releases from SunOS 4.1 through Solaris 2.4. It includes hard-to-find tuning information and offers insights that cannot be found elsewhere. This book is written for developers who want to design for performance and for system administrators who have a system running applications on which they want to improve performance.

1995, 288 pp., Paper,
0-13-149642-5 (14964-1)

Get Café 1.0 at a Special Price

The full version of Symantec Café contains the latest Java Development Kit and many exciting new features and tools:

✔ Debug your Java applets with the Café Visual Java Debugger

✔ Design your forms and menus with the Café Studio

✔ Navigate and edit your classes and methods with the Hierarchy Editor and Class Editor

✔ Compile your Java applets and applications 20 times faster with the Café native compiler

✔ Double the speed of your Java applications with the Café native Java virtual machine

SYMANTEC.

http://www.Café.Symantec.com

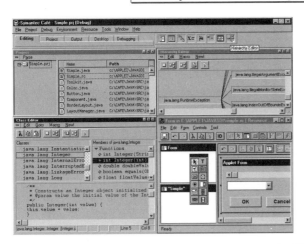

Symantec Café includes all the components found in Café Lite, plus a 2-way hierarchy editor, a class editor, a GUI multi-thread debugger, a visual menu and form designer, a native compiler which compiles the .class files up to 20 times faster, a new Java virtual machine for Windows which doubles the speed of your applications, 85 samples, a tutorial, and the API docs in help.

Get more information on Café automatically sent to you via e-mail. Send an email to **info@bedford.symantec.com** with no subject line, and an overview document will be sent to you along with a description of the other documents available and how to get them.

State Sales/Use Tax

In the following states, add sales/use tax: CO-3%; GA, LA, NY-4%; VA-4.5%; KS-4.9%; AZ, IA, IN, MA, MD, OH, SC, WI-5%; CT, FL, ME, MI, NC, NJ, PA, TN-6%; CA, IL, TX-6.25%; MN, WA-6.5%;DC-5.75%.

Please add local tax for AZ, CA, FL, GA, MO, NY, OH, SC, TN, TX, WA, WI.

Order Information:

- Please allow 2-4 weeks for processing your order.
- Please attach the order form with your payment.
- No P.O. boxes and no C.O.D.s accepted.
- Order form good in the U.S. only.
- If you are tax exempt, please include exemption certificate or letter with tax-exempt number.
- Resellers not eligible.
- Offer not valid with any other promotion.
- One copy per product, per order.

LICENSE AGREEMENT AND LIMITED WARRANTY

READ THE FOLLOWING TERMS AND CONDITIONS CAREFULLY BEFORE OPENING THIS DISK PACKAGE. THIS LEGAL DOCUMENT IS AN AGREEMENT BETWEEN YOU AND PRENTICE-HALL, INC. (THE "COMPANY"). BY OPENING THIS SEALED DISK PACKAGE, YOU ARE AGREEING TO BE BOUND BY THESE TERMS AND CONDITIONS. IF YOU DO NOT AGREE WITH THESE TERMS AND CONDITIONS, DO NOT OPEN THE DISK PACKAGE. PROMPTLY RETURN THE UNOPENED DISK PACKAGE AND ALL ACCOMPANYING ITEMS TO THE PLACE YOU OBTAINED THEM FOR A FULL REFUND OF ANY SUMS YOU HAVE PAID.

1. **GRANT OF LICENSE:** In consideration of your payment of the license fee, which is part of the price you paid for this product, and your agreement to abide by the terms and conditions of this Agreement, the Company grants to you a nonexclusive right to use and display the copy of the enclosed software program (hereinafter the "SOFTWARE") on a single computer (i.e., with a single CPU) at a single location so long as you comply with the terms of this Agreement. The Company reserves all rights not expressly granted to you under this Agreement.

2. **OWNERSHIP OF SOFTWARE:** You own only the magnetic or physical media (the enclosed disks) on which the SOFTWARE is recorded or fixed, but the Company retains all the rights, title, and ownership to the SOFTWARE recorded on the original disk copy(ies) and all subsequent copies of the SOFTWARE, regardless of the form or media on which the original or other copies may exist. This license is not a sale of the original SOFTWARE or any copy to you.

3. **COPY RESTRICTIONS:** This SOFTWARE and the accompanying printed materials and user manual (the "Documentation") are the subject of copyright. You may not copy the Documentation or the SOFTWARE, except that you may make a single copy of the SOFTWARE for backup or archival purposes only. You may be held legally responsible for any copying or copyright infringement which is caused or encouraged by your failure to abide by the terms of this restriction.

4. **USE RESTRICTIONS:** You may not network the SOFTWARE or otherwise use it on more than one computer or computer terminal at the same time. You may physically transfer the SOFTWARE from one computer to another provided that the SOFTWARE is used on only one computer at a time. You may not distribute copies of the SOFTWARE or Documentation to others. You may not reverse engineer, disassemble, decompile, modify, adapt, translate, or create derivative works based on the SOFTWARE or the Documentation without the prior written consent of the Company.

5. **TRANSFER RESTRICTIONS:** The enclosed SOFTWARE is licensed only to you and may not be transferred to any one else without the prior written consent of the Company. Any unauthorized transfer of the SOFTWARE shall result in the immediate termination of this Agreement.

6. **TERMINATION:** This license is effective until terminated. This license will terminate automatically without notice from the Company and become null and void if you fail to comply with any provisions or limitations of this license. Upon termination, you shall destroy the Documentation and all copies of the SOFTWARE. All provisions of this Agreement as to warranties, limitation of liability, remedies or damages, and our ownership rights shall survive termination.

7. **MISCELLANEOUS:** This Agreement shall be construed in accordance with the laws of the United States of America and the State of New York and shall benefit the Company, its affiliates, and assignees.

8.   **LIMITED WARRANTY AND DISCLAIMER OF WARRANTY:** The Company warrants that the SOFTWARE, when properly used in accordance with the Documentation, will operate in substantial conformity with the description of the SOFTWARE set forth in the Documentation. The Company does not warrant that the SOFTWARE will meet your requirements or that the operation of the SOFTWARE will be uninterrupted or error-free. The Company warrants that the media on which the SOFTWARE is delivered shall be free from defects in materials and workmanship under normal use for a period of thirty (30) days from the date of your purchase. Your only remedy and the Company's only obligation under these limited warranties is, at the Company's option, return of the warranted item for a refund of any amounts paid by you or replacement of the item. Any replacement of SOFTWARE or media under the warranties shall not extend the original warranty period. The limited warranty set forth above shall not apply to any SOFT-WARE which the Company determines in good faith has been subject to misuse, neglect, improper installation, repair, alteration, or damage by you. EXCEPT FOR THE EXPRESSED WARRANTIES SET FORTH ABOVE, THE COMPANY DISCLAIMS ALL WARRANTIES, EXPRESS OR IMPLIED, INCLUDING WITHOUT LIMITATION, THE IMPLIED WARRANTIES OF MERCHANTABILITY AND FITNESS FOR A PARTICULAR PURPOSE. EXCEPT FOR THE EXPRESS WARRANTY SET FORTH ABOVE, THE COMPANY DOES NOT WARRANT, GUARANTEE, OR MAKE ANY REPRESENTATION REGARDING THE USE OR THE RESULTS OF THE USE OF THE SOFTWARE IN TERMS OF ITS CORRECTNESS, ACCURACY, RELIABILITY, CURRENTNESS, OR OTHERWISE.

IN NO EVENT, SHALL THE COMPANY OR ITS EMPLOYEES, AGENTS, SUPPLIERS, OR CONTRACTORS BE LIABLE FOR ANY INCIDENTAL, INDIRECT, SPECIAL, OR CONSEQUENTIAL DAMAGES ARISING OUT OF OR IN CONNECTION WITH THE LICENSE GRANTED UNDER THIS AGREEMENT, OR FOR LOSS OF USE, LOSS OF DATA, LOSS OF INCOME OR PROFIT, OR OTHER LOSSES, SUSTAINED AS A RESULT OF INJURY TO ANY PERSON, OR LOSS OF OR DAMAGE TO PROPERTY, OR CLAIMS OF THIRD PARTIES, EVEN IF THE COMPANY OR AN AUTHORIZED REPRESENTATIVE OF THE COMPANY HAS BEEN ADVISED OF THE POSSIBILITY OF SUCH DAMAGES. IN NO EVENT SHALL LIABILITY OF THE COMPANY FOR DAMAGES WITH RESPECT TO THE SOFTWARE EXCEED THE AMOUNTS ACTUALLY PAID BY YOU, IF ANY, FOR THE SOFTWARE.

SOME JURISDICTIONS DO NOT ALLOW THE LIMITATION OF IMPLIED WARRANTIES OR LIABILITY FOR INCIDENTAL, INDIRECT, SPECIAL, OR CONSEQUENTIAL DAMAGES, SO THE ABOVE LIMITATIONS MAY NOT ALWAYS APPLY. THE WARRANTIES IN THIS AGREEMENT GIVE YOU SPECIFIC LEGAL RIGHTS AND YOU MAY ALSO HAVE OTHER RIGHTS WHICH VARY IN ACCORDANCE WITH LOCAL LAW.

ACKNOWLEDGMENT

YOU ACKNOWLEDGE THAT YOU HAVE READ THIS AGREEMENT, UNDERSTAND IT, AND AGREE TO BE BOUND BY ITS TERMS AND CONDITIONS. YOU ALSO AGREE THAT THIS AGREEMENT IS THE COMPLETE AND EXCLUSIVE STATEMENT OF THE AGREEMENT BETWEEN YOU AND THE COMPANY AND SUPERSEDES ALL PROPOSALS OR PRIOR AGREEMENTS, ORAL, OR WRITTEN, AND ANY OTHER COMMUNICATIONS BETWEEN YOU AND THE COMPANY OR ANY REPRESENTATIVE OF THE COMPANY RELATING TO THE SUBJECT MATTER OF THIS AGREEMENT.

Should you have any questions concerning this Agreement or if you wish to contact the Company for any reason, please contact in writing at the address below.

Robin Short
Prentice Hall PTR
One Lake Street
Upper Saddle River, New Jersey 07458

The SunSoft Press Java Series CD-ROM is a standard ISO-9660 disc. Software on this CD-ROM requires Windows 95, Windows NT, Solaris 2 or Macintosh (System 7.5).

Windows 3.1 IS NOT SUPPORTED